D1614240

Bloom's Modern Critical Views

African-American Poets: Volume 1
African-American Poets: Volume 2
Aldous Huxley
Alfred, Lord Tennyson
Alice Munro
Alice Walker
American Women Poets
Amy Tan
Anton Chekhov
Arthur Miller
Asian-American Writers
August Wilson
The Bible
The Brontës
Carson McCullers
Charles Dickens
Christopher Marlowe
Contemporary Poets
Cormac McCarthy
C.S. Lewis
Dante Aligheri
David Mamet
Derek Walcott
Don DeLillo
Doris Lessing
Edgar Allan Poe
Émile Zola
Emily Dickinson
Ernest Hemingway
Eudora Welty
Eugene O'Neill
F. Scott Fitzgerald
Flannery O'Connor
Franz Kafka
Gabriel García Márquez
Geoffrey Chaucer
George Orwell
G.K. Chesterton
Gwendolyn Brooks
Hans Christian Andersen
Henry David Thoreau
Herman Melville
Hermann Hesse
H.G. Wells
Hispanic-American Writers
Homer
Honoré de Balzac
Jamaica Kincaid
James Joyce
Jane Austen
Jay Wright
J.D. Salinger
Jean-Paul Sartre
John Donne and the Metaphysical Poets
John Irving
John Keats
John Milton
John Steinbeck
José Saramago
Joseph Conrad
J.R.R. Tolkien
Julio Cortázar
Kate Chopin
Kurt Vonnegut
Langston Hughes
Leo Tolstoy
Marcel Proust
Margaret Atwood
Mark Twain
Mary Wollstonecraft Shelley
Maya Angelou
Miguel de Cervantes
Milan Kundera
Nathaniel Hawthorne
Native American Writers
Norman Mailer
Octavio Paz
Paul Auster
Philip Roth
Ralph Ellison
Ralph Waldo Emerson
Ray Bradbury
Richard Wright
Robert Browning
Robert Frost
Robert Hayden
Robert Louis Stevenson
The Romantic Poets
Salman Rushdie
Samuel Taylor Coleridge
Stephen Crane
Stephen King
Sylvia Plath
Tennessee Williams
Thomas Hardy
Thomas Pynchon
Tom Wolfe
Toni Morrison
Tony Kushner
Truman Capote
Twentieth-Century British Poets
Walt Whitman
W.E.B. Du Bois
William Blake
William Faulkner
William Gaddis
William Shakespeare: Comedies
William Shakespeare: Histories
William Shakespeare: Romances
William Shakespeare: Tragedies
William Wordsworth
Zora Neale Hurston

Bloom's Modern Critical Views

TWENTIETH-CENTURY BRITISH POETS

Edited and with an introduction by
Harold Bloom
Sterling Professor of the Humanities
Yale University

Bloom's Literary Criticism
An imprint of Infobase Learning
132 West 31st Street
New York NY 10001

Library of Congress Cataloging-in-Publication Data
Twentieth-century British poets / edited and with an introduction by Harold Bloom.
p. cm. — (Bloom's modern critical views)
Includes bibliographical references and index.
ISBN 978-1-60413-990-7 (hardcover)
1. English poetry—20th century—History and criticism. 2. Poetics—History—20th century. I. Bloom, Harold.
PR603.T95 2011
821'.909—dc23
2011017007

Contributing editor: Pamela Loos
Cover designed by Alicia Post
Composition by IBT Global, Troy NY
Cover printed by Yurchak Printing, Landisville PA
Book printed and bound by Yurchak Printing, Landisville PA
Date printed: September 2011
Printed in the United States of America

10 9 8 7 6 5 4 3 2 1

This book is printed on acid-free paper.

Contents

Editor's Note

My introduction traces the range of poetic lights produced in Britain in the twentieth century, from the skeptical laments of Thomas Hardy to the severe and urgent work of Seamus Heaney.

Dominic Hibberd remains the leading Owen scholar and here notes the poet's combining of romantic notions of pity with the war subjects he knew so well. Robert Langbaum follows with a deft rendering of Hardy's precarious position on the cusp of modernism.

Helen Vendler explores the contradictory imperatives informing Heaney's eighth volume, followed by Stan Smith's exploration of Yeats, who, like Milton, Wordsworth, and Coleridge before him, attempted to rewrite the "book of the people."

Andrew Swarbrick takes up the final collection Philip Larkin published in his lifetime, after which Rainer Emig examines the philosophical strain in W.H. Auden's late works.

Lawrence Rainey returns us to the enduring appeal of *The Waste Land*, followed by Jane Dowson and Alice Entwistle's overview of the dialogic practices of some of Britain's leading women poets.

Tim Kendall offers a reading of war as an abiding concern in the poetry of Ted Hughes. Keith Sagar concludes the volume with a look at D.H. Lawrence's rich final phase.

HAROLD BLOOM

Introduction

Thomas Hardy

O*nly a poet challenges a poet as poet*, and so only a poet makes a poet. To the poet-in-a-poet, a poem is always *the other man*, the precursor, and so a poem is always a person, always the father of one's second birth. To live, the poet must *misinterpret* the father, by the crucial act of misprision, which is the rewriting of the father.

But who, what is the poetic father? The voice of the other, of the *daimon*, is always speaking in one; the voice that cannot die because already it has survived death—*the dead poet lives in one*. In the last phase of strong poets, they attempt to join the undying by living in the *dead poets* who are already alive in them. This late return of the dead recalls us, as readers, to a recognition of the original motive for the catastrophe of poetic incarnation. Vico, who identified the origins of poetry with the impulse toward divination (to foretell but also to become a god by foretelling), implicitly understood (as did Emerson and Wordsworth) that a poem is written to escape dying. Literally, poems are refusals of mortality. Every poem therefore has two makers: the precursor and the ephebe's rejected mortality.

A poet, I argue in consequence, is not so much a man speaking to men as a man rebelling against being spoken to by a dead man (the precursor) outrageously more alive than himself. A poet dare not regard himself as being *late* yet cannot accept a substitute for the first vision he reflectively judges to have been his precursor's also. Perhaps this is why the poet-in-a-poet *cannot marry*, whatever the person-in-a-poet chooses to have done.

Poetic influence, in the sense I give to it, has almost nothing to do with the verbal resemblances between one poet and another. Hardy, on the surface, scarcely resembles Shelley, his prime precursor, but then Browning, who resembles Shelley even less, was yet more fully Shelley's ephebe than even Hardy was. The same observation can be made of Swinburne and of Yeats in relation to Shelley. What Blake called the spiritual form, at once the aboriginal poetical self and the true subject, is what the ephebe is so dangerously obliged to the precursor for even possessing. Poets need not *look* like their fathers, and the anxiety of influence more frequently than not is quite distinct from the anxiety of style. Since poetic influence is necessarily misprision, a taking or doing amiss of one's burden, it is to be expected that such a process of malformation and misinterpretation will, at the very least, produce deviations in style among strong poets. Let us remember always Emerson's insistence as to what it is that makes a poem:

> For it is not meters, but a meter-making argument that makes a poem,—a thought so passionate and alive that like the spirit of a plant or an animal it has an architecture of its own, and adorns nature with a new thing. The thought and the form are equal in the order of time, but in the order of genesis the thought is prior to the form. The poet has a new thought; he has a whole new experience to unfold; he will tell us how it was with him, and all men will be the richer in his fortune. For the experience of each new age requires a new confession, and the world seems always waiting for its poet. . . . ("The Poet")

Emerson would not acknowledge that meter-making arguments themselves were subject to the tyrannies of inheritance, but that they are so subject is the saddest truth I know about poets and poetry. In Hardy's best poems, the central meter-making argument is what might be called a skeptical lament for the hopeless incongruity of ends and means in all human acts. Love and the means of love cannot be brought together, and the truest name for the human condition is simply that it is loss:

> And brightest things that are theirs. . . .
> Ah, no; the years, the years;
> Down their carved names the raindrop plows.

These are the closing lines of "During Wind and Rain," as good a poem as our century has given us. The poem, like so many others, is a grandchild of the "Ode to the West Wind," as much as Stevens's "The Course of a Particular" or any number of major lyrics by Yeats. A carrion eater, old style, would challenge my observations, and to such a challenge I could offer, in its own terms, only the first appearance of the refrain:

Ah, no; the years O!
How the sick leaves reel down in throngs!

But such terms can be ignored. Poetic influence, among strong poets, works in the depths, as all love antithetically works. At the center of Hardy's verse, whether in the early *Wessex Poems* or the late *Winter Words*, is this vision:

And much I grieved to think how power and will
In opposition rule our mortal day,

And why God made irreconcilable
Good and the means of good; and for despair
I half disdained mine eyes' desire to fill

With the spent vision of the times that were
And scarce have ceased to be—

Shelley's *The Triumph of Life* can give us also the heroic motto for the major characters in Hardy's novels: "For in the battle Life and they did wage, / She remained conqueror." The motto would serve as well for the superb volume *Winter Words in Various Moods and Metres*, published on October 2,1928, the year that Hardy died on January 11. Hardy had hoped to publish the book on June 2, 1928, which would have been his eighty-eighth birthday. Though a few poems in the book go back as far as the 1860s, most were written after the appearance of Hardy's volume of lyrics, *Human Shows*, in 1925. A few books of twentieth-century verse in English compare with *Winter Words* in greatness but very few. Though the collection is diverse and has no central design, its emergent theme is a counterpoise to the burden of poetic incarnation and might be called the Return of the Dead, who haunt Hardy as he faces toward death.

In his early poem "Shelley's Skylark" (1887), Hardy, writing rather in the style of his fellow Shelleyan, Browning, speaks of his ancestor's "ecstatic heights in thought and rhyme." Recent critics who admire Shelley are not particularly fond of "To a Skylark," and it is rather too ecstatic for most varieties of modern sensibility, but we can surmise why it so moved Hardy:

We look before and after,
And pine for what is not:
Our sincerest laughter
With some pain is fraught;
Our sweetest songs are those that tell of saddest thought.

> Yet if we could scorn
> Hate, and pride, and fear;
> If we were things born
> Not to shed a tear,
> I know not how thy joy we ever should come near.

The thought here, as elsewhere in Shelley, is not so simple as it may seem. Our divided consciousness, keeping us from being able to unperplex joy from pain and ruining the presentness of the moment, at least brings us an aesthetic gain. But even if we lacked our range of negative affections, even if grief were not our birthright, the pure joy of the lark's song would still surpass us. We may think of Shelleyan ladies like Marty South, and even more Sue Bridehead, who seems to have emerged from the *Epipsychidion*. Or perhaps we may remember Angel Clare as a kind of parody of Shelley himself. Hardy's Shelley is very close to the most central of Shelleys, the visionary skeptic, whose head and whose heart could never be reconciled, for they both told truths but contrary truths. In *Prometheus Unbound*, we are told that in our life the shadow cast by love is always ruin, which is the head's report, but the heart in Shelley goes on saying that if there is to be coherence at all, it must come through Eros.

Winter Words, as befits a man going into his later eighties, is more in ruin's shadow than in love's realm. The last poem, written in 1927, is called "He Resolves to Say No More" and follows directly on "We Are Getting to the End," which may be the bleakest sonnet in the language. Both poems explicitly reject any vision of hope and are set against the Shelleyan rational meliorism of *Prometheus Unbound*. "We are getting to the end of visioning / The impossible within this universe," Hardy flatly insists, and he recalls Shelley's vision of rolling time backward only to dismiss it as the doctrine of Shelley's Ahasuerus: "(Magians who drive the midnight quill / With brain aglow / Can see it so)." Behind this rejection is the mystery of misprision, of deep poetic influence in its final phase, which I have called *Apophrades* or the return of the dead. Hovering everywhere in *Winter Words*, though far less explicitly than it hovers in *The Dynasts*, is Shelley's *Hellas*. The peculiar strength and achievement of *Winter Words* is not that we are compelled to remember Shelley when we read in it, but rather that it makes us read much of Shelley as though Hardy were Shelley's ancestor, the dark father whom the revolutionary idealist failed to cast out.

Nearly every poem in *Winter Words* has a poignance unusual even in Hardy, but I am moved most by "He Never Expected Much," the poet's reflection on his eighty-sixth birthday, where his dialogue with the "World" attains a resolution:

"I do not promise overmuch,
Child; overmuch;
Just neutral-tinted haps and such,"
You said to minds like mine.
Wise warning for your credit's sake!
Which I for one failed not to take,
And hence could stem such strain and ache
As each year might assign.

The "neutral-tinted haps," so supremely hard to get into poems, are the staple of Hardy's achievement in verse and contrast both to Wordsworth's "sober coloring" and Shelley's "deep autumnal tone." All through *Winter Words* the attentive reader will hear a chastened return of High Romantic Idealism but muted into Hardy's tonality. Where Yeats malformed both himself and his High Romantic fathers, Blake and Shelley, in the violences of *Last Poems and Plays*, Hardy more effectively subdued the questing temperaments of his fathers, Shelley and Browning, in *Winter Words*. The wrestling with the great dead is subtler in Hardy and kinder both to himself and to the fathers.

Hardy's Shelley was essentially the darker poet of *Adonais* and *The Triumph of Life*, though I find more quotations from *The Revolt of Islam* scattered through the novels than from any other single work by Shelley, and I suppose *Hellas* and *Prometheus Unbound* were even more direct, technical influences on *The Dynasts*. But Hardy was one of those young men who went about in the 1860s carrying a volume of Shelley in his pocket. Quite simply, he identified Shelley's voice with poetry itself, and though he could allow his ironic sense to touch other writers, he kept Shelley inviolate, almost as a kind of secular Christ. His misprision of Shelley, his subversion of Shelley's influence, was an unconscious defense, quite unlike the overt struggle against Shelley of Browning and Yeats.

American poets, far more than British, have rebelled overtly against ancestral voices, partly because of Whitman's example and also because of Emerson's polemic against the very idea of influence, his insistence that going alone must mean refusing even the good models and so entails reading primarily as an inventor. Our greater emphasis on originality has produced inversely a more malevolent anxiety of influence, and our poets consequently misinterpret their precursors more radically than do the British. Hardy's was a gentler case of influence anxiety than that of any other modern strong poet for reasons allied, I think, to the astonishing ease of Hardy's initial entrance into his poethood.

William Butler Yeats

From an early twenty-first-century perspective, William Butler Yeats (1865–1939) appears to be the major Anglo-Irish poet in the long tradition that goes from Thomas Moore to our contemporary Seamus Heaney and beyond. No English poet of the last century, not even Thomas Hardy, D.H. Lawrence, or Geoffrey Hill, can be judged equal to Yeats in eminence. A handful of modern American poets—Robert Frost, Wallace Stevens, T.S. Eliot, Hart Crane—are of Yeats's stature but cannot be said to surpass him. Time's revenges have been unkind to many of Yeats's social and political ideals and to his occult enthusiasms, but his powers as a dramatic lyricist remain undiminished. Yeats recognized that Robert Browning was always a dangerous influence on him, partly because both Yeats and Browning had swerved away from Shelley as prime precursor.

Robert Browning is now unfashionable but is too great a poet not to return, once we get beyond the institutional politics of our bad moment, which prefers Browning's wife to him and also exalts Mrs. Felicia Hemans as John Keats's equal and Lady Mary Chudleigh as a rival to John Milton. But no one as yet prefers Charlotte Mew or Lady Dorothy Wellesley to W. B. Yeats, who thus seems in little danger of being demoted, except perhaps by the lunatic fringe of feminist critics, who after all do not flinch at castigating Shakespeare and Dante. Yeats's stance toward women is certainly archaic, being a curious blend of chivalry and brutality. But no one need take such attitudes seriously, since they are akin to Yeats's fascist eugenics and his credulous table rappings.

Yeats, as a poet, craved either ecstasy or wisdom but luckily achieved something very different: a personal myth that plied him with powerful metaphors for his poetry. A convinced supernaturalist yet not a Christian, Yeats invoked spirits as so many variant muses, to enable his access to realms of vision where Shelley and William Blake had preceded him. He enters visionary space with less confidence than his romantic precursors and, oddly enough, also with less irony. The skeptical Shelley and the polemical Blake employ biblical ironies to sound out their prophecies, but Yeats had little enough concern for the Bible, preferring the sacred scriptures of the East. Again, this benefited Yeats, for he was no prophet but a phantasmagorist. The intensity of Yeats's greatest lyrics is extraordinary and is sustained by an intricate personal mythology, systematized in the two versions of *A Vision* (1925, 1937), in which the dead and history are reconciled as a cosmological dance of contraries.

Because of *A Vision*, Yeats is likely to seem a more difficult poet than he actually is. "The Second Coming," a chant of astonishing force, perplexes many readers because they assume the poem's title refers to Christ, which it does not. What is reborn and so comes again in Yeats's litany is the one-eyed male Egyptian Sphinx, god of the Sun. The poet hails him cognitively (though with a certain emotional revulsion) because this rough beast heralds the end of Christian revelation and its replacement by the counter-revolutionary tide of fascism. I don't know that a visionary fascism is any more acceptable humanly than the terrifying brutalities of an actual fascism, but "The Second Coming" is unquestionably a sublime poem, a triumph of language and of controlled turbulence.

Yeats makes legitimate demands on his readers: We need always to pay close attention to his own relationship to what he sees and shows. As a dramatist of the self, Yeats towers above every other poet in the English language in the twentieth century. We go back to his poetry incessantly, because we need that drama, and because its cognitive and passionate music overcomes all resistances.

D.H. Lawrence

As a judicial critic, R.P. Blackmur approximates the Arnold of our day. He ranks poets. His essay "Lord Tennyson's Scissors: 1912–1950" creates a new scriptural canon out of modern poetry in English. Class I: Yeats, Pound, and Eliot. Plenty of other classes, but all their members standing below Pound and Eliot. In a rather sad class, the violent school, lumped in with Lindsay, Jeffers, Roy Campbell, Sandburg, etc., are D.H. Lawrence and Hart Crane. Lawrence and Crane "were outside the tradition they enriched. They stood at the edge of the precipice which yawns to those who lift too hard at their bootstraps."

Presumably, Blackmur bases this judgment on two of his own more influential essays: "D. H. Lawrence and Expressive Form" and "New Thresholds New Anatomies: Notes on a Text of Hart Crane." Both essays will be sizable relics when most specimens of currently fashionable analysis are lost. But because they attempt so little description and so much value judgment, they will be relics at best. By their documentation we will remember what illusions were prevalent at a particular moment in the history of taste.

Blackmur is a critic of the rhetorical school of I.A. Richards. The school is spiritually middle-aged to old; it is in the autumn of its emblematic body. Soon it will be dead. "Lord Tennyson's Scissors" is only an episode in the school's dying. But, as criticisms die so grudgingly, the essay is worth clinical attention.

Northrop Frye has recently said that all selective approaches to tradition invariably have some ultracritical joker concealed in them. A few sentences from Frye's *Anatomy of Criticism* are enough to place Blackmur's pseudodialectics as false rhetoric:

> The dialectic axis of criticism, then, has as one pole the total acceptance of the data of literature, and as the other the total acceptance of the potential values of those data. This is the real level of culture

> and liberal education, the fertilizing of life by learning, in which the systematic progress of scholarship flows into a systematic progress of taste and understanding. On this level there is no itch to make weighty judgments, and none of the ill effects which follow the debauchery of judiciousness, and have made the word critic a synonym for an educated shrew. Comparative estimates of value are really inferences, most valid when silent ones, from critical practice, not expressed principles guiding its practice.

What I propose to do here is to examine Blackmur's "debauchery of judiciousness" in his criticism of Lawrence and to suggest where it is inadequate to the poetry.

Poetry is the embodiment of a more than rational energy. This truth, basic to Coleridge and Blake, and to Lawrence as their romantic heir, is inimical to Blackmur's "rationally constructed imagination," which he posits throughout his criticism. Eliot's, we are to gather, is a rational imagination, Lawrence's is not. Eliot is orderly; the lines beginning "Lady of silences" in "Ash Wednesday" convey a sense of controlled hysteria. Lawrence is merely hysterical: The concluding lines of "Tortoise Shout" are a "ritual frenzy." The great mystics, and Eliot as their poetic follower, saw their ultimate vision "within the terms of an orderly insight." But Lawrence did not. Result: "In them, reason was stretched to include disorder and achieved mystery. In Lawrence, the reader is left to supply the reason and the form; for Lawrence only expresses the substance."

The underlying dialectic here is a social one; Blackmur respects a codified vision, an institutionalized insight, more than the imaginative word of an individual romantic poet, be he Blake or Lawrence or Crane. In fairness to Blackmur, one remembers his insistence that critics are not the fathers of a new church, as well as his quiet rejoinder to Eliot's "After Strange Gods": "The hysteria of institutions is more dreadful than that of individuals." But why should the order of institutions be more valid for poetry than the order of a gifted individual? And why must order in poetry be "rational," in Blackmur's minimal sense of the word? Lawrence's poetry, like Blake's, is animate with mental energy: It does not lack mind. For it is precisely in a quality of mind, in imaginative invention, that Lawrence's poetry excels. Compared to it, the religious poetry of Eliot suggests everywhere an absence of mind, a poverty of invention, a reliance on the ritual frenzy of others.

Blackmur, who is so patient an exegete of verse he admires, will not even grant that Lawrence's poetry is worth descriptive criticism:

> You cannot talk about the art of his poetry because it exists only at the minimum level of self-expression, as in the later, more important

poems, or because, as in the earlier accentual rhymed pieces written while he was getting under way, its art is mostly attested by its badness.

Neither half of this confident judgment is true, but Blackmur has a thesis about Lawrence's poetry that he wants very much to prove. The poetry does not matter if the essay can be turned well to its despite. For Lawrence, according to this critic who denies his fatherhood in a new faith, is guilty of the "fallacy of expressive form." Blackmur's proof of guilt is to quote Lawrence external to his poetry, analyze the quotation, and then to quote without comment some fragments of Lawrence's verse ripped from context. But the fact is that Lawrence was a bad critic of his own poetry. Lawrence may have believed in "expressive form"; his poetry largely does not.

Blackmur quotes the final lines of "Medlars and Sorb Apples":

Orphic farewell, and farewell, and farewell
And the ego sum of Dionysos
The sono io of perfect drunkenness.
Intoxication of final loneliness.

Here, for Blackmur, "the hysteria is increased and the observation becomes vision, and leaves, perhaps, the confines of poetry." We can begin by restoring the context, so as to get at an accurate description of these "hysterical" lines. For the tone of "Medlars and Sorb Apples" is very quiet, and those final lines that Blackmur would incant as "ritual frenzy" are slow with irony, if that word is still available in the discussion of poetry. The Orphic farewell is a leave-taking of a bride left in the earth, and no frenzy accompanies it here.

"Medlars and Sorb Apples" might be called a natural emblem poem, as are most of the *Birds, Beasts and Flowers* sequence, one of the signatures of all things. In the "brown morbidity" of the medlar, as it falls through its stages of decay, Lawrence tastes the "delicious rottenness" of Orphism, the worship of the "Dionysos of the Underworld," god of isolation and of poetry. For the retorts of medlars and sorb apples distill the exquisite odor of the autumnal leave-taking of the year, essence of the parting in Hades of Orpheus and Eurydice. The intoxication of this odor, mingled with Marsala, provides that gasp of further isolation that imaginatively completes the loneliness of the individual soul. The poem is an invocation of this ultimate loneliness as the best state of the soul. The four final lines are addressed directly to medlar and sorb apples as an Orphic farewell, but different in kind from the Eurydice parting, because of Lawrence's identification of Orpheus with Dionysos. This Orphic farewell is a creative vivification, a declaration of Dionysiac being, a perfect, lonely, intoxicated finality of the isolated self of the poet. What smells of death in the autumnal fruit is life to him. Spring will mean inevitable division, crucifixion into sex, a genuine Orphic farewell to solipsistic wholeness. The poem is resolved finally as two overlapping cycles, both ironically treated.

"Tortoise Shout" is Blackmur's prime example of "the hysteria of expression" in Lawrence, where "every notation and association, every symbolic suggestion" possible is brought to bear upon "the shrieking plasm of the self." In contrast, Eliot's "Rose Garden with Virgin" is our rational restorative to invocatory control.

Eliot's passage is a simple, quite mechanical catalogue of clean Catholic contradictions, very good for playing a bead game but not much as imaginative meaning. The Virgin is calm and distressed, torn and most whole, exhausted and life-giving, etc. To Blackmur, these ritualistic paradoxes inform "nearly the same theme" as "Tortoise Shout." Unless "Ash-Wednesday" takes all meaning as its province, I am at a loss to know what Blackmur thinks he means. He invites us to "examine the eighteen pages of the poems about tortoises" with him, but as he does not do any examining, we ought perhaps to read them for ourselves.

The Tortoise poems, a continuous sequence, communicate a homely and humorous, if despairing, love for the tortoise, in itself and as emblematic of man and all created nature involved in sexual division and strife. The Tortoise-Christ identifications have throughout them a grim unpretentious joy, which Blackmur, on defensive grounds, takes as hysteria.

"Baby Tortoise," the first poem, celebrates the infant creature as Ulyssean atom, invincible and indomitable. The best parallel is Whitman, in his praise of animals who do not whine about their condition. "No one ever heard you complain." The baby tortoise is a life-bearer, a Titan against the inertia of the lifeless. But he is a Titan circumscribed by a demiurge like Blake's Urizen; this is the burden of the next poem, "Tortoise Shell," which seems to me closer to Blake than anything else by Lawrence or by Yeats. Blake's Urizen, the Old Man of the Compasses, draws horizons (as his name and its derivation indicate). The Nobodaddy who made the Tortoise in its fallen condition circumscribes with the cross:

> The Cross, the Cross
> Goes deeper in than we know,
> Deeper into life;
> Right into the marrow
> And through the bone.

On the back of the baby tortoise Lawrence reads the terrible geometry of subjection to "the mystic mathematics of the city of heaven." Under all the eternal dome of mathematical law, the tortoise is subjected to natural bondage; he exhibits the long cleavage of division. An arbitrary division, a Urizenic patterning, has been made, and the tortoise must bear it eternally. Lawrence's earlier tone of celebration is necessarily modulated into a Blakean and humanistic bitterness:

> The Lord wrote it all down on the little slate
> Of the baby tortoise.
> Outward and visible indication of the plan within,
> The complex, manifold involvedness of an individual creature
> Plotted out.

Against this natural binding the tortoise opposes his stoic individuality, his slow intensity. In "Tortoise Family Connections" his more-than-human independence is established, both as against Christ:

> He does not even trouble to answer: "Woman, what have I to do with thee?"
> He wearily looks the other way.

and against Adam:

> To be a tortoise!
> Think of it, in a garden of inert clods
> A brisk, brindled little tortoise, all to himself—
> Adam!

The gentle homeliness that follows, in "Lui Et Elle" and "Tortoise Gallantry," is punctuated by a purely male bitterness, in preparation for the great and climactic poem of the series, "Tortoise Shout."

This last poem is central in romantic tradition, deriving ultimately as much from Wordsworth as from Whitman. Parallel to it is Melville's enigmatic and powerful "After The Pleasure Party":

> For, Nature, in no shallow surge
> Against thee either sex may urge,
> Why hast thou made us but in halves—
> Co-relatives? This makes us slaves.
> If these co-relatives never meet
> Self-hood itself seems incomplete.
> And such the dicing of blind fate

Few matching halves here meet and mate.
What Cosmic jest or Anarch blunder
The human integral clove asunder
And shied the fractions through life's gate?

Lawrence also is not concerned with asking the question for the answer's sake:

Why were we crucified into sex?
Why were we not left rounded off, and finished in ourselves,
As we began,
As he certainly began, so perfectly alone?

The subject of "Tortoise Shout" is initially the waking of the tortoise into the agony of a fall into sexual division, a waking into life as the heretofore silent creature screams faintly in its arousal. The scream may be just audible, or it may sound "on the plasm direct." In the single scream Lawrence places all cries that are "half music, half horror," in an instructive ordering. The cry of the newborn, the sound of the veil being rent, the "screaming in Pentecost, receiving the ghost." The ultimate identity, achieved in an empathy dependent upon Wordsworthian recollection, is between the tortoise cry in orgasm, and Christ's Passion on the Cross, the connecting reference being dependent upon the poem "Tortoise Shell."

The violence of expression here, obscene blasphemy to the orthodox, has its parallels in Nietzsche and in Yeats when they treat the Passion. Lawrence structures this deliberate violence quite carefully. First, a close account of the tortoise in coition, emphasizing the aspects of the act beyond the tortoise's single control. Then a startling catalogue (the form from Whitman, the mode from Wordsworth) of memories of boyhood and youth, before the major incantation assigned by Blackmur to the realm of the hysterical.

The passage of reminiscence works by positing a series of similitudes that are finally seen as a composite identity. The cries of trapped animals, of animals in passion, of animals wounded, animals newborn, are all resolved on the human plane as the infant's birth pang, the mother singing to herself, the young collier finding his mature voice. For all of these represent:

The first elements of foreign speech
On wild dark lips.

The voice of the solitary consciousness is in each case modified, usually by pain, into the speech of what is divided, of what is made to know its own separateness. Here, as in Wordsworth's great ode, the awareness of separateness is equated to the first intimations of mortality.

The last protesting cry of the male tortoise "at extremity" is "more than all these" in that it is more desperate, "less than all these" in that it is faintest. It is a cry of final defeat:

> Tiny from under the very edge of the farthest far-off horizon of
> life.

One sees why Lawrence has chosen the tortoise; the horizon of separateness-in-sexual-division could not be extended further and still be manageable in a poem of this kind. From this extreme Lawrence carries us to the other pole of human similtude, Christ or Osiris being divided, undergoing ultimate dismemberment:

> The cross,
> The wheel on which our silence first is broken,
> Sex, which breaks up our integrity, our single inviolability, our
> deep silence,
> Tearing a cry from us.
> Sex, which breaks us into voice, sets us calling across the deeps,
> calling, calling for the complement,
> Singing, and calling, and singing again, being answered, having
> found.
> Torn, to become whole again, after long seeking for what is lost,
> The same cry from the tortoise as from Christ, the Osiris-cry of
> abandonment,
> That which is whole, torn asunder,
> That which is in part, finding its whole again throughout the
> universe.

Much of the meaning in this is conveyed through rhythmical mastery; the scattering and reuniting of the self is incanted successively, now widening, now narrowing.

The cross here is the mechanical and mathematical body, the fallen residue of Blake's Human Form Divine. It is also the circumscribed tortoise body, as adumbrated in "Tortoise Shell." As such, the cross is a demonic image, symbolizing enforced division (into male and female, or in the self, or self kept from another self) and torture (tearing on the wheel, crucifixion). The tortoise, torn asunder in coming together, and perpetually caught in that cyclic paradox, utters the same cry as the perpetually sacrificed Osiris in his vegetative cycle. Christ's cry of forsakenness, to Lawrence, is one with these, as the divine nature is torn apart in the Passion. The sexual reduction in this last similitude is imaginatively unfortunate but as interpretation does not issue from Lawrence alone.

Blackmur, defending Eliot as a dogmatic critic and poet, has written that "conviction in the end is opinion and personality, which however greatly valuable cannot satisfy those who wrongly expect more." The remark is sound, but Blackmur has been inconsistent in its application.

Lawrence, as a romantic poet, was compelled by the conventions of his mode to present the conceptual aspect of his imagery as self-generated. I have borrowed most of this sentence from Frye's *Anatomy of Criticism*, where it refers to Blake, Shelley, Goethe, and Victor Hugo. What Frye calls a mode of literature, mythopoeia, is to Blackmur "that great race of English writers whose work totters precisely where it towers, collapses exactly in its strength: work written out of a tortured Protestant sensibility." We are back in a social dialectic external to criticism being applied to criticism. Writers who are Protestant, romantic, radical exemplify "the deracinated, unsupported imagination, the mind for which, since it lacked rational structure sufficient to its burdens, experience was too much." This dialectic is out of Hulme, Pound, and Eliot, and at last we are weary of it. Under its influence Blackmur has tried to salvage Wallace Stevens as a late Augustan, while Allen Tate has asserted that Yeats's romanticism will be invented by his critics. That the imagination needs support can perhaps be argued; that a structure properly conservative, classical, and Catholic enough is its necessary support is simply a social polemic and irrelevant to the criticism of poetry.

Lawrence himself, if we allow ourselves to quote him out of context, can be left to answer his judicious critic:

> What thing better are you, what worse?
> What have you to do with the mysteries
> Of this ancient place, of my ancient curse?
> What place have you in my histories?

Lawrence, whom the older Yeats so deeply and understandably admired, is in much of his poetry and many of his novels and polemical writings another prophet of irrationalism, but his central poems and novels are well within the most relevant aspects of the romantic tradition and make their own highly individual contribution to the romantic vision of a later reason. The insights of his finest novels, *The Rainbow* and *Women in Love,* are condensed in the relatively early and very Blakean "Under the Oak," while the blind vitalism and consequent irrationalism of the later novels like *Lady Chatterley's Lover* and *The Plumed Serpent* are compensated for by the sane and majestic death poems, like "Bavarian Gentians" and "Ship of Death," and particularly by the poem called "Shadows," which moves me as much as any verse of our century.

The speaker of "Under the Oak" is experiencing a moment of vision, a moment so intense and privileged that the whole natural context in which he stands becomes a confinement set against him, a covering that must be ripped asunder though his life run out with it. He speaks to the reader, the "you" of the poem, his rational, his too-rational companion underneath the sacrificial Tree of Mystery, and his impatience chastises our rationalizations and hesitations, our troubled refusal to yield ourselves to a moment of vision. Like Balder slain by the mistletoe, the poet is sacrificed to the chthonic forces and struggles against a Druidic adversary, as in Blake's tradition. We are excluded, unless we too can break the barrier of natural and rational confinement:

Above me springs the blood-born mistletoe
In the shady smoke.
But who are you, twittering to and fro
Beneath the oak?

What thing better are you, what worse?
What have you to do with the mysteries
Of this ancient place, of my ancient curse?
What place have you in my histories?

At the end, Lawrence felt the full strength of that ancient curse. The marvel of his death poems is that they raise the ancient blessing of the Romantic Later Reason against the curse, the triumph over it. So, in the sublime opening of "Shadows":

And if tonight my soul may find her peace
in sleep, and sink in good oblivion,
and in the morning wake like a new-opened flower
then I have been dipped again in God, and new created.

The poem turns on an imagistic contrast between the new-opened flowers of a still-unfolding consciousness and the lengthening and darkening shadows of mortality. The imagination's antagonist in the poem is not to be found in the actual shadows but in a reasonable conception of mortality, a conception that would make what Lawrence calls "good oblivion" impossible. In a related death poem, "The End, The Beginning," Lawrence writes:

If there were not an utter and absolute dark
of silence and sheer oblivion
at the core of everything,
how terrible the sun would be,
how ghastly it would be to strike a match, and make a light.

But the very sun himself is pivoted
upon a core of pure oblivion,
so is a candle, even as a match.

And if there were not an absolute, utter forgetting
and a ceasing to know, a perfect ceasing to know
and a silent, sheer cessation of all awareness
how terrible life would be!
how terrible it would be to think and know, to have
consciousness!

But dipped, once dipped in dark oblivion
the soul has peace, inward and lovely peace.

Renewal depends on the expunging of self-consciousness, as much as it did in "Resolution and Independence." Lawrence's death poem, "Shadows," is finally a hymn of renovation, of the privileged moments becoming "a new morning."

T.S. Eliot

One can fight a long war against T.S. Eliot's criticism and still confess a lifelong fascination with his best poems: *The Waste Land* and a group that certainly includes "The Love Song of J. Alfred Prufrock," "La Figlia Che Piange," "The Hollow Men," and "The Journey of the Magi." Probably one could add "Gerontion" and "Little Gidding" to any short list of Eliot's most lasting poetry, but these five poems can be called his essential achievement in verse.

The perpetual freshness of "Prufrock" is a surprise each time I return to the poem. Actually, reading "Prufrock" (preferably out loud to oneself) is never quite the experience I expect it to be. Christopher Ricks charmingly demonstrates the incongruity of "Love Song" and the outrageous name J. Alfred Prufrock, and yet this dramatic monologue remains something of a defeated erotic reverie. In his very useful *Inventions of the March Hare* (1996), Ricks gives us a richly annotated version of Eliot's poems of 1909–1917 and includes an unpublished passage of the "Love Song." The missing middle, "Prufrock's Pervigilium," plays in its title on the Latin poem "Pervigilium

Veneris" (fourth century CE), the "Eve of Venus," which had a great vogue in the era of the splendid critic Walter Pater. Eliot had nothing good to say of Pater, probably because his own sensibility was essentially Paterian, but Prufrock seems to have read Pater's historical novel, *Marius the Epicurean*. Pater, the prophet of the Aesthetic movement in England, exalted perception and sensation and deprecated dogmatic belief of any sort. *Marius the Epicurean* has a memorable scene in which the authorship of the "Pervigilium" is ascribed to Marius's dying friend, Flavian. Ricks shrewdly notes Pater's hint that Flavian's illness is venereal, and something otherwise obscure in Prufrock's dramatic monologue is illuminated when we intuit that J. Alfred's erotic timidity is allied to his obsessive fear of venereal infection.

The "Love Song" is a perpetual "dying fall," its "hundred indecisions" a series of erotic evasions. Brooding on the arms of women, which have for him an overwhelming sexual power, Prufrock will never bring any of his incipient relationships to the moment of crisis. His poem continues to pulsate with a barely repressed energy and may be the most remarkable instance in the language of a deferred eroticism transfiguring itself into a sublime eloquence.

Even as a boy, I fell in love with "La Figlia Che Piange," which remains one of Eliot's incantory triumphs and the poem he chose to conclude the volume *Prufrock and Other Observations* (1917). Eliot's weeping girl is far more intense than the alluring women of the "Love Song," but the chanter of "La Figlia" is very like Prufrock: another obsessed evader of the sexual experience. Nearly 60 years of reciting the lyric to myself have only enhanced its aura for me; few poems in the language so evoke erotic longing, the sense of an unrealized relationship.

And yet the voice of this lyric is in one respect not Prufrockian; its imaginative sympathy adheres to the weeping girl and hardly at all to her departing lover. Something very like a Paterian privileged moment, or secularized epiphany, is being celebrated, even as the voice retreats into detachment, the autumn weather of the soul. The Paterian flesh of radiance against a darkening background is the sunlight woven in the girl's hair. Eliot, notoriously unsympathetic to John Milton's poetry, vies with Milton as the poet in English most celebratory of the erotic glory of a woman's hair.

Despite himself, Eliot always remained a high romantic lyric poet, with profound affinities to Shelley (whom he professed to dislike) and Tennyson (to whom he condescended). Any vision of romantic love poetry would be impoverished if it excluded "La Figlia Che Piange."

The Waste Land, though something less than a unified poem, is Eliot's masterwork, by common agreement. Where few agree is on the question as to just what *The Waste Land* is doing, as a poetic performance. Is it a lament for Western cultural decline, for a Europe in retreat from Christianity? Or is it a very American elegy for the self, in direct descent from Walt Whitman's magnificent "When Lilacs Last in the Dooryard Bloom'd." Clearly the second, I would insist, though mine remains a minority view.

Eliot's own "Notes" to *The Waste Land* are frequently outrageous, never more so than when they explicate the song of the hermit-thrush by remarking, "Its 'water-dripping song' is justly celebrated." Why yes, particularly when the hermit thrush sings its song of death in Whitman's "Lilacs" elegy. Ostensibly mourning the martyred Lincoln, "Lilacs" more pervasively both celebrates and laments the Whitmanian poetic self. Eliot's poethood, and not Western civilization, is the elegiac center of *The Waste Land*. Personal breakdown is the poem's true subject, shrewdly masked as the decline and fall of Christian culture in post–World War I Europe.

Such a judgment, on my part, hardly renders *The Waste Land* a less interesting or aesthetically eminent poem (or series of poems, or fragments). Hardly an escape from either emotion or from personality, *The Waste Land*, three-quarters of a century after its publication, seems a monument to the emotional despair of a highly individual romantic personality, one in full continuity with Shelley, Tennyson, and Whitman, who are far closer to the poem than are Eliot's chosen precursors: Dante, Baudelaire, Jules Laforgue.

Northrop Frye followed Eliot himself in reading *The Waste Land* as a poem of Christian redemption. I think that Eleanor Cook is more accurate in her subtle emphasis on the poem as a representation of exile and of private grief. No one is saved in *The Waste Land*, any more than Lincoln or Whitman is saved in "When Lilacs Last in the Dooryard Bloom'd." Both grand elegies for the self are American songs of death, including the death-in-life of poetic crisis.

"The Hollow Men" (1925) is the culmination of early (and major) Eliot, a grim and permanent achievement, indeed a parodic masterpiece. Though the chant is overtly Dantesque, I hear in it Shakespeare's Brutus of *Julius Caesar*, a drama replete with "hollow" Roman patriots, who protest their endless sincerity, only to be subtly exposed by the playwright. Brutus, no Hamlet, but dominated by a Macbeth-like proleptic imagination, kills himself, still blind to his own hollowness. Eliot, who perhaps unconsciously was more affected by *Julius Caesar* than his beloved *Coriolanus*, parodies saints as well as "patriots." The power of "The Hollow Men" is its universality. Though some critics interpret the poem as a portrait of a world without belief, waiting for the return of Christian revelation, scarecrows hardly seem candidates for any redemption. Eliot himself was moving toward conversion (two years later, in 1927), but nothing in "The Hollow Men" intimates that such movement is possible.

Eliot's poetry of belief—in "Ash Wednesday," "The Rock," and *Four Quartets*—seems to me considerably less persuasive than his visions of the waste land. "The Journey of the Magi" is Eliot's most effective "religious" poem because its speaker dramatizes the poignance of exile, always Eliot's true mode. The Magus speaks for Eliot the poet and not for Eliot the Anglo-Catholic. Like Tennyson, whom Eliot had praised for the quality of his doubt, the Magus stands between two worlds, never to be at home in either. At his best, the poet Eliot remained dispersed.

Wilfred Owen

Killed in action at twenty-five, the age when tuberculosis ended his precursor, John Keats, Owen nevertheless established himself as a major poet. Owen's best work would include "Insensibility," "Greater Love," "Arms and the Boy," and the early, very Keatsian "From My Diary, July 1914." Other critics might choose additional poems, with reason, since Owen's poignance and eloquence are unceasing. Though William Butler Yeats was a considerable influence on Owen, the great Anglo-Irish poet manifested a singular blindness toward Owen's work. Omitting Owen from *The Oxford Book of Modern Verse*, Yeats defended his decision by calling Owen "unworthy of the poet's corner of a country newspaper" because "he is all blood, dirt, and sucked sugar stick." That is mere abuse, but Yeats's more formal explanation is still a shocker:

> . . . passive suffering is not a theme for poetry. In all the great tragedies, tragedy is a joy to the man who dies. . . . If war is necessary in our time and place, it is best to forget its suffering as we do the discomfort of fever . . .

In the foreword to his anthology, *War Poems* (1999), John Hollander observes rather that war poetry represents a "tremendously varied response to an age-old human theme." For Wilfred Owen, the poetry was in the pity, distinctly not a Yeatsian attitude. I wonder though if a complex irony, rather than pity, is not Owen's true mode:

> I went hunting wild
> After the wildest beauty in the world,
> Which lies not calm in eyes, or braided hair,
> But mocks the steady running of the hour,
> And if it grieves, grieves richlier than here.
>
> For his teeth seem for laughing round an apple.
> There lurk no claws behind his fingers supple;

> And God will grow no talons at his heels,
> Nor antlers through the thickness of his curls.
>
> Friend, be very sure
> I shall be better off with plants that share
> More peaceably the meadow and the shower.
> Soft rains will touch me,—as they could touch once,
> And nothing but the sun shall make me ware.

Perhaps a fatal irony is the essence of war poetry. Simonides (556–468 BCE) achieves ironic perfection in his elegy for the Spartan heroes:

> Go tell the Spartans, thou that passest by
> That here obedient to their laws we lie.
> (Translated by W. L. Bowles)

W.H. Auden

> Attacking bad books is not only a waste of time but also bad for the character.
>
> —Auden
>
> While an author is yet living we estimate his powers by his worst performance, and when he is dead we rate them by his best.
>
> —Johnson

Secondary Worlds is a bad book and Auden's worst performance. These four lectures in memory of T.S. Eliot deal in turn with *Thomas Cranmer*, a pious verse drama by Charles Williams; Icelandic sagas; the three opera libretti by Auden and Chester Kallman; and the relation between Christian belief and the writing of poetry. Since the title, *Secondary Worlds*, refers to works of art as against "the primary world of our everyday social experience," the rationale for printing these four talks as a book must be their linked relevance to what has long been Auden's overt polemic against the romantic view of poetry. Coleridge's ill-chosen terms, primary and secondary imagination, are here subverted by Auden's wit, since by secondary, Auden, unlike Coleridge, does mean "inferior."

Of all Auden's writings, *Secondary Worlds* comes most directly out of the neo-Christian matrix of modern Anglo-Catholic letters: Eliot, Williams, C.S. Lewis, Tolkien. I search in vain only for references to Dorothy Sayers. Auden compensates with a quotation from *The Future of Belief*, by Leslie Dewart, a book one might not otherwise know:

> The Christian God is not *both* transcendent and immanent. He is a reality other than being Who is present to being, by which presence He makes being to be.

"To believe this," Auden modestly says, "is to call into question the art of poetry and all the arts." In *The Dyer's Hand*, an admirable performance, Auden remarked that "the imagination is a natural human faculty and therefore retains the same character whatever a man believes." In his new book, the imagination of a humane man of letters and talented comic poet appears to be hardening, which would be a loss.

Johnson definitively stated the difficulties of devotional verse when he observed that the good and evil of eternity were too ponderous for the wings of wit. The mind sinks under them and must be content with calm belief and humble adoration, attitudes admirable in themselves but perhaps not conducive to the writing of poems. One of Auden's many virtues is that, unlike Eliot and other literary Christians, he has spared us and mostly refrained from devotional verse. *For the Time Being*, a work dear to many churchwardenly critics, is a long and unhappy exception, but even it, unlike much Eliot, does not offer us the disciplined humility of the poet as our aesthetic experience.

It is of course one thing to deprecate the possibility of Christian poetry, or of poetry being Christian, and quite another to deprecate poetry itself, all poetry. In Auden's criticism, and particularly *Secondary Worlds*, the two are not always kept apart. When this happens, I find it is bad for my character. On a higher level, the experience of reading Auden then becomes rather like reading Kilmer's *Trees*. "Poems are made by fools like me," yes, and by Dante, Milton, Blake, and Homer, but only God makes primary worlds. Or, as Auden says:

> it is possible that artists may become both more modest and more self-assured, that they may develop both a sense of humour about their vocation and a respect for that most admirable of Roman deities, the god *Terminus*. No poet will then produce the kind of work which demands that a reader spend his whole life reading it and nothing else. The claim to be a "genius" will become as strange as it would have seemed to the Middle Ages.

It is possible that other artists may become more like Auden. It is likelier that other critics may become more like him for, with Arnold and Eliot, he is a poet-critic who appeals greatly to critics, little as the splendor of becoming a "poet of professors" appeals to him. Books about Auden all tend to be fairly good, just as books about, say Wallace Stevens, tend to be quite bad. This is probably not because admirers of Stevens love him less well than the lovers of Auden, but because more genuinely difficult poets do not reduce to structures of ideas and images so readily as Auden does.

Auden's poetry now maintains a general esteem among academic critics. If one's judgment of Auden's poetry is more eccentric, one needs to take up the sad burden of literary dissent. Auden has been accepted as not only a great poet but also a Christian humanist sage not because of any conspiracy among moralizing neo-Christian academicians, but because the age requires such a figure. Eliot is gone, and Auden now occupies his place, though with a difference. The difference is refreshing; Auden is wittier, gentler, much less dogmatic, and does not feel compelled to demonstrate the authenticity of his Christian humanism by a judicious anti-Semitism. He has more wisdom and more humor than Eliot, and his talent is nowhere near so sparse, as the enormous range of his lyrics shows. I think it unfortunate that he should find himself in apostolic succession to Eliot, but *Secondary Worlds* seems to indicate that the succession is not unwelcome to him.

Much of *The Dyer's Hand*, despite its generosity as criticism, is darkened by Auden's obsessive doubts about the value of art in the context of Christianity. Similar doubts have maimed many writers, Tolstoy and Hopkins in particular. Insofar as Auden's uneasiness has prevented him from devotional poetry, he has gained by it, but unfortunately the effect on him has been larger and has resulted in a trivialization of his art. As a songwriter he remains supreme, being certainly the best in English in the century, but as a reflective poet he suffers from the continual evanescence of his subject matter. As a satirist, he may have been aided, yet the staple of his poetry is neither song nor satire but rumination on the good life, and his notion of the relation between Christianity and art has troubled that rumination. Auden is one of the massive modern sufferers from the malady of poetic influence, a variety of melancholy or anxiety principle that our studies have evaded. Poetic influence, in this sense, has little to do with the transmission of ideas and images from an earlier poet to a later one. Rather, it concerns the poet's sense of his precursors and of his own achievement in relation to theirs. Have they left him room enough, or has their priority cost him his art? More crucially, where did they go wrong, so as to make it possible for him to go right? In this revisionary sense, in which the poet creates his own precursors by necessarily misinterpreting them, poetic influence forms and malforms new poets and aids their art at the cost of increasing, finally, their already acute sense of isolation. Auden, like Byron, gives the continual impression of personal sincerity in his poetry, but again like Byron this sincerity is the consequence of a revisionary swerve away from the sincerity of the precursor. In Byron's case of poetic influence, the great precursor was Pope, with his highly dialectical sincerity; with Auden the prime precursor is Hardy, and the poetic son's sincerity is considerably more dialectical than the father's.

Auden, in his very fine *New Year Letter* (January 1, 1940, at the height of his poetic power), wrote an important poem about poetic influence. His precursors are invoked there as a summary tribunal sitting in perpetual session:

> Though
> Considerate and mild and low
> The voices of the questioners,
> Although they delegate to us
> Both prosecution and defence,
> Accept our rules of evidence
> And pass no sentence but our own,
> Yet, as he faces them alone,
> O who can show convincing proof
> That he is worthy of their love?

He names these fathers and judges: Dante, Blake, Rimbaud, Dryden, Catullus, Tennyson, Baudelaire, Hardy, and Rilke, connecting this somewhat miscellaneous ninefold (except for Dryden, there for his mastery of the middle style) by their common sense of isolation, fit companions "to one unsocial English boy." Of all these, Auden's most characteristic poetry is closest to Hardy's, not merely in its beginnings, and like Hardy, Auden remains most convincing as a ruminator upon human incongruities, upon everything valuable that somehow will not fit together. Auden's best poems, such as the justly esteemed "In Praise of Limestone," brood on incongruities, swerving from Hardy's kind of poem into a more double-natured sense of ruinous circumstance and thwarted love, yet retaining their family resemblance to Hardy. But where Hardy's strenuous unbelief led him to no worse redundancies than an occasional sharp striving after too palpable an irony, Auden's self-conscious belief and attendant doubt of poetry mar even "In Praise of Limestone" with the redundancy of uneasy and misplaced wit:

> But if
> Sins can be forgiven, if bodies rise from the dead,
> These modifications of matter into
> Innocent athletes and gesticulating fountains,
> Made solely for pleasure, make a further point;
> The blessed will not care what angle they are regarded from,
> Having nothing to hide,

The blessed, as Auden says so often in prose, need neither to read nor to write poems, and poems do not describe their sanctity with much success, as Auden also sadly notes, contemplating the verse of Charles Williams. Close thy Auden, open thy Stevens, and read:

> If, then, when we speak of liberation, we mean an exodus; if when we speak of justification, we mean a kind of justice of which we had not known and on which we had not counted; if when we experience a sense of purification, we can think of the establishing of a self, it is certain that the experience of the poet is of no less a degree than the experience of the mystic and we may be certain that in the case of poets, the peers of saints,t hose experiences are of no less a degree than the experiences of the saints themselves. It is a question of the nature of the experience. It is not a question of identifying or relating dissimilar figures; that is to say, it is not a question of making saints out of poets or poets out of saints.

Seamus Heaney

At thirty-nine, Wallace Stevens wrote "Le Monocle de Mon Oncle"; at about the same age, Yeats wrote "Adam's Curse." Texts of the fortieth year form a remarkable grouping; I can think immediately of Browning's "Childe Roland" and Poe's "Eureka," and I invite every reader to add more (Whitman's "Out of the Cradle" and "As I Ebb'd" suddenly come to mind, but there are many others). I would not say that the Northern Irish poet Seamus Heaney, at forty, has printed any single poem necessarily as fine as "Adam's Curse," but the lyric called "The Harvest Bow" in *Field Work* may yet seem that strong, against all of time's revenges. There are other poems in *Field Work* worthy of comparison to the Yeats of *In the Seven Woods* (1904), and it begins to seem not far-fetched to wonder how remarkable a poet Heaney may yet become, if he can continue the steady growth of an art as deliberate, as restrained, and yet as authoritative and universal as the poems of *Field Work*—his fifth and much his best volume in the years since his first book, *Death of a Naturalist* (1966).

That book, praised for its countryman's veracity and vividness of soil sense, reads in retrospect as a kind of dark hymn of poetic incarnation, a somber record of the transgression of having been a Clare-like changeling. Heaney's first poems hold implicit his central trope, *the vowel of earth*, and move in a cycle between the guilt of having forsaken spade for pen and the redemption of poetic work: "I rhyme. To see myself, to set the darkness echoing." *Door into the Dark* (1969) seems now, as it did to me a decade ago, mostly a repetition, albeit in a finer tone, and I remember putting the book aside with the sad reflection that Heaney was fixated in a rugged but minimalist lyrical art. I was mistaken and should have read more carefully the book's last poem, "Bogland," where Heaney began to open both to the Irish and to his own abyss. Reading backward from *Field Work* (and the two other, intervening books), I am taught now by the poet how he passed from description to a visionary negation:

> Our pioneers keep striking
> Inwards and downwards,
>
> Every layer they strip
> Seems camped on before.
> The bogholes might be Atlantic seepage.
> The wet centre is bottomless.

Such a center indeed could not hold, and Heaney was poised on the verge of becoming a poet of the Northern Irish Troubles, a role he now wisely seeks to evade, but in a morally rich sense of "evade," as I will try to show later. *Wintering Out* (1972) seems stronger than it did seven years ago, when it began to change my mind about Heaney's importance. It is a book about nearing the journey's center and takes as its concern the poet's severe questioning of his own language, the English at once his own and not his own, since Heaney is of the Catholic Irish of Derry. Few books of poems brood so hard on names or touch so overtly on particular words as words. No single poem stands out, even upon rereading, for this is the last volume of Heaney's careful apprenticeship as he works toward his deferred glory. *North* (1975) begins that glory, a vital achievement by any standards, perhaps a touch dimmed for American critics by the accident of its appearance so close to Geoffrey Hill's *Somewhere Is Such a Kingdom*, which gathered, for American readers, Hill's first three volumes. But the power of *North* is that four years of reading have enhanced it, while *Field Work* seems to me the only recent British book of poems worthy of sustained comparison to the magnificence of Hill's *Tenebrae*, published in 1978.

Heaney's first three books sparred gently with local and contemporary precursors; the alert reader could find the colors and flavors of Kavanagh and Montague, of Ted Hughes and R.S. Thomas. Like the deliberate touches of the late Robert Lowell, in *Field Work* these are all "screen-memories," of interest only as tactical blinds. What emerges in *North* and stands clear in *Field Work* is the precursor proper, the middle Yeats, with whom the agon of the strong Irish poet must be fought, as much by Heaney in his maturity as it is by Kinsella, with the agon itself guaranteeing why Heaney and Kinsella are likely to become more memorable than Kavanagh and Clarke, among the Irish poets following Yeats.

I hear behind the poems of *North* the middle Yeats of *The Green Helmet* and of *Responsibilities*, a hearing reinforced by *Field Work*. This is the Yeats of a vision counting still its human cost and so not yet abandoned to daemonic presences and intensities:

> I passed through the eye of the quern,
>
> Grist to an ancient mill,
> And in my mind's eye saw
> A world-tree of balanced stones,
> Querns piled like vertebrae,
> The marrow crushed to grounds.

That is Heaney's "Belderg" from *North*, but I do not think Yeats would have disowned it. The enduring poems in *North* include the majestic title piece, as well as "Funeral Rites," "Kinship," "Whatever You Say Say Nothing," and, best of all, the sequence of poetic incarnation with the Yeatsian title, "Singing School." The poem "North" gave and still gives Heaney his poetics, as a mythic voice proclaims what must be this new poet's relation to the Irish past:

> It said, 'Lie down
> in the word-hoard, burrow
> the coil and gleam
> of your furrowed brain.
>
> Compose in darkness.
> Expect aurora borealis
> in the long foray
> but no cascade of light.
>
> Keep your eye clear
> as the bleb of the icicle,
> trust the feel of what nubbed treasure
> your hands have known.'

The reader of *Field Work* comes to realize that Heaney's eye is as clear, through discipline, as the air bubble in an icicle, as clear, say, as the American eye of the late Elizabeth Bishop. "Funeral Rites" inaugurates what seems doomed to be Heaney's central mode, whether he finally chooses Dublin or Belfast. "Kinship," a more difficult sequence, salutes the bog country as the "outback of my mind" and then flows into a grander trope:

> This is the vowel of earth
> dreaming its root
> in flowers and snow,
>
> mutation of weathers
> and seasons,
> a windfall composing the floor it rots into.
> I grew out of all this
>
> like a weeping willow
> inclined to
> the appetites of gravity.

Such inevitability of utterance would be more than enough if it were merely personal; it would suffice. Its grandeur is augmented in the last section of "Kinship" when Heaney acquires the authentic authority of becoming the voice of his people:

> Come back to this
> 'island of the ocean'
> where nothing will suffice.
> Read the inhumed faces
>
> of casualty and victim;
> report us fairly,
> how we slaughter
> for the common good
>
> and shave the heads
> of the notorious,
> how the goddess swallows
> our love and terror.

The problem for Heaney as a poet henceforward is how not to drown in this blood-dimmed tide. His great precedent is the Yeats of "Meditations in Time of Civil War" and "Nineteen Hundred and Nineteen," and it cannot be said in *North* that this precedent is met, even in "Whatever You Say Say Nothing," where the exuberance of the language achieves a genuine phantasmagoria. But "Singing School," with its queerly appropriate mix of Wordsworth and Yeats, does even better, ending poem and book with a finely rueful self-accepting portrait of the poet, still waiting for the word that is his alone:

> I am neither internee nor informer;
> An inner émigré, grown long-haired
> And thoughtful; a wood-kerne
>
> Escaped from the massacre,
> Taking protective colouring
> From bole and bark, feeling
> Every wind that blows;
>
> Who, blowing up these sparks
> For their meagre heat, have missed
> The once-in-a-lifetime portent,
> The comet's pulsing rose.

That is true eloquence but fortunately not the whole truth, as *Field Work* richly shows. Heaney is the poet of the vowel of earth and not of any portentous comet. In *Field Work*, he has gone south, away from the Belfast violence, heeding the admonition that Emerson addressed to himself in the bad year 1846, when the American slaveholders made war against Mexico:

> Though loath to grieve
> The evil time's sole patriot,
> I cannot leave
> My honied thought
> For the priest's cant,
> Or statesman's rant.
>
> If I refuse
> My study for their politique,
> Which at the best is trick,
> The angry Muse
> Puts confusion in my brain.

Like Emerson, Heaney has learned that he has imprisoned thoughts of his own that only he can set free. No poem in *Field Work* is without its clear distinction, but I exercise here the critic's privilege of discussing those poems that move me most: "Casualty," "The Badgers," "The Singer's House," the lovely sequence of ten "Glanmore Sonnets," "The Harvest Bow" (Heaney's masterpiece so far), and the beautiful elegy "In Memoriam Francis Ledwidge," for the Irish poet killed on the western front in 1917. All of these lyrics and meditations practice a rich negation, an art of excluded meanings, vowels of earth almost lost between guttural consonants of history. Heaney's Irish sibyl warns him that "The ground we kept our ear to for so long / Is flayed or calloused." The muted elegy "Casualty," which cunningly blends the modes of Yeats's "The Fisherman" and "Easter 1916," concludes in a funeral march giving us the sea's version of Heaney's vowel of earth:

> They move in equal pace
> With the habitual
> Slow consolation
> of a dawdling engine,
> The line lifted, hand
> Over fist, cold sunshine
> On the water, the land
> Banked under fog: that morning
> I was taken in his boat,
> The screw purling, turning
> Indolent fathoms white,
> I tasted freedom with him.
> To get out early, haul
> Steadily off the bottom,
> Dispraise the catch, and smile
> As you find a rhythm
> Working you, slow mile by mile,
> Into your proper haunt
> Somewhere, well out, beyond . . .

Even as the slain fisherman's transcendence fuses with Heaney's catch of a poem to send the poet also "beyond," so Heaney has revised Yeats's ambition by having written an elegy as passionate as the perpetual night of the Troubles. Even stronger is "The Badgers," an oblique poem of deepest self-questioning, in which the elegiac strain is evaded and all simple meanings are thwarted. Sensing "some soft returning," whether of the murdered dead or of the badgers, Heaney places upon his reader the burden of difficult interpretation:

> Visitations are taken for signs.
> At a second house I listened

> for duntings under the laurels
> and heard intimations whispered
> about being vaguely honoured.

The first line of this passage does not reach back to Lancelot Andrewes through Eliot's "Gerontion" but rather itself boldly revises John 4:48, "Except ye see signs and wonders, ye will not believe" and perhaps even Matthew 12:38–39, "An evil and adulterous generation seeketh after a sign." The duntings are at once the dull sounds of badgers and, more crucially, the Wordsworthian "low breathings" of *The Prelude* 1,323. Though an external haunting, testifying to the laurels of poetic election "vaguely honoured," they are also Heaney's hard-drawn breaths, in this text and out of it, in a murderous Northern Ireland. Heaney, once so ruggedly simplistic in his only apparent stance, has entered upon the agonistic way of a stronger poetry, necessarily denser, more allusive, and persuasively difficult.

I read this entrance as the triumph of "The Singer's House," a poem I will forebear quoting entire, though I badly want to, and give only the superb three stanzas of the conclusion, where Heaney laments the loss of everything in his land that should be "crystal" and discovers an inevitable image for his audacious and determined art that would reverse lament and loss:

> People here used to believe
> that drowned souls lived in the seals.
> At spring tides they might change shape.
> They loved music and swam in for a singer
>
> who might stand at the end of summer
> in the mouth of a whitewashed turf-shed,
> his shoulder to the jamb, his song
> a rowboat far out in evening.
>
> When I came here first you were always singing,
> a hint of the clip of the pick
> in your winnowing climb and attack.
> Raise it again, man. We still believe what we hear.

The verve of that final line is a tonic even for an American reader like myself, cut off from everything local that inspires and appalls Heaney. Closer to ordinary evenings in New Haven are the universal concerns that rise out of the local in the distinguished "Glanmore Sonnets" that open, again, with Heaney's central trope: "Vowels ploughed into other: opened ground."

Confronting an image of the good life as field work, with art redeemed from violence and so "a paradigm" of new-ploughed earth, Heaney finds even in the first sonnet that his ghosts come striding back. Against the ghosts he seeks to set his own story as a poet who could heed Moneta's admonition to Keats, or Nietzsche's to all of us: "Think of the earth."

> Then I landed in the hedge-school of Glanmore
> And from the backs of ditches hoped to raise
> A voice caught back off slug-horn and slow chanter
> That might continue, hold, dispel, appease:
> Vowels ploughed into other, opened ground,
> Each verse returning like the plough turned round.

Yet the ninth sonnet is driven to ask with true desperation: "What is my apology for poetry?" and the superb tenth sonnet ends the sequence overtly echoing Wyatt's most passionate moment, while more darkly and repressively alluding to the Yeatsian insight of the perpetual virginity of the soul: "the lovely and painful / Covenants of flesh; our separateness." More hopeful, but with a qualified hope, is the perfect lyric "The Harvest Bow," which I quote in its entirety:

> As you plaited the harvest bow
> You implicated the mellowed silence in you
> In wheat that does not rust
> But brightens as it tightens twist by twist
> Into a knowable corona,
> A throwaway love-knot of straw.
>
> Hands that aged round ashplants and cane sticks
> And lapped the spurs on a lifetime of game cocks
> Harked to their gift and worked with fine intent
> Until your fingers moved somnambulant:
> I tell and finger it like braille,
> Gleaning the unsaid off the palpable,
>
> And if I spy into its golden loops
> I see us walk between the railway slopes
> Into an evening of long grass and midges,
> Blue smoke straight up, old beds and ploughs in hedges,
> An auction notice on an outhouse wall—
> You with a harvest bow in your lapel,

Me with the fishing rod, already homesick
For the big lift of these evenings, as your stick
Whacking the tips off weeds and bushes
Beats out of time, and beats, but flushes
Nothing: that original townland
Still tongue-tied in the straw tied by your hand.

The end of art is peace
Could be the motto of this frail device
That I have pinned up on our deal dresser
Like a drawn snare
Slipped lately by the spirit of the corn
Yet burnished by its passage, and still warm.

Heaney could not have found a more wistful, Clare-like emblem than the love knot of straw for this precariously beautiful poem, or a sadder, gentler motto than: "*The end of art is peace.*" Certainly the oversong of the poem, its stance as love lyric, seems to sing against Yeats's Paterian ringers in the tower, who have appointed for the hymeneal of the soul a passing bell. But the end of married love may be peace; the end of art is agonistic, against time's "it was" and so against anterior art.

The hands that plait the harvest bow are masculine and hardened, but delicate in the office of marriage, which brings in harvest. Implicated in the making is the knowable corona of mellowed silence, not the unreliable knowledge of poetry; and Heaney as poet must both love and stand back and away from this wisdom, paternal and maternal. The fingers that follow a human tradition can move as if moving in sleep—"asleep in its own life," as Stevens said of the child. But Heaney must "tell and finger it like braille," for that is the poet's field of work: "Gleaning the unsaid off the palpable," the slender pickings after the granary is full.

Though his vision, *through her emblem*, in the third stanza approximates a true peace, it breaks into something both richer and more forlorn in what comes after. The young Yeats sang of "The Happy Townland," where "Boughs have their fruit and blossom / At all times of the year" and "all that are killed in battle / Awaken to life again." Heaney, leaving youth, hears in recollections of innocent venery a music that "Beats out of time, and beats, but flushes / Nothing." There is nothing for it to start up since the happy or original townland belongs only to those "still tongue-tied" in the frail device of the harvest bow. Heaney's genius is never surer than in his all but undoing of this emblem in his final trope, where the love knot becomes a drawn snare recently evaded by the corn king, an evasion that itself both burnishes and animates the knowable corona of achieved marriage. Obliquely but firmly, the struggle of poetry displaces the lover's stance, and the undersong finds a triumph in the poem's closure.

I verge on saying that Heaney approaches the cunning stance of the strong poet, evasion for which I cite not its American theorists and bards, from Emerson through Whitman and Dickinson to Frost and Stevens, but the central British master of the mode:

> Know ye not then the Riddling of the Bards?
> Confusion, and illusion, and relation,
> Elusion, and occasion, and evasion?

That is Tennyson's Seer, not Emerson's Merlin, and must become Heaney's poetic, if like Yeats he is to transcend the vowel of earth. It will be a painful transition for a poet whose heart is with the visionary naturalism of Wordsworth and Keats and Clare (and Kavanagh, Montague, R.S. Thomas) rather than with a vision fighting free of earth. But there are signs in *Field Work* that the transition is under way. Heaney ends the book with a grim rendition of Dante's Ugolino, too relevant to the Irish moment, and with his not altogether successful title poem, which invokes the Gnostic doubloon of Melville's Ahab. I end here by reading in the noble quatrains of Heaney's "In Memoriam Francis Ledwidge" a powerful evasion of a fate that this poet will never accept as his own:

> In you, our dead enigma, all the strains
> Criss-cross in useless equilibrium
> And as the wind tunes through this vigilant bronze
> I hear again the sure confusing drum
>
> You followed from Boyne water to the Balkans
> But miss the twilit note your flute should sound.
> You were not keyed or pitched like these true-blue ones
> Though all of you consort now underground.

Not my way to go, as Heaney tells us, for he is keyed and pitched unlike any other significant poet now at work in the language, anywhere. The strains crisscross in him in so useful an equilibrium that all critics and lovers of poetry must wish him every cunning for survival. To this critic, on the other side of the Atlantic, Heaney is joined now with Geoffrey Hill as a poet so severe and urgent that he compels the same attention as his strongest American contemporaries and indeed as only the very strongest among them.

DOMINIC HIBBERD

Wilfred Owen
The Pity of War

In the early months of 1918 Owen decided on the subject of his poetry, stating it in his Preface in the spring as 'War, and the pity of war'. In settling on the subject of 'pity' he was returning to the beliefs of the Romantics, although he was no doubt also influenced by Hardy and the new direction in Sassoon's work. His 1918 poetry has a resonance of feeling, language and ideas which comes from his knowledge of the Romantic poets; whereas his pleasure in being 'held peer by the Georgians' at the end of 1917 soon ceased to represent an ambition to write in an exclusively Georgian way, his allegiance to his first masters had never faltered. His thoughts about the subject and function of his poetry in 1918 are reflected in his plans for publishing a book; the fragmentary Preface and two lists of contents which he drafted in the spring can be seen as a commentary on the poems he was writing at the time.

There was little fighting on the Western Front between mid December and mid March, so that he began to feel more optimistic about his future, even starting to buy furniture for use after the war. His months in Scarborough were busy and sociable. But in February things looked 'stupefyingly catastrophic on the Eastern Front' as Russia collapsed and Germany began to assemble her forces for a final attack in the west. On 12 March Owen was posted to a training-camp at Ripon, one tiny movement in the Army's efforts to gather

---

reinforcements. 'An awful Camp—huts—dirty blankets—in fact WAR once more. Farewell Books, Sonnets, Letters, friends, fires, oysters, antique-shops.' Nine days later the German offensive opened, throwing the British line into desperate retreat. As in 1914, national opinion rallied behind the war effort, leaving only the most dedicated pacifists still demanding peace negotiations. By the end of March Owen was 'trying to get fit', 'Permanent Home Service' having ceased to be either possible or desirable. His writing-career might have ended here, had camp routine been less generous in its allowance of free time, but on the 23rd he found a room in a cottage in Borrage Lane which he was able to rent for use during his long free evenings. Almost all his finest poems (except 'Spring Offensive') and his plans for a book seem to have been composed or revised in this secret 'workshop'. He reported on the 31st:

> Outside my cottage-window children play soldiers so piercingly that I've moved up into the attic, with only a skylight. It is a jolly Retreat. There I have tea and contemplate the inwardness of war, and behave in an owlish manner generally.

Fine spring weather, secrecy and an attic room being the ideal conditions for his poetry to grow, 1918 brought the last and by far the most fruitful of the creative springs of his poethood.[1]

Despite his lightness of tone, that 'owlish' process of contemplating 'the inwardness of war' was a strict, intensely serious discipline, learned, one may guess, from Wordsworth's account of composing from 'emotion recollected in tranquillity'. Owen was 'haunted by the vision of the lands about St Quentin crawling with wounded', the very ground he had advanced over in 1917. 'They are dying again at Beaumont Hamel, which already in 1916 was cobbled with skulls.' Meanwhile the children played soldiers and 'all the Lesser Celandines opened out together' in the lane '(my Lane)'. It was now that Owen earned Murry's later description of him as 'not a poet who seized upon the opportunity of war, but one whose being was saturated by a strange experience, who bowed himself to the horror of war until his soul was penetrated by it, and there was no mean or personal element remaining unsubdued in him'. In order to achieve this imaginative state, Owen trained himself in the impersonal, poetic insensibility which he describes in the poem of that title; he had been working towards this throughout the winter ('Insensibility' may have been in draft before he went to Ripon) but the process was completed at Borrage Lane. Wordsworth had said,

> poetry is the spontaneous overflow of powerful feelings; it takes its origin from emotion recollected in tranquillity; the emotion is

> contemplated till by a species of reaction the tranquillity gradually disappears, and an emotion, kindred to that which was before the subject of contemplation, is gradually produced and does itself actually exist in the mind.

Owen had been working on similar lines in February when he had willingly brought on war dreams in order to perform his 'duty . . . towards War'. The task was both painful and dangerous for a poet of strong imaginative sensations such as he was, but the first draft of 'Insensibility' shows him working out a solution. Poets cannot shirk their 'duty', but since a mere 'hint', 'word' or 'thought' can smother their souls in blood they must acquire the vision of the common soldier, his senses dulled by the 'scorching cautery of battle'. Owen commented in March that the 'enormity of the present Battle numbs me' and said later in the year after returning to the front that his senses were 'charred'. This dullness of sensation became a necessary preliminary to writing poetry, a means of keeping control over bloodiness and more than shadowy crimes. That 'blindfold look . . . like a dead rabbit's' of the troops was not only a petrifying memory but also a clue to the way in which a poet could still function. However 'great' or otherwise Owen's Borrage Lane poems may be judged to be, his method of working deserves to be recognised as an extraordinary undertaking—a young subaltern training by day for the fighting that would almost certainly kill him, and in the warm spring evenings walking down a country lane to shut himself away in a windowless room and open his 'inward eye' to the intensity of those feelings and experiences that had brought him close to madness a year before.[2]

That his guide in all this was Wordsworth is confirmed by the deliberate literary references in 'Insensibility'. Like Wordsworth's 'Intimations of Immortality' the poem is a 'Pindaric' ode, a form developed in the eighteenth century, and is concerned with the loss of poetic imagination.[3] Several of the key words ('imagination', 'feeling', 'simplicity') belong to late eighteenth-century critical debate, while the opening phrase, 'Happy are men who', is the classical *Beatus ille* construction used, for example, by Pope in 'Happy the man whose wish and care / A few paternal acres bound'.[4] The sanity and order of eighteenth-century literature is used as ironic contrast, showing up the inverted values of war. As the simple Augustan swain was 'happy' in his little world, so the modern soldier is 'happy' when he is back at home 'with not a notion / How somewhere, every dawn, some men attack'. Wordsworth had lamented his own blunted vision but for Owen such a limitation was essential in 1918, when the problem for the 'wise' was an excess of imagination rather than a lack of it.[5] Nevertheless, the aim of poetry was still as Wordsworth had stated it, to reach and ennoble the human heart. Wordsworth ends his ode by claiming that the 'meanest flower that blows' could still give him 'Thoughts that do often lie too deep for tears'. Owen echoed the language but broadened the statement, making it more Shelleyan than Wordsworthian; thoughts about men who 'fade' and 'wither' in war should arouse 'The eternal reciprocity of tears'.

'Insensibility' seems to refer to two great Romantic manifestos, not only Wordsworth's Preface to *Lyrical Ballads* but also Shelley's *Defence of Poetry*. The last stanza contains Owen's first use in a war poem of the word 'pity'. Shelley argues that poetry should arouse man's imagination, making him understand other people and sympathise with them, putting himself 'in the place of another and of many others'. Poetry promotes love, which develops from sympathy and is the key to all moral goodness. Furthermore the power of poetry is such that it 'turns all things to loveliness; it exalts the beauty of that which is most beautiful, and it adds beauty to that which is most deformed; it marries exultation and horror, grief and pleasure, eternity and change; it subdues to union under its light yoke all irreconcilable things'. In the intensity of poetry even the most terrible subjects can be beautiful. One can see how this can be applied to Owen's work; in 'Disabled', for example, the mutilated soldier has lost all his physical beauty, yet the poem 'adds beauty to that which is most deformed' until the reader becomes aware of the man as a fellow human being still fit to be loved. The word 'exultation' occurs in 'Apologia', where it is 'married' with horror. This imaginative process is not to be confused with what Owen dismisses in 'Insensibility' as 'poets' tearful fooling', the sentimental versifying of writers who are more interested in being poetic than in their subject ('Above all I am not concerned with Poetry'). Yet even the true poets could not reach all hearts. The last stanza of his ode condemns civilian 'dullards' (originally 'these old') who, like the 'wise' but for very different reasons, make themselves insensible by choice. This Romantic distinction between the 'wise' and dullards follows that made by Shelley in the Preface to *Alastor* between poets, who suffer from too acute a consciousness of humanity, and men, 'who, deluded by no generous error, . . . loving nothing on this earth, . . . yet keep aloof from sympathies with their kind, rejoicing neither in human joy nor mourning with human grief; these, and such as they, have their apportioned curse'. Owen delivers the curse in one of his most elaborately composed stanzas, using pararhyme and other sound-patterns now with practised ease:

> But cursed are dullards whom no cannon stuns,
> That they should be as stones.
> Wretched are they, and mean
> With paucity that never was simplicity.

> By choice they made themselves immune
> To pity and whatever moans in man
> Before the last sea and the hapless stars;
> Whatever mourns when many leave these shores;
> Whatever shares
> The eternal reciprocity of tears.

In my judgment, this stanza is not quite as successful as some modern critics have made it out to be. Its technical complexity is remarkable—only Owen could have written it—but the imagery lacks substance. The 'last sea' and the 'hapless stars' are no more than clichés, as in Arthur Symons's 'Beyond the last land where the last sea roars' (and Owen's own 'Timeless, beyond the last stars of desire', a line which he had tried out as an ending for 'My Shy Hand').[6] The rest of 'Insensibility' is much more solid, the images coming from hard experience—'Their spirit drags no pack', 'alleys cobbled with their brothers' (a memory of bones frozen into the streets of Beaumont Hamel[7])—but in attempting to articulate a fullness of emotion which any twentieth-century poet would have found difficult to handle the last stanza comes too close to Tennysonian cadences and nineteenth-century vagueness. He was to be more successful, and no less original in his technique, in later 1918 poems.

He had probably begun to think about the poetry of 'pity' before the end of 1917, since it is clear that he set himself to read several famous elegies during the winter and following spring. He may have had no very scholarly idea of what an elegy was, remembering only from reference books that it originally meant a song of grief over a dead man and from Tailhade's example that *élégiaque* meant something other than *aristophanesque*, but when he described his war poems at 'These elegies' in his Preface he did not use the word at random. In December he read Lang's translation of the elegies by Bion and Moschus that had been Shelley's model for *Adonais*. In the spring he considered calling his book 'English Elegies' or 'With Lightning and with Music' (a phrase from *Adonais*). Dr Bäckman has pointed out some convincing parallels between the rhetorical structure of 'Asleep' (late 1917) and that of Milton's 'Lycidas', and between the tramp in 'The Send-Off' (Ripon) and the swain in Gray's 'Elegy Written in a Country Churchyard'. 'Futility' (probably Ripon) seems to reflect a famous passage in *In Memoriam*, while Tennyson's description of Hallam as 'strange friend' may be the source of that paradoxical phrase in 'Strange Meeting'.[8] 'Hospital Barge' (December) was written after a 'revel in "the Passing of Arthur"' and is a less serious effort in Tennyson's elegiac mode. Some of Owen's other poems have affinities with the elegies in *A Shropshire Lad* and *The Dynasts*. As early as November 1917 he was aware of a difference between his own verse and Sassoon's, saying that Sassoon wrote 'so acid' while he wrote 'so big'.[9] He described 'Miners' in January as 'sour' but the poem also has a 'bigness' which Sassoon had not attempted, a largeness of expression which is elegiac rather than satirical, universal rather than immediate, even though the poem was inspired by an actual event. His readings in elegy are reflected particularly clearly in the oddly undistinguished 'Elegy in April and September',[10] composed in those months in 1918. On the back of the April draft he made a note about Matthew Arnold, including the titles of two elegies, 'Thyrsis' and 'The Scholar-Gipsy', and '1. lofty, restrained, dignified. / 2. wistful agnostic'. His own 'Elegy', with its search for a lost poet-friend among woods and fields, is an imitation of Arnold's two poems; indeed, the five adjectives which he attached to Arnold could be applied to much of his own 1918 work, which conforms to 'a solemn dignity in the treatment' like the sonnets he had thought of collecting under the title 'With Lightning and with Music' some three years earlier. These traces of Shelley, Tennyson, Arnold and Gray in his late work are a reminder that these were the four poets he had reverently described in a verse letter from Dunsden in 1911. His reading in the winter of 1917–18 was not only in new writers such as the Georgians but also in old ones studied long before.

Critics have argued that elegy is a false response to war because it offers consolation. Although Owen's poems are not wholly devoid of consolation, he said firmly in his Preface that 'These elegies are to this generation in no sense consolatory'. One value of elegy was that it could provoke pity, appealing to hearts which might have been unmoved by satirical attacks. Having read Sassoon's book of press-cuttings, he knew that some contemporary reviewers had dismissed Sassoon's acidity as the product of immaturity and nervous strain. Edmund Gosse had remarked disapprovingly in October 1917 that such verse would tend to weaken the war effort, quite failing to see that that was precisely what it was intended to do.[11] It was possible to miss the target entirely with poems in Sassoon's style, devastating though they seemed to be. In any case, the elegiac convention allowed for protest; if Milton had attacked priests in 'Lycidas' and Shelley had savaged critics in *Adonais*, it was legitimate to attack civilians in war 'elegies'. To accept the elegiac element in Owen's 1918 poems is not to deny that they contain social criticism, but it is to recognise that their subject is indeed 'pity' and that in defining it they make extensive use of literary tradition.[12]

At Borrage Lane he returned to 'Wild with all Regrets', expanding it into 'A Terre'. He had originally imagined the dying officer in the poem as bookish ('But books were what I liked. Dad called me moony')[13] but in the finished December 1917 draft the man is given a thoughtless, sporting past. In the 1918 version the bookishness is restored, the officer quoting from

Adonais to a friend who seems himself to be the author of a 'poetry book'. The reference to Shelley suggests that the officer's viewpoint is Shelleyan throughout in its condemnation of class distinction, blood sports and war. His somewhat obscure remark that his soul is 'a little grief lodging for a short time in his friend's chest' may be compared with the lament in *Adonais* (xxi):

> Alas! that all we loved of him should be,
> But for our grief, as if it had not been,
> And grief itself be mortal!

The hope of becoming one with nature after death, the state which Shelley claimed for Keats, is a 'poor comfort' in the cruel, impoverished world of war but it is nevertheless the 'philosophy of many soldiers'. Although Shelley did not mean it in the sense in which the 'dullest Tommy' holds it, as a democrat he might have been pleased to find it so widely valued. There is a scepticism about poetry in 'A Terre', Owen's as well as Shelley's (a typically Owenish metaphor is scornfully relegated to the friend's 'poetry book'), but this is not so much a condemnation of Romanticism as a Romantic unease like the doubts about the poet's usefulness which Keats had expressed in *The Fall of Hyperion*. Perhaps poetry *was* mere 'tearful fooling'; the poet could only assert his faith by continuing to write, not for the sake of 'Poetry' but for the sake of humanity.

Some of the poems which Owen wrote at Borrage Lane are less concerned than his earlier war pieces had been with conveying realistic detail to civilians. Instead he takes a subject which a civilian could see or imagine and reveals its significance. Thus, for example, 'The Send-Off' describes a draft of soldiers setting out for France and suggests that they are victims of a 'hushed-up' conspiracy. The situations in these poems are representative rather than specific, sometimes entirely without topical reference so that they become applicable to any war, although they remain in origin 'matters of experience'. 'Arms and the Boy', for instance, may have been suggested by the irony of the children's playing soldiers outside the cottage. Since a boy is not armed by nature, society must provide him with man-made weapons:

> Lend him to stroke these blind, blunt bullet-leads,
> Which long to nuzzle in the hearts of lads,
> Or give him cartridges whose fine zinc teeth
> Are sharp with sharpness of grief and death.
>
> For his teeth seem for laughing round an apple.
> There lurk no claws behind his fingers supple;

And God will grow no talons at his heels,
Nor antlers through the thickness of his curls.

This is Owen's 1918 voice, no longer that of Georgian realism though still ironic towards the older generation. War's greatest cruelty is seen to be its destruction of youth and beauty. Its relationship to the young soldier is presented in sexual terms, consumingly urgent on one side ('long to nuzzle', 'famishing for flesh') and innocently exploring on the other ('try', 'stroke'). The imagery is strongly physical, with particular emphasis on parts of the body; the title literary; the language rich but dissonant in the manner of 'advanced composers' of contemporary music. Yet the universality of the statement does not weaken its bitterness, for the boy and the 'blind, blunt' bullets are not mere generalities. In the Easter Sunday letter which mentions children playing soldiers, Owen refers to two boys whom he often remembered:

> I wonder how many a *frau, fräulein, knabe und mädchen* Colin will kill in his time?
>
> Johnny de la Touche leaves school this term, I hear, and goes to prepare for the Indian Army.
>
> He must be a creature of killable age by now.
>
> God so hated the world that He gave several millions of English-begotten sons, that whosoever believeth in them should not perish, but have a comfortable life.

The feeling in 'Arms and the Boy' comes from that kind of reflection, but it is rendered into impersonal terms as a result of deliberate contemplation of the 'inwardness of war'.

Like earlier poems, Borrage Lane work demonstrates how strongly Owen was moved by the waste of young life. One of his first attempts there, 'As bronze may be much beautified', which was begun on Good Friday but never finished, seems to have been first conceived as a lament for a particular youth:

As women's pearls needs [be refreshed in deep sea,]

There he found brightness for his tiring eyes
And the old beauty of his young strength returned—

Dropped back for ever down the abysmal war.

Perhaps a young soldier, Antaeus-like, was to have been pictured as regaining contact with earth and sea, only to be killed by the war machine and lost underground. In 'Futility' the loss of potential new life is related to all natural renewal, just as Antaeus was the embodiment of all life in nature:

> Move him into the sun—
> Gently its touch awoke him once,
> At home, whispering of fields half-sown.
> Always it woke him, even in France,
> Until this morning and this snow.
> If anything might rouse him now
> The kind old sun will know.
> Think how it wakes the seeds—
> Woke once the clays of a cold star.
> Are limbs, so dear achieved, are sides
> Full-nerved, still warm, too hard to stir?
> Was it for this the clay grew tall?
> —O what made fatuous sunbeams toil
> To break earth's sleep at all?

F. W. Bateson (1979) condemned 'Futility' as an elegant technical exercise in which 'prosodic gadgets' count for more than truth. The 'Hell of trench warfare was already becoming . . . an abstraction' to Owen, according to Bateson, whereas in 'the great war poems' of 1917 grief is an 'authentic' 'personal experience'. It is true that the 1918 poems are less immediately 'realistic' and colloquial than those of 1917, becoming boldly original in technique and firmly grafted into literary tradition, but there is no fault here unless one is determined that all war poems must be of the Georgian kind. Bateson's comments rest on careless reading and a very hazy notion of the dates of Owen's poems. He understands 'Move him into the sun' as a 'curiously inhumane' order to carry a dead or dying man out of a hospital bed into the snow; were that correct, Owen would indeed be shown to have lost touch with true feeling and experience. The setting of the poem seems clear enough: the man has just died from exposure after a night in the open (like 'Exposure', 'Futility' may draw on an actual memory) and his body is to be moved out of the shadow of a parapet or some other object into the light and warmth of the rising sun. Bateson also complains that the second stanza is scientifically nonsense and that it puts the blame for war on the sun rather than on man, but Owen is making use of myth not science (according to ancient legend the sun's rays brought living creatures out of mud). The sun symbolises the source of life; if Owen is blaming it, he is blaming God, which was at least a defensible position to hold in 1918. Much literature has to be dismissed if poets are not to be permitted to question the Creator or to conclude that life is futile. The questions in the poem are not answered, however, so the blame may still be humanity's: Man was made for life and for sowing seed which the sun can ripen; when he turns to killing, nature has to reject him, his potency is lost and he dies. This is consistent with the mythic pattern which Owen had been working on for years. In the 'Perseus' sequence the young lover, 'full-nerved', commits some strange 'Wrong' which results in his being cut off from fertilising sunlight and paralysed (or, as it were, frozen) in darkness. The powerful cadence of the last lines of 'Futility' is passionately felt and far from mere elegance. As Owen felt his young strength returning in the sunlight of the Yorkshire spring while men died again at Beaumont Hamel, his memories of the 'Hell of trench warfare' were very far from becoming an 'abstraction'.

* * *

The way in which 'the pity of war' could be evoked, and the relationship between it and anger and disgust, are suggested in the organisation which Owen planned for the book of war poems which was his immediate objective at Ripon. All that remains of this plan is a fragmentary Preface and two rough lists of contents, together with a note of some possible titles ('Disabled and Other Poems' being his preferred choice).[14] The earlier list, written on the same type of paper as the final drafts of 'Insensibility' and 'Strange Meeting' and the first draft of 'Exposure', probably dates from April or early May.[15] It gives an idea of the stage his work had reached after perhaps a month's labour in the cottage. 'Strange Meeting' is included among nineteen or so 'Finished' poems; 'The Send-Off' and 'Mental Cases' await their final titles, as does the first version of 'Exposure'; 'The Sentry' is still 'Only Fifty Yards', the phrase with which the 1917 draft ends. Except for 'Spring Offensive', 'Training', 'The Kind Ghosts' and 'Smile, Smile, Smile', which were written later, almost all his war poems were by now either complete or in draft. It follows that much of his effort in May must have been devoted to polishing existing poems, producing the numerous fair copies overlaid with massive revisions that have been such a minefield for his editors. It was probably in late May or early June that he drew up his second, more detailed list and roughed out a Preface.

The Preface has become so famous that its fragmentary nature is often forgotten. The following version of it attempts to show some of Owen's first thoughts and revisions.[16]

Preface

This book is not about heroes. English Poetry is not yet fit to speak of them.
Nor is it about [battles, and glory of battles or lands, or] deeds or lands nor anything about glory or honour any might, majesty, dominion or power [whatever] except War.
[Its This book] is Above all I am not concerned with Poetry.
[Its The] My subject is War, and the pity of [it] War. The Poetry is in the pity.

[I have no hesitation in making public
publishing such]
[My] Yet These elegies are [not for the consolation] to this generation in no sense consolatory to this [a bereaved generation]. They may be to the next. [If I thought the letter of this book would last, I woul might have used proper names;] All a poet can do today is [to] warn [children] That is why the true [War] Poets must be truthful.

If I thought the letter of this book would last, I [wo] might have used proper names: but if the spirit of it survives—survives Prussia—[I] my ambition and those names will [be content; for they] have achieved [themselves ourselves] fresher fields than Flanders,
far be, not of war
would be
sing

A following sheet bears the words 'in those days remembers' (perhaps a continuation of the Preface) and the second table of contents. Owen's declaration of poetic intent is in the tradition of the Preface to *Lyrical Ballads* and the *Defence of Poetry*. (It also contains an echo of Keats's poem about art, the 'Ode on a Grecian Urn': 'These elegies are to this generation in no sense consolatory . . . They may be to the next' / 'When old age shall this generation waste, / Thou shalt remain. . . . a friend to man'.) As Wordsworth, Shelley and Keats required, the poet rejects 'Poetry' for its own sake and dedicates himself to the betterment of humanity. There were requirements peculiar to 1918, including the need to refrain from consoling the older generation. It was perhaps because most existing poetic language was consolatory in its effect that Owen considered English poetry to be not 'yet' fit to describe the heroism of soldiers, but the word 'yet' implies that he would have liked to see a kind of poetry fit to speak of heroes and in 'Spring Offensive' he was to move towards a poetry of that kind. The later part of the Preface shows him reaching out to 'children', the future generations who were in the event to be his audience.

The list of contents which accompanies the Preface is arranged in a careful sequence, each poem being given a 'Motive' and each group of poems a further label. The first group, which seems in the manuscript to consist of thirteen titles, is 'Protest', beginning with 'Miners' and including 'Dulce et Decorum Est', 'S. I. W.' and 'The Dead-Beat', as well as some newer work such as 'Aliens' (a title for 'Mental Cases' which was suggested by Owen's friend Charles Scott Moncrieff at the end of May[17]). The fourteenth poem, 'The Show', is at the halfway point, its Motive of 'Horrible beastliness of war' sharply contrasting with the next two, 'Cheerfulness' ('The Next War') and 'Cheerfulness & Description & Reflection' ('Apologia'). Two more 'Description' poems follow, then five of 'Grief' and four which all seem to be included under 'Philosophy'. This arrangement was devised to take the reader through a developing, coherent experience. He would begin with 'Miners', a poem based on a civil disaster but leading into the subject of war, then move on to 'Arms and the Boy', a statement of the 'unnaturalness of weapons' and the exploitation of the younger generation. Then comes a series of angry protests at the madness, lies and callousness of war. 'The Show' brings the first half of the book to a climax of horror. Then the mood changes. Having been taught to protest, the reader may now see in 'The Next War' and 'Apologia' that war has a cheerfulness understood only by those who have faced its true nature. 'Exposure' and 'The Sentry' provide more description but check any inclination to make light of the troops' suffering. Then the poems of 'Grief', which include 'Anthem' and 'Futility', establish the mood of elegy, introducing the final 'Philosophy' section ('Strange Meeting', 'Asleep', 'A Terre', 'The Women and the Slain'). The reader was thus to proceed from protest through grief to meditation, a pattern Owen himself had gone through since meeting Sassoon. No stage was invalid but none was complete in itself. Protest was unproductive unless it led to grief, and grief in turn had to bear fruit in new attitudes. Owen seems to have thought of the entire experience as 'pity'—not grief alone but grief arising from re-educated knowledge and feeling, producing a positive, active frame of mind.

'Disabled and Other Poems' was never put together and Owen's notes for it should not be taken as his final thoughts about his poetry. He was never entirely convinced that publishing in wartime would be useful, and his cousin's precipitate rush into print had persuaded him that poetry could not be hurried. He said at the end of May that he could 'now write so much better than a year ago that for every poem I add to my list I subtract one from the beginning of it. You see I take myself solemnly now, and that is why, let me tell you, once and for all, I refrain from indecent haste in publishing.'[18] His departure from Ripon on 5 June perhaps prevented his taking his plans for a book any further but what mattered was to write rather than to publish. His audience was posterity. Poems such as 'Exposure' and 'Strange Meeting' show that he lost hope for the war generation, concluding that civilians could never understand and soldiers could never explain. All that a true war poet could do was to warn children, who might find consolation later in the knowledge that a true voice had managed to speak. His poems might prove that there was something indestructible in the human spirit, but that would be consolation only if future generations acted on his warning and loved their fellow men. On the whole we have not so acted, which may be why we find his 1917 poems of protest more immediately forceful than his later work; prevented by conscience from discovering any kind of consolation in his poems, we are ill at ease when he introduces them as 'elegies'. Nevertheless he meant us to see that protest is an essential stage, but not a final one, in the process of perceiving that 'pity of war' which he described in a draft of 'Strange Meeting' as 'the one thing war distilled'. The task of poetry was the Shelleyan one of arousing imagination, enabling people to share in the experience of others, to sympathise with them and love them, for war was above all a failure of love.

Notes

1. *CL*, 535 (catastrophic), 538 (Farewell), 543 (get fit, cottage-window). WO, *CL* and JS spell 'Borage'; WO probably never saw it written down but then as now it was apparently 'Borrage' (from 'burgherage', not 'borage'). 'No one here knows of my retreat' (*CL*, 547): JS, 259, may be mistaken in implying WO actually lived in the cottage, since he would presumably have had to inform his superiors. He was free daily from about 3 p.m. to Lights Out. Borrage Lane compositions probably include 'As bronze', 'Arms and the Boy', 'The Send-Off', 'Strange Meeting', 'Futility', 'Mental Cases', 'Elegy in April' (four stanzas). Many poems begun earlier were extensively revised, including 'Exposure', 'A Terre' and 'Insensibility'.

2. Wordsworth, Preface to *Lyrical Ballads* (1802). *CL*, 544 (public attention was on the German breakthrough at St Quentin), 524 (Hamel), 542 (Wordsworth wrote three poems to the 'small' celandine). Murry (1921). *CL*, 543 (numbs), 581 (charred).

3. *Pace CPF*, 147, 'Insensibility' is hardly a reply to Wordsworth's 'Happy Warrior', which is not a Pindaric ode and contains little that WO would have disagreed with (cf. Ch. 11, n. 23, below).

4, 'Happy': a key word in Keats's odes but also in wartime propaganda (cf. 'Smile, Smile, Smile', and Plates 13, 14).

5. The 'wise' in 'Insensibility' are poets (cf. Ch. 7, n. 29, above, and *Adonais*, line 312). WO does not imply any comment on class or education as some critics have supposed.

6. Symons, 'To the Merchants of Bought Dreams', *Poems* (1906) II, 175. BL1, 15.

7. The first draft (*CPF*, 304) refers to frozen bodies underfoot. Cf. *CL*, 542.

8. *English Elegies*, etc.: titles on verso of first list of contents (*CPF*, 538; cf. JS, 265, and *CL*, 561 n. 3, an inaccurate note). Lang: see Ch. 6., n. 32, above. Milton, Gray: Bäckman (1979) 40–3. Tennyson: DH, WO (1975) 32–3; *In Memoriam*, cxxix.

9. *CL*, 511 (acid). EB, 125 (sour).

10. MSS, like 'An Imperial Elegy', have musical annotations. At one stage entitled 'Ode for a Poet reported Missing: later, reported killed', this may be the 'Ode' in the 1918 lists of contents (*CPF*, 147 headnote). Subtitle, '(jabbered among the trees)', from SS, 'Repression of War Experience'. In stanzas 1–4 (Apr) the poet seeks a companion missing in spring; in stanzas 5–7 (Sep) he laments him killed in autumn. Presumably the poem was meant for SS, but who is its subject?

11. *CL*, 526. Gosse in *Casebook*, 44–5.

12. Some careless remarks of mine years ago on protest and elegy have been rebuked. DW (1978) 167–8 rescues me from an absurd position with characteristic generosity. Silkin (1980) seems less persuasive.

13. '[And have I shut the last book I shall read?]' OEF 339–42, not in *CPF*.

14. For both lists, see *CPF*, 538–9. They are of war poems only, but WO continued to plan work unconnected with war, assembling sonnets at Scarborough ('Farewell . . . Sonnets'—*CL*, 538). A note of 5 May 1918 (OEF; *CL*, 551 n. 1) lists four 'Projects': verse plays on old Welsh themes, like Tennyson's English and Yeats's Irish dramas (so WO envisaged a role as a Welsh poet); *Collected Poems* (1919); 'Perseus'; 'Idylls in Prose'. But he would have been less old-fashioned than this if he had lived; he had yet to encounter Modernism.

15. For the date of Society Bond MSS, see Appendix B.

16. MS reproduced as frontispiece to *CPF* and in DH (1975).

17. CKSM to WO, 26 May 1918 (OEF).

18. *CL*, 554.

ROBERT LANGBAUM

The Issue of Hardy's Poetry

When I told the American poet Theodore Weiss that I was writing on Hardy's poetry, he snorted contemptuously saying Hardy was being used nowadays as a stick with which to beat the modernists, such as Yeats, Eliot, and Pound. Weiss argues this view powerfully in the *Times Literary Supplement* of February 1, 1980. Irving Howe, instead, in the *New York Times Book Review* of May 7, 1978, defends the taste for Hardy's poetry in just the terms feared by Weiss:

> As we slowly emerge from the shadowing power of the age of modernism, Hardy's poems can be felt as more durable . . . than those of, say, T. S. Eliot. . . . Reading Eliot (or even Yeats) one may say, "ah, here in fulfillment is the sensibility that formed us." Reading Hardy one may say, "but this is how life is, has always been, and probably will remain." (p. 11)

In his book *Thomas Hardy*, Howe says that Hardy "through the integrity of his negations" helps make possible the twentieth-century "sensibility of problem and doubt," but "he is finally not of [this century]. That his poems span two cultural eras while refusing to be locked into either is a source of his peculiar attractiveness."[1]

Donald Davie, in his *Thomas Hardy and British Poetry* (1972), most acutely defines the crisis for modernism represented in Britain by the "conversion" to Hardy. Davie begins by declaring that "in British poetry of the last fifty years (as not in American) the most far-reaching influence, for good and ill, has been not Yeats, still less Eliot or Pound, not Lawrence, but *Hardy*." Davie cites as the model for post–World War II British poetry Philip Larkin's significant "conversion . . . from Yeats to Hardy in 1946, after his very Yeatsian first collection."[2] The post–World War II British poets renounced the grand resonances emerging from the modernists' allegiances to the tradition and to various myths—the "common myth-kitty," as Larkin put it (Davie, p. 42)—settling for the smaller, drier tones of a precisely noted quotidian reality. In learning to read the great modernists we had to assent to mysticisms, religious orthodoxies, and reactionary politics most of us would not dream of living by. But we thought only such views could in our time supply the symbols necessary for great poetry. Here, says Davie, lies Hardy's importance as "the one poetic imagination of the first magnitude in the present century who writes out of . . . political and social attitudes which a social democrat recognizes as 'liberal.'" Hardy shows that poetry can be made out of the commonsense working ethic of most English-speaking readers—an ethic Davie aptly describes as "scientific humanism" (pp. 6, 5), a scientific world-view tempered by humanitarianism, by what Hardy in the "Apology" to *Late Lyrics* (1922) calls "loving-kindness."[3] In the "Apology" Hardy decries the "present, when belief in witches of Endor is displacing the Darwinian theory" (2:324). Hardy is probably responding to Yeats's occultism.

Most contemporary American poets seem able to reconcile admiration for the modernists with a taste for Hardy. Even in Britain, pre–World War II poets like W. H. Auden and Cecil Day Lewis could admire Eliot without repudiating their earlier passions for Hardy (Day Lewis' passion remained so strong that he had himself buried near Hardy in Stinsford churchyard). Auden tells how Hardy first gave him the sense of modernity: "Besides serving as the archetype of the Poetic, Hardy was also an expression of the Contemporary Scene." Hardy "was my poetical father."[4] A generation earlier Ezra Pound declared the same filial relation to Browning ("Ich stamm aus Browning. Pourquoi nier son père?"),[5] who educated him in the rough diction, broken syntax, and difficult music of modern lyricism. In a generation still earlier Hardy, as we shall see, learned the same things from Browning, while from Swinburne he learned modern ideas delivered in classic meters ("New words, in classic guise"[6]).

Davie, however, insists that for post–World War II poets "the choice cannot be fudged" between mythical and realistic poetry. The contemporary poet must decide whether like Yeats to try "to transcend historical time by seeing it as cyclical, so as to leap above it into a realm that is visionary, mythological," or like Hardy to confine himself to "the world of historical contingency [linear time], a world of specific places at specific times" (pp. 4, 3). While mainly agreeing with Davie, I find difficulties in his position which I will try to puzzle out.

Having begun by saying that Hardy is the one twentieth-century poet "of the first magnitude" to express the liberal ethos, Davie subsequently casts doubt on whether Hardy's poetry is indeed "of the first magnitude." He goes on to criticize Hardy's too obvious symmetries, attributing them to the hand of an engineer influenced by Victorian technology or to a poet educated in the regularities of architecture (though Hardy spoke of having learned from his experience with Gothic the art of irregularity). Davie uses the question of symmetry as a criterion of evaluation, showing that the best poems display asymmetries that have slipped past the surveillance of the poet's "imperious" will (p. 25). Despite his high evaluation at the beginning, Davie seems subsequently to approve of Blackmur's argument that Hardy's successes are "isolated" cases, that he had expertise but lacked "technique in the wide sense" because he lacked "the structural support of a received imagination."[7] "Hardy is not a great poet," writes Davie, "because, except in *The Dynasts*, he does not choose to be" (p. 39). Davie proposes Hardy as a precursor of Larkin and the other contemporary British poets who in reaction against modernism deliberately set out to be precise and minor. Is the implication then that liberal, realistic poets are not first-rate?

While admitting that Hardy is a much larger figure than Larkin, Davie still considers him minor because his poems deliver an untransformed reality. This, however, is the characteristic of Hardy's poetry which, after the transcendentalizing nineteenth century, later poets took over as particularly modern. Thus Yeats, in the one sentence he devotes to Hardy in the Introduction to his *Oxford Book of Modern Verse*, belittles Hardy's "technical accomplishment" but praises "his mastery of the impersonal objective scene."[8] Italy's leading modernist poet, Eugenio Montale, finds Hardy's relation to objects congenial to his own art, as we see by his translation into Italian of Hardy's "The Garden Seat," but Montale wonders at Hardy's "rigidly closed" forms and "impeccably traditional" stanzas.[9] Davie concludes his discussion of Hardy's poems as follows:

> And so his poems, instead of transforming and displacing quantifiable reality or the reality of common sense, are on the contrary just so many glosses on that reality, which is conceived of as unchallengeably "given" and final. . . . He sold the vocation short, tacitly surrendering the proudest claims traditionally made for the act of poetic imagination. (p. 62)

Yet for an atheistic realist Hardy populates his poems with a surprising number of ghosts. And if he does not draw on the "myth-kitty," he does in his poems and fiction draw on observed folklore which, as the mythology of the illiterate, is older and more fundamental than the myths available through the literary tradition. Hardy's ghosts are not only the folklore ghosts of his ballads, but in his lyrics they are also psychological ghosts of Wordsworthian involuntary memory, wrapping the poems in mystery, dissolving fixities of place and time. Even "The Garden Seat," a realistic portrayal of the abandoned garden seat, evokes the ghosts of those who used to sit upon it (2:331). The ghost of Hardy's dead wife Emma flits through these pages, as in "After a Journey" (which Davie calls a "phantasmagoria"), where the ghost is placeless: "Hereto I come to view a voiceless ghost; / Whither, O whither will its whim now draw me?" (2:59); or in "The Voice" where Emma's ghost is a timeless, placeless auditory experience:

> Woman much missed, how you call to me, call to me, . . .
>
> Or is it only the breeze, in its listlessness
> Travelling across the wet mead to me here,
> You being ever dissolved to wan wistlessness,
> Heard no more again far or near?
> Thus I; faltering forward,
> Leaves around me falling,
> Wind oozing thin through the thorn from norward,
> And the woman calling. (2:56–57)

"Or is it only the breeze" continues the romantic tradition of natural-supernaturalism; while the shortened lines and changed meters of the last stanza produce the break in symmetry which by Davie's criteria (and mine) mark this poem as major.

The ghost of involuntary memory is best exemplified in "During Wind and Rain," where scenes from the past rush back with unbearable poignancy to overwhelm a present represented only by wind and rain: "Ah, no; the years O! / How the sick leaves reel down in throngs" (2:239). In "Wessex Heights" (2:25–27), a ghost poem of eschatological magnitude, the heights, realistically evoked by place names, seem to represent a detached state of existence comparable to the afterlife:

> and at crises when I stand,
> Say, on Ingpen Beacon eastward, or on Wylls-Neck westwardly,
> I seem where I was before my birth, and after death may be. (ll. 2–4)

"In the lowlands," instead, "I have no comrade." "Down there I seem to be false to myself, my simple self that was" (l. 13). It seems misleading to try to identify, as does J. O. Bailey in his *Commentary*,[10] the people being accused of betraying him since he accuses himself as well. "Too weak to mend" and "mind-chains do not clank where one's next neighbour is the sky" suggest self-accusation; so does "I am tracked by phantoms" and "I cannot go to the great grey Plain; there's a figure against the moon, / Nobody sees it but I, and it makes my breast beat out of tune" (ll. 17–18). The ghosts who enter the powerful penultimate stanza seem to represent a purgatorial experience:

> There's a ghost at Yell'ham Bottom chiding loud at the
> fall of the night,
> There's a ghost in Froom-side Vale, thin lipped and
> vague, in a shroud of white,
> There is one in the railway-train whenever I do not
> want it near,
> I see its profile against the pane, saying what I would
> not hear. (ll. 21–24)

The speaker saves himself through the liberating perspective achieved through loneliness on the heights: "And ghosts then keep their distance; and I know some liberty" (l. 32).

There are also poems in which Hardy portrays himself through the analogy to ghostliness. "He Revisits His First School" (2:258–259) begins:

> I should not have shown in the flesh,
> I ought to have gone as a ghost;
> It was awkward, unseemly almost,
> Standing solidly there. (ll. 1–4)

as though, Hardy says, I still belonged to the same vigorously living species that inhabits this classroom. I should have waited and returned from the tomb. In the comparable "Among School Children," Yeats's strong presence takes over the scene; whereas Hardy projects his relative absence: his ghost would have made a stronger presence. Absence is again projected in "The Strange House (Max Gate, A.D. 2000)," in which future inhabitants sense only faint ghostly stirrings of the Hardys' life there. The most uncanny of the ghostly self-portrayals is the early poem, "I Look into My Glass" (1:106), in which the aged speaker, seeing himself wasted in body and wishing his "heart had shrunk as thin" so he could wait his "endless rest / With equanimity," is horrified by the youthful passions that still shake his "fragile frame"—as though he were a ghost who could not find rest. One wonders how much Hardy's sense of himself as ghostly emerged from his knowledge that he was at birth taken for dead. "For my part," he wrote in his diary,

> if there is any way of getting a melancholy satisfaction out of life it lies in dying, so to speak, before one is out of the flesh; by which I mean putting on the manners of ghosts, wandering in their haunts, and taking their views of surrounding things. . . . Hence even when I enter into a room to pay a simple morning call I have unconsciously the habit of regarding the scene as if I were a spectre not solid enough to influence my environment.[11]

I have cited all these examples to show, in answer to Davie, that many of Hardy's poems do transform reality, even if the poems of commonsense reality, poems like "A Commonplace Day" (1:148–149) are admittedly most characteristic. Yet even that poem, which contains such finely realistic lines as "Wanly upon the panes / The rain slides," begins with the line, "The day is turning ghost," and opens out in the end to a cosmic speculation that accounts for the speaker's regret over the dying of so commonplace a day. In the "Apology" to *Late Lyrics*, Hardy tries to reconcile the two sides of his work by dreaming of "an alliance between religion . . . and complete rationality . . . by means of the interfusing effect of poetry" (2:325). And in the *Life* he speaks of his "infinite trying to reconcile a scientific view of life with the emotional and spiritual, so that they may not be interdestructive" (p. 153).

We cannot classify Hardy the poet simply as an antimythic, commonsense realist when his great novels are wrapped in the mystery noted by Virginia Woolf, who, in her essay on him in *The Common Reader*, describes him as a novelist of unconscious intention, and when so many of his plots are modeled on the mythic patterns of Greek and Shakespearean drama. We cannot finally assess Hardy's poems without remembering that he began publishing his poems when already an elderly successful novelist and that readers were first drawn to the poems because of the novels. Too many critics of the poems (Davie included) write as though the novels did not exist.[12]

Davie describes the difficulty of assessing Hardy's poetry. "Affection for Hardy the poet is general," he writes, " . . . but it is ruinously shot through with protectiveness, even condescension. Hardy is not thought of as an intellectual force." "None of Hardy's admirers have yet found how to make Hardy the poet *weigh* equally with Eliot and Pound and Yeats" (pp. 5, 4). Davie does not try to accomplish this end. He and other critics have in effect withdrawn Hardy from the competition by judging him according to another scale—as, though most critics avoid the term, a first-rate *minor* poet. John Crowe Ransom, in the *Southern Review* Hardy issue, calls him "a great minor poet" (p. 14).

Most critics note in Hardy's prodigious output an inevitable number of bad poems, a majority of interesting, well-made poems comprising a refreshing variety of subjects, verse forms, and tones, and a dozen or two major poems. But there is no agreed upon Hardy canon for the poems as there is for the novels. Everyone, of course, agrees upon a few poems as major; otherwise each critic chooses different poems for discussion. Most critics (Yeats is an exception) praise Hardy's craftsmanship, and the question arises whether the major poems are to be viewed as happy accidents or as a main criterion for evaluating his poetry. In speaking of Hardy as ambitious technically but, except in *The Dynasts*, unambitious in every other way, Davie is suggesting that Hardy *chose* to work on a minor scale and that the major poems are happy accidents, moments when the creative impulse escaped from the watchful eye of the technician and the willful self: hence the chapter titles, "Hardy as Technician" and "Hardy Self-Excelling."

Before proposing my own different evaluation, I want to see how far Hardy can be considered minor in a nonpejorative sense, since many minor poets have become classics. The minor scale of Hardy's poetry makes him useful as an influence. His admirers display an intimate affection for him differing from the awe inspired by the great modernists. More recent poets have found Hardy supportive because he points a direction without preempting their own ideas and feelings. He is, in other words, a precursor from whom much can be learned, but not a competitor.

Auden speaks of his debt to Hardy for "technical instruction." Hardy's faults "were obvious even to a schoolboy, and the young can learn best from those of whom, because they can criticize them, they are not afraid." Hardy was useful as a teacher because no other English poet "employed so many and so complicated stanza forms," and because his rhymed verse kept Auden from too early an excursion into free verse which to a beginner looks easy but is really the most difficult of verse forms. Hardy "taught me much about direct colloquial diction, all the more because his directness was in phrasing and syntax, not in imagery"—for example, "'I see what you are doing: you are leading me on'" ["After a Journey"] and "'Upon that shore we are clean forgot'" ["An Ancient to Ancients"]. "Here was a 'modern' rhetoric which was more fertile and adaptable to different themes than any of Eliot's gasworks and rats' feet [imagery] which one could steal but never make one's own" (Guerard, pp. 141–142). Actually "An Ancient to Ancients," which was first published in 1922, the year of *The Waste Land*, contains modern imagery comparable to Eliot's:

> Where once we danced, where once we sang,
> Gentlemen,
> The floors are sunken, cobwebs hang,
> And cracks creep; worms have fed upon
> The doors. . . .
> . . . .
> The bower we shrined to Tennyson,
>   Gentlemen,
> Is roof-wrecked; damps there drip upon
> Sagged seats, the creeper-nails are rust,
> The spider is sole denizen. (2:481–483)

But Auden's point is that the apprentice can take what he wants from a minor poet while still calling his style his own.

What then is the difference between major and first-rate minor poetry? The difference does not lie in Hardy's unevenness; Wordsworth is more uneven, yet most of us would agree that he is major. Auden, in introducing his anthology of nineteenth-century British minor poets, says that the major poet is likely to "write more bad poems than the minor." As for enjoyment, he says, "I cannot enjoy one poem by Shelley and am delighted by every line of William Barnes, but I know perfectly well that Shelley is a major poet, and Barnes a minor one."[13]

What then is the difference? A major poet seems to me to be one whose world-view and personal character determine each other and determine the diction, imagery, and central myth running through all his poetry. His poetry is thus characteristic down to its unconscious elements; its originality of content and form emerges from its characteristicness or inner compulsion. That is why major poetry gives the impression of unfathomed depths, leaving us with the desire to reread as soon as we have read. Not so minor poetry, which, deriving from the poet's will, can usually be understood and enjoyed with one or two readings, though we may return to it many times to enjoy its clarity of meaning and form. The symmetries of minor poems are obvious, sometimes too obvious; whereas major poems favor asymmetries and leave a final impression of openness even though the older poems employ formal closures.[14]

T. S. Eliot tries to define minor poetry in writing about another poet-novelist, Rudyard Kipling, whom Eliot calls a writer of "*great* verse." Kipling exhibits

> that skill of craftsmanship which seems to enable him to pass from form to form, though always in an identifiable idiom, and from

> subject to subject, so that we are aware of no inner compulsion to write about this rather than that—a versatility which may make us suspect him of being no more than a performer. . . . I mention Yeats at this point because of the contrast between his development, which is very apparent in the way he writes, and Kipling's development, which is only apparent in what he writes about. We expect to feel, with a great writer, that he *had* to write about the subject he took, and in that way. With no writer of equal eminence to Kipling is this inner compulsion . . . more difficult to discern.[15]

Auden, too, employs the criterion of development. "In the case of the major poet," he says in his Introduction to *Minor Poets*,

> if confronted by two poems of his of equal merit but written at different times, the reader can immediately say which was written first. In the case of a minor poet, on the other hand, however excellent the two poems may be, the reader cannot settle their chronology on the basis of the poems themselves. (p. 16)

If we judge by these criteria, most of Hardy's poems would count as minor, but a significant number would count as major. The New Critics—if we take as an example the contributors to the *Southern Review*'s Hardy Centennial issue (Summer 1940)—divide evenly between on the one side Ransom and Tate, who praise Hardy's poetry with qualifications, and on the other Blackmur and Leavis, who have hardly a good word to say about the poetry. Critics of note nowadays, instead, are unqualified in their praise, beginning with Pound, who in *Guide to Kulchur* asks: "When we, if we live long enough, come to estimate the 'poetry of the period,' against Hardy's 600 pages we will put what?" (p. 285). Philip Larkin "would not wish Hardy's *Collected Poems* a single page shorter, and regards it as many times over the best body of poetic work this century so far has to show."[16] "It is generally agreed today," writes J. Hillis Miller, "that Thomas Hardy is one of the greatest of modern poets writing in English."[17] Harold Bloom calls Hardy a *strong* (i.e., a major) poet, "Shelley's ephebe."[18] Christopher Ricks describes "the recovery of the conviction of Hardy's greatness as a poet," but speaks of him as "the poet who owed so much to Browning."[19]

We might reconcile these varying judgments by saying that Hardy is a major poet who chose for long stretches to work in the minor mode, probably because (now that he had given himself the luxury of writing poetry after all the years of writing fiction for money) he wanted to test his skill at as many poetic forms as possible, wanted to indulge in the craft of poetry.

Most Hardy poems are successes in the minor mode, in that they make their points completely with symmetries that are obvious, sometimes too obvious. The symmetries of thought and form in "The Convergence of the Twain" are in my opinion too obvious. A successful poem like "His Immortality" (1:180) establishes in an unvarying stanza of obvious symmetry a quickly predictable pattern of thought. The poem begins:

> I saw a dead man's finer part
> Shining within each faithful heart
> Of those bereft. Then said I: "This must be
> His immortality." (ll. 1–4)

Clearly, the dead man's immortality must diminish as the friends who remember him die. Each stanza describes another step in this diminution until in the final stanza the dead man finds "in me alone, a feeble spark, / Dying amid the dark" (ll. 15–16). The imagery, however, springs a surprise in suggesting ironically that the speaker's immortality is equally vulnerable. The completeness of the ironical statement and the fulfillment of our expectations of thought and form make this poem successful in a minor mode.

As for the question of development, it is a commonplace that Hardy the poet—in contrast to Hardy the novelist—shows no *development*, that his volumes of verse mix earlier and later poems with no discernible differences of period, unless dated or distinguished by a subject such as the Boer War. Hardy dated his early poems, suggesting that in his view they differed from the later poems. Yet if an early success like "Neutral Tones" were not dated, could we discern its period? Looking back over Hardy's poems in the *Sunday Times* of May 28, 1922, Edmund Gosse concluded that the poetry had "suffered very little modification in the course of sixty years."

Dennis Taylor, however, in his *Hardy's Poetry 1860–1928*, argues for development, finding it in Hardy's development of the meditative lyric and in the flowering of pastoral poems in his last volumes. While conceding that Hardy's "poetry does not display the obvious and clearly defined stages" of "other poets," Taylor shows that Hardy himself thought his volumes of verse displayed development, writing in his preface to *Time's Laughingstocks* (1909) of the first-person lyrics in that volume: "'As a whole they will, I hope, take the reader forward, even if not far, rather than backward.'"[20] By the criterion of development Hardy's poetry falls on the border between major and minor poetry. Having myself discerned little development in Hardy's poetry, I did note in my latest reading a steady increase in plain colloquial diction and syntax. Hardy developed, as Samuel Hynes puts it, "toward a more consistent and more effective control of that tone which we recognize as uniquely his."[21]

Most importantly I noted, beginning so late as *Human Shows* (1925), the last volume published during Hardy's lifetime, a new imagist style which projects emotion entirely through closely observed objective correlatives. "Snow in the Suburbs" (3:42–43) is the best known example: "Every branch big with it, / Bent every twig with it" (ll. 1–2). Objective correlatives to emotion appear later: "Some flakes have lost their way, and grope back upward, when / Meeting those meandering down they turn and descend again" (ll. 5–6). Although written in couplets throughout, the stanzas vary in line lengths and in the last stanza in number of lines, suggesting a freeing up of the verse.

Other examples are "Green Slates" (3:19–20), an "East-End Curate" (3:20–21), and "Coming up Oxford Street: Evening" (1925) (3:25), which could be early Eliot:

> A city-clerk, with eyesight not of the best,
> Who sees no escape to the very verge of his days
> From the rut of Oxford Street into open ways;
> And he goes along with head and eyes flagging forlorn,
> Empty of interest in things, and wondering why he was born. (ll. 15–20)[22]

These couplets vary in number of syllables, and are much longer than the lines in the previous longer stanza, which vary in number of syllables and rhyme scheme—suggesting again a freeing up of the verse, already seen in such early poems as "My Cicely" and "The Mother Mourns" with their many unrhymed lines.

Still other examples are "The Flower's Tragedy" (3:103) and "At the Aquatic Sports" (3:104), which sound like Frost ("So wholly is their being here / A business they pursue" [ll. 13–14]), and in the posthumous *Winter Words* (1928) the admirably restrained "The New Boots" (3:243–244). In the moving poem "Bereft" (1:263; dated 1901), a workingman's widow laments his death with the balladlike refrain:

> Leave the door unbarred,
> The clock unwound,
> Make my lone bed hard—
> Would 'twere underground! (ll. 5–8)

In "The New Boots," instead, the widow's grief is projected through a neighbor's description of the boots which the husband bought joyfully but never lived to wear. The widow's grief is all the more apparent because of her muteness: "'And she's not touched them or tried / To remove them . . . '" (ll. 19–20).

It is not clear whether Hardy's imagism developed from his own objective realism (already evident in "On the Departure Platform," 1909), or whether he was influenced by the Imagist poets. He appears to have read volumes sent him by Ezra Pound in 1920–21 and by Amy Lowell in 1922, but his responses to these young Imagists do not suggest influence.[23] The phrase in his last volume, "Just neutral-tinted haps" ("He Never Expected Much" [3:225]), explains what he always aimed to convey, so that the neutrality characteristic of imagism was incipient in his early poems "Neutral Tones" and "Hap." Hardy's objective realism or metonymy is more characteristic of his poetry than are metaphor and symbol.[24]

If we apply to Hardy Eliot's remark about Kipling's variety, we find that as poet Hardy exhibits even more variety than Kipling, in that he passes not only from form to form and subject to subject but also from level to level. For he mixes with humorous verse and melodramatic balladry poems that are serious philosophically and others that are in the full sense "poetry." The difference between Hardy and his older friend, the Dorsetshire dialect poet William Barnes, exemplifies Hardy's ambiguous position between minor and major poet. According to Samuel Hynes, Barnes's poetry is idyllic whereas Hardy introduces into the regional setting modern ideas: "Darwin stands between them" (*Pattern of Hardy's Poetry*, p. 25).

Yet we do not feel in reading through a Hardy volume the assured pitch of intensity that we feel with indubitably major poets, or the equally assured lightness of versifiers. Hardy's variousness can be entertaining if we are alive to his shifts of tone; otherwise we may become impatient with his skillful ballads and narratives because our standards have been determined by the greater depths of emotion and psychological insights offered in the major poems. When an indubitably major poet relaxes into light verse—as does Eliot in his charming little book on cats—we feel that the playful excursion need not be taken into account for understanding him. But Hardy establishes no such criterion for exclusion. He himself recognized this problem when complaining in the "Apology" to *Late Lyrics*,

> that dramatic anecdotes of a satirical and humorous intention following verse in a graver voice, have been read as misfires because they raise the smile that they were intended to raise, the journalist, deaf to the sudden change of key, being unconscious that he is laughing with the author, and not at him. I admit that I did not foresee such contingencies as I ought to have done, and that people might not perceive when the tone altered. (2:321–322)

Eliot's remark that Kipling's poetry "does not revolutionize" (*On Poetry and Poets*, p. 293) is inapplicable to Hardy as evidenced by his influence on succeeding poets. Although Hardy did not innovate in verse forms, he did innovate in diction, tone, and above all in subject matter. As novelist Hardy was a major innovator, having developed sex and the unconscious as subjects and mythical rendition as technique. These innovations appear also in the poetry, though less conspicuously. To the extent that Hardy innovated, he might be considered a major poet; to the extent that he modernized and transmitted what was usable in nineteenth-century poetry, Hardy might be considered a first-class minor poet.

What is the use, one might well ask, of the distinction I am trying to draw between major and minor poetry? I am, first of all, trying to develop a standard for evaluating Hardy as against the classic modernist poets and to give him his fair place in the competition by showing that he is in most cases successful on another scale. I am also trying to develop criteria for dealing with the great variety of levels and tones in Hardy's poems. To use the word "major" for the best of them is to make clear the extent and mode of their success. To use the words "first-class minor" for many of the others is to recognize their success on another scale. Finally I want to distinguish between Hardy's poems and novels, to argue for the great novels as his most consistently major work, containing, albeit in prose, his most massively major poetry.

Notes

1. Irving Howe, *Thomas Hardy* (New York, 1967), p. 161.
2. Donald Davie, *Thomas Hardy and British Poetry* (New York, 1972), pp. 3–4.
3. *The Complete Poetical Works of Thomas Hardy*, ed. Samuel Hynes (Oxford, 1982–85), 2:319.
4. W. H. Auden, "A Literary Transference," in *Hardy: A Collection of Critical Essays*, ed. Albert J. Guerard (Englewood Cliffs, New Jersey, 1987), pp. 136, 142.
5. Ezra Pound, *Selected Letters 1907–1941*, ed. D. D. Paige (New York, 1971), p. 218. In the Appendix to his anthology *Confucius to Cummings*, Pound traces a succession from Browning, through Hardy and Ford, to himself (ed. with Marcella Spann, New York, 1964), pp. 326–327.
6. Thomas Hardy, "A Singer Asleep," elegy for Swinburne, Hynes, 2:31, l. 16.
7. R. P. Blackmur, "The Shorter Poems of Thomas Hardy," in *Southern Review* 6 (Summer 1940): 44, 28, 20.
8. W. B. Yeats, ed., *Oxford Book of Modern Verse 1892–1935* (London, 1936), Introduction, p. xiv.
9. Eugenio Montale, "A Note on Hardy the Poet," with translations into Italian by Montale and others, *Agenda* 10 (Spring–Summer 1972): 77, 79.
10. J. O. Bailey, *The Poetry of Thomas Hardy: A Handbook and Commentary* (Chapel Hill, 1970), pp. 274–279.

11. Thomas Hardy, *The Life and Work of Thomas Hardy*, ed. Michael Millgate (Athens, Georgia, 1985), p. 218.

12. Ezra Pound did not ignore Hardy's novels. "20 novels," he wrote, "form as good a gradus ad Parnassum as does metrical exercise" (*Guide to Kulchur* [New York, 1970], p. 293).

13. W. H. Auden, ed., *19th Century British Minor Poets* (New York, 1966), Introduction, p. 15.

14. In her influential book *Poetic Closure* (Chicago, 1968), Barbara Herrnstein Smith draws a line from the strong closure of Renaissance and Augustan poetry to the deliberately weak closure of Romantic poetry and the anti-closure of much modern poetry. Smith uses the felicitous phrase "the sense of a lingering suspension" (p. 245) to describe the endings of successful modern poems. I am arguing that that sense, or an enigmatic suggestiveness, characterizes major lyrics, even when their closures and symmetries are relatively formal.

15. T. S. Eliot, "Rudyard Kipling," *On Poetry and Poets* (New York, 1957), pp. 294, 274–275.

16. Philip Larkin, "Wanted: Good Hardy Critic," *Critical Quarterly* 8 (Summer 1966): 179.

17. J. Hillis Miller, "Hardy," *The Linguistic Moment: From Wordsworth to Stevens* (Princeton, 1985), p. 269.

18. Harold Bloom, *A Map of Misreading* (New York, 1975), pp. 9, 19.

19. Christopher Ricks, ed., *The New Oxford Book of Victorian Verse* (New York, 1987), Introduction, p. xxx.

20. Dennis Taylor, *Hardy's Poetry 1860–1928* (London, 1981), pp. xiv–xv, also chap. 1 and Epilogue. See also Taylor's *Hardy's Metres and Victorian Prosody* (Oxford, 1988).

21. Samuel Hynes, "The Question of Development," *The Pattern of Hardy's Poetry* (Chapel Hill, 1961), p. 131.

22. According to Trevor Johnson, Hardy read *The Waste Land* from 1922 on, making "extracts and notes upon it for his commonplace book" (*A Critical Introduction to the Poems of Thomas Hardy* [London, 1991], p. 7). *The Literary Notebooks of Thomas Hardy* (ed. Lennart A. Björk [New York, 1985], vol. 2) show extracts from "Prufrock" (pp. 226–227) and "Miss Helen Slingsby" (p. 441, where Hardy expresses preference for Eliot over Pound and the other vers libre poets).

23. Thomas Hardy, *The Collected Letters*, ed. Richard L. Purdy and Michael Millgate (Oxford, 1978–88), 6: 49, 77–78, 186.

24. See Patricia O'Neill, "Thomas Hardy: Poetics of a Postromantic," *VP* 27 (1989): 129–145. Although Paul Zietlow, in *Moments of Vision: The Poetry of Thomas Hardy* (Cambridge, Massachusetts, 1974), shows how Hardy's realism sometimes opens out to epiphany, Hardy is not notably an epiphanic poet.

HELEN VENDLER

Seamus Heaney
Second Thoughts: The Haw Lantern

Here are thirty-two poems by Seamus Heaney—the yield since *Station Island* (1985). Heaney is a poet of abundance who is undergoing in middle age the experience of natural loss. As the earth loses for him the mass and gravity of familiar presences—parents and friends taken by death—desiccation and weightlessness threaten the former fullness of the sensual life.

The moment of emptiness can be found in other poets. "Already I take up less emotional space / Than a snowdrop," James Merrill wrote at such a point in his own evolution. Lowell's grim engine, churning powerfully on through the late sonnets, did not quite admit the chill of such a moment until *Day by Day*:

> We are things thrown in the air alive in flight . . .
> our rust the color of the chameleon.

It is very difficult for poets of brick and mortar solidity, like Lowell, or of rooted heaviness, like Heaney, to become light, airy, desiccated. In their new style they cannot abandon their former selves. The struggle to be one's old self and one's new self together is the struggle of poetry itself, which must accumulate new layers rather than discard old ones.

Heaney must thus continue to be a poet rich in tactile language, while expressing emptiness, absence, distance. *The Haw Lantern*, poised between these contradictory imperatives of adult life, is almost penitentially faithful to each, determined to forsake neither. Here is the earlier Heaney writing fifteen years ago about moist clay:

> They loaded on to the bank
> Slabs like the squared-off clots
> Of a blue cream . . .
>   Once, cleaning a drain
> I shovelled up livery slicks
> Till the water gradually ran
> Clear on its old floor.
> Under the humus and roots
> This smooth weight. I labour
> Towards it still. It holds and gluts.[1]

Image and sound both bear witness here to the rich fluidity of the natural world. Now, in *The Haw Lantern*, Heaney finds he must, to be truthful to his past, add manufacture to nature. When he looks with adult eyes at his natal earth, he finds machinery there as well as organic matter; and he writes not with fluidity but with aphoristic brevity:

> When I hoked there, I would find
> An acorn and a rusted bolt.
>
> If I lifted my eyes, a factory chimney
> And a dormant mountain.
>
> If I listened, an engine shunting
> And a trotting horse.
> . . .
> My left hand placed the standard iron weight.
> My right tilted a last grain in the balance.

"Is it any wonder," the poet asks, "when I thought / I would have second thoughts?" ('Terminus').

The Haw Lantern is a book of strict, even stiff, second thoughts. Such analytical poetry cannot permit itself a first careless rapture. No longer (at least, not often) do we follow the delightful slope of narrative: "And then, and then." Instead, we see the mind balancing debits and credits. "I balanced all, brought all to mind," said Yeats, using a scale to weigh years behind and years to come. A poet who began as luxuriously as Heaney could hardly have dreamed he would be called to such an audit. The need for adult reckoning must to some degree be attributed to his peculiar internal exile. Born among the Catholic minority in British Protestant Ulster, he came young to social awareness; now removed to the Catholic Republic of Ireland, he is part of an Ulster-bred minority substantially different in culture and upbringing from the majority.

The poetry of second thoughts has its own potential for literary elaboration. *The Haw Lantern* is full of parables and allegories, satires of Irish religious, social and political life. The blank verse of these allegories is as far from the opulent rhymed stanzas of Heaney's sensual, Keatsian aspect as from the slender trimeters and dimeters of his "Irish" side. The strangest poem in *The Haw Lantern*, a blank verse piece called 'The Mud Vision', arises from Heaney's desire to respect amplitude, even in an analytic poem. I don't find the effort wholly successful, but I see in it the way Heaney is willing to flail at impossibility rather than divide his believing youth from his skeptical middle age.

This religious-political-social poem begins with a bitter satiric portrait of an unnamed country dithering between atavistic superstition and yuppie modernity. The landscape displays a thin layer of industrial modernization over a desolate rural emptiness; in a typical scene, terrorist casualties are carried, in a heliport, past the latest touring rock star:

> Statues with exposed hearts and barbed-wire crowns
> Still stood in alcoves, hares flitted beneath
> The dozing bellies of jets, our menu-writers
> And punks with aerosol sprays held their own
> With the best of them. Satellite link-ups
> Wafted over us the blessings of popes, heliports
> Maintained a charmed circle for idols on tour
> And casualties on their stretchers. We sleepwalked
> The line between panic and formulae, . . .
> Watching ourselves at a distance, advantaged
> And airy as a man on a springboard
> Who keeps limbering up because the man cannot dive.

In that last image, Heaney catches the "advantaged and airy" complacency of an impotent nation congratulating itself on political flexibility as a way of concealing indecisiveness. The despair brilliantly hidden in this sketch casts up a compensatory vision. What if a dispossessed country could believe not in its useless statues of the Sacred Heart nor in its modern veneer of restaurants and heliports, but in its own solid earth? In the "mud vision" of the title, a whirling rainbow-wheel of transparent mud appears in the foggy midlands of this unnamed country, and a fine silt of earth spreads from it to touch every cranny. Heaney tries to catch the vision and its effect on those who see it:

> And then in the foggy midlands it appeared,
> Our mud vision, as if a rose window of mud
> Had invented itself out of the glittery damp,
> A gossamer wheel, concentric with its own hub
> Of nebulous dirt, sullied yet lucent
> . . . We were vouchsafed
> Original clay, transfigured and spinning.

The poem runs out of steam trying to imagine how the "mud vision" banishes traditional religion (bulrushes replace lilies on altars, invalids line up for healing under the mud shower, and so on). Eventually, of course, the vision disappears in the "*post factum* jabber" of experts. "We had our chance," says the speaker, "to be mud-men, convinced and estranged," but in hesitation, all opportunity was lost.

"Vision" is meant in the entirely human sense, as we might say Parnell had a vision of a free Ireland, or Gandhi a vision of a free India, but 'The Mud Vision' puts perhaps a too religious cast on clay. Can a vision of the earthly borrow its language from the conventional "vision" of the heavenly ("a rose window . . . lucent . . . original . . . transfigured")?

'The Mud Vision' puts many of Heaney's qualities on record—his territorial piety, his visual wit, his ambition for a better Ireland, his reflectiveness, his anger—and attempts somehow to find a style that can absorb them all. However, 'The Mud Vision' has none of the *sprezzatura* and firm elegance of other poems in *The Haw Lantern*, such as 'Wolfe Tone'. In this posthumous self-portrait, the speaker is the Irish Protestant revolutionary (1763–1798) who attempted a union of Catholics and Protestants against England, and was captured in 1798 after his invading fleet was defeated off Donegal. Tone committed suicide in prison before he could be executed for treason. He symbolizes the reformer estranged by his gifts, his style and his daring from the very people he attempts to serve:

> Light as a skiff, manoeuvrable yet outmanoeuvred,
> I affected epaulettes and a cockade,
> wrote a style well-bred and impervious

to the solidarity I angled for . . .
I was the shouldered oar that ended up
far from the brine and whiff of venture,
like a scratching post or a crossroads flagpole,
out of my element among small farmers.

Though the first two lines of 'Wolfe Tone' owe something to Lowell's *Day by Day*, the poem has a dryness and reticence all its own. The force of the poem lies in the arid paradox—for reformers—that authentic style is often incompatible with political solidarity with the masses (a paradox on which Socialist Realism foundered). The desolate alienation of the artist/revolutionary is phrased here with the impersonality and obliqueness of Heaney's minimalist style (of which there was a foretaste in *Station Island*'s 'Sweeney Redivivus'). I hope I have said enough to suggest where Heaney finds himself morally at this moment, poised between the "iron weight" of analysis and "the last grain" of fertile feeling, between cutting satire and a hopeful vision of possibility. Besides the blank-verse political parables I have mentioned, *The Haw Lantern* contains several notable elegies, among them a sequence of eight sonnets ('Clearances') in memory of Heaney's mother, who died in 1984. To make this hardest of genres new, Heaney moves away from both stateliness and scepticism. Borrowing from Milosz's 'The World', a poem in which luminous past is evoked in the simplest, most childlike terms, Heaney writes a death-sonnet that imagines all Oedipal longings fulfilled:

It is Number 5, New Row, Land of the Dead,
Where grandfather is rising from his place
With spectacles pushed back on a clean bald head
To welcome a bewildered homing daughter
Before she even knocks, 'What's this? What's this?'
And they sit down in the shining room together.

Such felicity brings Milosz's 'naive' effect fully into our idiom, and displays the self-denying capacity of the son to write about his mother as ultimately her father's daughter.

But 'Clearances' also touches on the irritability, the comedy, and the dailiness of the bond between sons and mothers. In one of its best sonnets son and mother are folding sheets together: and here I recall Alfred Kazin's recent memoir of his youth in the Thirties, when he wrote for a freshman English class at City College "an oedipal piece about helping my mother carry ice back to our kitchen, each of us holding one end of a towel":

> This was such a familiar and happy experience for me in the summer that I was astonished by the young instructor's disgust on reading my paper. He was a vaguely British type, a recent Oxford graduate . . . who openly disliked his predominantly Jewish students. My loving description of carrying ice in partnership with my mother seemed to him, as he tightly put it, "impossible to comprehend."[2]

It is useful to be reminded how recently literature has been open to such experiences. Here is Heaney with his mother folding the sheets:

> The cool that came off sheets just off the line
> Made me think the damp must still be in them
> But when I took my corners of the linen
> And pulled against her, first straight down the hem
> And then diagonally, then flapped and shook
> The fabric like a sail in a cross-wind,
> They made a dried-out undulating thwack.

Petrarch or Milton could hardly have imagined that this might be the octave of a sonnet. Yet the pretty 'rhymes' echo tradition, as *line* stretches to *linen* (the clothesline and the sheets), and as *them* shrinks to *hem* (a folded sheet in itself). Frost, Heaney's precursor here, would have recognized the unobtrusive sentence-sounds; the line "Made me think the damp must still be in them" could slip into 'Birches' without a hitch. (The "dried-out undulating thwack" though, is pure Heaney; Frost's eye was more on Roman moral epigram than on sensual fact.)

The seven-line "sestet" of the sonnet closes with a muted reference to the writing of the poem (the poet is now inscribing his family romance on a different set of folded sheets), but this literary marker is almost invisible in Heaney's intricately worked plainness:

> So we'd stretch and fold and end up hand to hand
> For a split second as if nothing had happened
> For nothing had that had not always happened
> Beforehand, day by day, just touch and go,
> Coming close again by holding back
> In moves where I was x and she was o
> Inscribed in sheets she'd sewn from ripped-out sacks.

Taut lines and folded sheets connect mother and son, in art as in life.

Like 'Clearances', the other elegies in this volume combine the density of living with the bleakness of loss, preserving the young, tender Heaney in the present stricken witness. 'The Stone Verdict' is an anticipatory elegy for Heaney's father, who has since died; other poems commemorate his young niece Rachel, dead in an accident; his wife's mother ('The Wishing Tree'); and his colleague at Harvard, Robert Fitzgerald. Heaney affirms that the space left in life by the absence of the dead takes on a shape so powerful that it becomes a presence in itself. In the elegy for his mother, Heaney's emblem for the shocking absence is a felled chestnut tree that was his "coeval"—planted in a jam jar the year he was born. Cut down, it becomes "utterly a source,"

> Its heft and hush become a bright nowhere,
> A soul ramifying and forever
> Silent, beyond silence listened for.

Heaney's sharply etched "nowhere" is a correction not only of Christian promises of heaven, but also of Yeats's exuberant purgatorial visions of esoteric afterlifes. It returns Irish elegy to truthfulness.

Heaney has said that because people of any culture share standards and beliefs, the artist's "inner drama goes beyond the personal to become symptomatic and therefore political."[3] To ascribe immense and unforgettable value to the missing human piece, simply because it is missing, is to put the power to ascribe value squarely in the human rather than in the religious sphere. Since institutional ideology everywhere reserves to itself alone the privilege of conferring value, it is all the more important for writers to remind us that control of value lies in individual, as well as in collective, hands.

Heaney directly addresses the question of value in 'The Riddle', the poem placed last in this self-questioning book. His governing image here is the ancient one of the sieve that separates wheat from chaff. Such sieves are no longer in use, but the poet has seen one:

> You never saw it used but still can hear
> The sift and fall of stuff hopped on the mesh,
> Clods and buds in a little dust-up,
> The dribbled pile accruing under it.
>
> Which would be better, what sticks or what falls through?
> Or does the choice itself create the value?

This is the poem of a man who has discovered that much of what he has been told was wheat is chaff, and a good deal that was dismissed as chaff turns out to be what he might want to keep. Coleridge, remembering classical myths of torment, wrote "Work without hope draws nectar in a sieve"; Heaney, rewriting Coleridge, thinks that the endless labors of rejection and choice might yet be a way to salvation. He asks himself, at the close of 'The Riddle', to

> . . . work out what was happening in that
> story
> Of the man who carried water in a riddle.
>
> Was it culpable ignorance, or was it rather
> A *via negativa* through drops and let-downs?

The great systems of dogma (patriotic, religious, ethical) must be abandoned, Heaney suggests, in favor of a ceaseless psychic sorting. Discarding treasured pieties and formed rules, the poet finds "drops and let downs," and he refuses to take much joy in the task of sifting, though a middle couplet shows it to be undertaken with good will:

> Legs apart, deft-handed, start a mime
> To sift the sense of things from what's imagined.

In Heaney's earlier work, this couplet would have been the end of the poem, breathing resolve and hope. Now he ends the poem asking whether his sifting should be condemned as "culpable ignorance" (the Roman Catholic phrase is taken from the penitentials) or allowed as a *via negativa*. The latter phrase, which is also drawn from Catholicism, is a theological term connected to mysticism, suggesting that we can know God only as he is not.

The elegiac absences and riddles of *The Haw Lantern* are balanced by powerful presences, none more striking than the emblematic winter hawthorn in the title poem. This poem, by dwelling throughout on a single allegorical image, displays a relatively new manner in Heaney's work. In the past, Heaney's imagery has been almost indecently prolific; readers of *North* (1975) will remember, for instance, the Arcimboldo-like composite of exhumed cadaver called Grauballe Man:

> The grain of his wrist
> is like bog oak,
> the ball of his heel
>
> like a basalt egg.
> His instep has shrunk

cold as a swan's foot
or a wet swamp root.

His hips are the ridge
and purse of a mussel,
his spine an eel arrested
under a glisten of mud.[4]

It is hard for a poet so fertile in sliding simile to stay put, to dwell on a single image until it becomes an emblem; it means going deeper rather than rippling on. 'The Haw Lantern', doing just this, fires on the one burning spot in the blank landscape of winter—the red berry, or haw, on the naked hawthorn branch. At first the poet sees the berry as an almost apologetic flame, indirectly suggesting his own quelled hopes as a spokesman. He goes deeper into self-questioning by transforming the haw into the lantern carried by Diogenes, searching for the one just man. The stoic haw, meditation reminds the poet, is both pith and pit, at once fleshy and stony. The birds peck at it, but it continues ripening. In this upside-down almost-sonnet, the stern haw lantern scrutinizes the poet scrutinizing it:

The wintry haw is burning out of season,
crab of the thorn, a small light for small people,
wanting no more from them but that they keep
the wick of self-respect from dying out,
not having to blind them with illumination.

But sometimes when your breath plumes in the frost
it takes the roaming shape of Diogenes
with his lantern, seeking one just man;
so you end up scrutinized from behind the haw
he holds up at eye-level on its twig,
and you flinch before its bonded pith and stone,
its blood-prick that you wish would test and clear you,
its pecked-at ripeness that scans you, then moves on.

Like other poems in Heaney's new volume, 'The Haw Lantern' reflects a new despair of country and of self.

Heaney's burning haw can bear comparison with Herbert's emblematic rose, "whose hue, angry and brave, Bids the rash gazer wipe his eye". Forsaking topical reference, the artist writing in such genres as the emblem poem ('The Haw Lantern') and allegory ('The Mud Vision') positions himself at a distance from daily events. Such analytic, generalized poetry hopes to gain in intelligence what it loses in immediacy of reference. (The greatest example of such an aesthetic choice is Milton's decision to write the epic of Puritan war, regicide, reform, and defeat by retelling Genesis.)

Heaney has several times quoted Mandelstam's "notion that poetry—and art in general—is addressed to . . . 'The reader in posterity'".

> It is not directed exploitatively towards its immediate audience—although of course it does not set out to disdain the immediate audience either. It is directed towards the new perception which it is its function to create.[5]

The social, historical, and religious perceptions of *The Haw Lantern*, if they should become general in Ireland, would indeed create a new psychic reality there. Such a prospect seems so unlikely now that it is only by believing in "the reader in posterity" that a writer can continue to address Irish issues at all.

I have saved the best of this collection for the last: two excellent poems about the life of writing. The first, 'Alphabets', written as the Phi Beta Kappa poem for Harvard, presents a series of joyous scenes that show the child becoming a writer. The alphabets of the title are those learned by the poet as he grew up: English, Latin, Irish and Greek. They stand for the widening sense of place, time, and culture gained as the infant grows to be a youth, a teacher, and a poet. Against Wordsworth's myth of childhood radiance lost, the poem sets a countermyth of imaginative power becoming fuller and freer with expanding linguistic and literary power.

With great charm, 'Alphabets' shows us the child in school mastering his first alphabet:

> First it is 'copying out', and then 'English'
> Marked correct with a little leaning hoe.
> Smells of inkwells rise in the classroom hush.
> A globe in the window tilts like a coloured O.

Learning Irish, with its prosody so different from those of English and Latin, awakens the boy's Muse:

> Here in her snooded garment and bare feet,
> All ringleted in assonance and woodnotes,
> The poet's dream stole over him like sunlight
> And passed into the tenebrous thickets.

The boy becomes a teacher, and the verse makes gentle fun of his self-conscious and forgivable vanity:

> The globe has spun. He stands in a wooden O.
> He alludes to Shakespeare. He alludes to Graves.

'Alphabets' closes with a hope for global vision, based on two exemplary human images. The first is that of a Renaissance humanist necromancer who hung from his ceiling "a figure of the world with colours in it", so that he could always carry it in his mind—

> So that the figure of the universe
> And 'not just single things' would meet his sight
>
> When he walked abroad.

The second figure is that of the scientist-astronaut, who also tries to comprehend the whole globe:

> . . . from his small window
> The astronaut sees all he has sprung from,
> The risen, aqueous, singular, lucent O
> Like a magnified and buoyant ovum.

Heaney implies that whatever infant alphabet we may start from, we will go on to others, by which we hope to encompass the world. Ours is the first generation to have a perceptual (rather than conceptual) grasp of the world as a single orbiting sphere—"the risen, aqueous, singular lucent O", and the almost inexpressible joy of sensuous possession lies in that line, a joy Heaney sees in the cultural and intellectual possession of the world, whether by humanist or scientist. 'Alphabets' combines a humorous tenderness of self-mockery with an undiminished memory of the vigilant vows of youth, proving that middle age need not mark a discontinuity in life or writing.

The other brilliant poem here, 'From the Frontier of Writing', offers a *vie de poète* altogether different from that of 'Alphabets'. Written in an adapted Dantesque *terza rima*, 'The Frontier' retells a narrow escape from a modern hell. It takes as its emblem the paralyzing experience—familiar even to tourists—of being stopped and questioned at a military roadblock in Ireland. The writer, however, has not only to pass through real roadblocks but to confront as well the invisible roadblocks of consciousness and conscience. In either case, you can lose your nerve: in life, you can be cowed:

in writing, you can be tempted to dishonesty or evasion. I quote this report from the frontier in full.

> The tightness and the nilness round that space
> when the car stops in the road, the troops inspect
> its make and number and, as one bends his face
>
> towards your window, you catch sight of more
> on a hill beyond, eyeing with intent
> down cradled guns that hold you under cover
>
> and everything is pure interrogation
> until a rifle motions and you move
> with guarded unconcerned acceleration—
>
> a little emptier, a little spent
> as always by that quiver in the self,
> subjugated, yes, and obedient.
>
> So you drive on to the frontier of writing
> where it happens again. The guns on tripods;
> the sergeant with his on-off mike repeating
>
> data about you, waiting for the squawk
> of clearance; the marksman training down
> out of the sun upon you like a hawk.
>
> And suddenly you're through, arraigned yet freed,
> as if you'd passed from behind a waterfall
> on the black current of tarmac road
>
> past armour-plated vehicles, out between
> the posted soldiers flowing and receding
> like tree shadows into the polished windscreen.

This poem is so expressive of the present armed tension in Ireland that it is political simply by being. It produces in us an Irish weather—menacing, overcast, electric—so intense that for a while we live in it. It has the allegorical solidity of the *déjà vu*, and the formal solidity of its two twelve-line roadblocks.

those women whose voices, according to Yeats, 'grew shrill with argument', turning into 'an old bellows full of angry wind'. She took an active part in organising support for the prolonged Dublin Transport Workers' strike of 1913 (which Yeats, under her influence, campaigned in support of).[3] Yeats's poetry acknowledges but mystifies all this. In it, she is the mindless militant, redeemed only by her storm-tossed beauty, who in 'No Second Troy' in *The Green Helmet*

> would of late
> Have taught to ignorant men most violent ways,
> Or hurled the little streets upon the great,
> Had they but courage equal to desire.

But he can forgive this, as he can forgive her filling his days with misery, because these are the mere froth of history through which a deeper meaning is expressed. Her 'nobleness' is 'not natural in an age like this'. It is, ultimately, a supernatural force linking her to the great mythic archetypes,

> What could have made her peaceful with a mind
> That nobleness made simple as a fire,
> With beauty like a tightened bow, a kind
> That is not natural in an age like this,
> Being high and solitary and most stern?
> Why, what could she have done, being what she is?
> Was there another Troy for her to burn?

'Being what she is' is not described except in terms of a metaphor which calls up other classical and mythological analogues, the virgin huntress Diana and Penthesilea and her Amazons.

'What she is', as a historical figure, however, is precisely *not* this. 'What she is' is a very Modern agitator, a stirrer-up of class hatred, seeking to bring down the very 'nobleness' Yeats in imagination attributes to her and to the 'great streets' she wishes to burn. Yeats's ennobling metaphors and analogies do violence to the actual historical figure, by casting the origins of all her activity precisely in the Ascendancy power she pits herself against. She is 'high and solitary and most stern', and thereby reappropriable to traditional cultural-political discourses and fantasies. The mythologising diminishes as it claims to aggrandise, making her actual courage and tenacity into one more instance of an effortless supernatural energy.

The literary means by which this is effected is simple. The whole poem is a series of rhetorical questions in the subjunctive mood. The first two questions insinuate a subjective motivation to external acts, and cast the external world as a mere stage for the expression of 'inner' power. 'Why should I blame her . . . ?' from the start gives priority to Yeats's viewpoint; 'What could have made her peaceful?' suggests that it is the inadequacy of the age which drives her to desperate acts. The second sentence moves away from the historical specificity of the first, which links the poet's misery with ignorant men and mean streets, to a realm speculatively in the interior of Maud Gonne's mind, a site remarkably like the *Anima Mundi*. Both of these sentences engage in, as they dissemble, acts of historical interpretation, as do the two one-line questions with which the poem ends.

The penultimate sentence repeats in miniature the doing and being antithesis of the first two questions. For such great figures, being issues directly in action, without prevarication. Grammatically a subordinate, participial qualification of deeds, 'being' in Yeats's rhetoric actually displaces deeds, which the past subjunctive reduces to a mere emanation of 'being'. Yet the tautological emptiness of the phrase 'being what she is' indicates how Yeats substitutes a hollow signifier for an actual signified. That signified in turn is pushed out of its historical particularity by the use of a merely conditional and speculative form of the verb. Gonne 'would have taught', 'would have . . . hurled'—*if* there had been a matching historical force in the masses. And, given her nature, what else 'could she have done' but what she did? The poem denies the possibility of historical agency and choice, with all its uncertainties and anxieties, to instate instead a kind of mythic determinism. It presents, in traditional terms, a woman driven by her nature, rather than by a sense of historical urgency and choice, existentially compelled to do what she has done. But if this is in her nature, then she is in a strange sense not responsible for it. The poet exonerates her of her grotesque politics. As another, later Amazon might have declaimed, there is no alternative.

Yeats's last question then answers itself. Gonne's problem—one of how tactics relate to strategy in a class struggle—is not that her *actual* projects found no matching correlative in the balance of class forces in Irish society. The problem instead becomes a *tragedy*: that the age was unworthy of her. Her 'real' being for Yeats is not her historical contingency at all, but that of a historically displaced mythic force.

Nevertheless, though the question answers itself (the answer is 'No'), it remains rather puzzling. What have Irish class and national politics in the 1900s got to do with Troy? And did Maud Gonne burn the first Troy? For that matter, did *Helen*, rather than her affronted cuckold husband and his gang of brigands? Or does Yeats simply mean that unfortunately in this degenerate world there are no more Troys and so Maud must degrade herself to put up with second-best, burning only an inferior Dublin? Behind this lies a further implication: that she is forgiven her vulgar actual politics on the grounds that she was driven, not by the urge to right injustice, abolish poverty and inequality, but by a *femme fatale's* desire to see civilisations burning. The eternal female gets her kicks from goading men to fight for her. Whatever else is going on in this poem, Yeats is engaged in a major act of ideological recuperation. It is a form of taming and domesticating at the very moment that it speaks through a fantasy of wildness.

We can see the same process at work in one of Yeats's last poems, 'A Bronze Head', about the bust of Gonne in old age in the Dublin Art Gallery. Here, the phrase 'not natural in an age like this' is replaced by an invocation of a supernatural linked, as in 'Leda and the Swan', to the bestial. The bust presents a head 'Human, superhuman, a bird's round eye'. Gonne is in some way *uncanny*, for such a concept alone can explain the intensity and persistence of her commitment. Once again, the rhetorical question allows Yeats to slide surreptitiously from history to myth, speculatively summoning up supernatural forces ostensibly to explain but actually to mystify the nature of historical agency. The plenitude of being he attributes to Gonne in youth, 'her form all full / As though with magnanimity of light', turns easily into an emptiness—one founded in 'terror'. This emptiness, as if in desperation, seeks relief in the *hysterica passio* of deeds, in a world which is also empty, for it 'finds there nothing to make its terror less'. The bronze bust catches in Gonne's old age the 'terror' that Yeats detected in her youth, though then she was a 'form all full', not empty, and 'a most gentle woman'. But youth and age, fleshly and bronze images are only superficial forms of a 'substance' that exists outside of history. The rhetorical question once more raises the relation between eternity's noumena and the mere phenomena of history. Gonne is subjected to the poem's authorial power in the very question, 'Which of her forms has shown her substance right?' This male interpreter can, in this present of retrospect, see her true substance, has a special insight:

> But even at the starting-post, all sleek and new,
>
> I saw the wildness in her and I thought
> A vision of terror that it must live through
> Had shattered her soul.

That terror can only be the 'terrible beauty' of contemporary Irish history, supposedly envisioned by Gonne but actually retrospectively attributed to her by the poet who is trying to remake her as an image, something intended, complete. That this is actually domestication is confirmed by the overt patriarchal appropriation which closes the stanza. Infected by her wildness, himself grown wild, he 'wandered murmuring everywhere, "My child, my child!"' 'Among School Children', almost two decades earlier, had performed the same recuperative act, summoning up as a mythical archetype the unapproachable Ledaean body of a Maud Gonne now, in the order of history, transformed into a crone, and then projecting her before him as a 'living child' who drives his heart 'wild'. There too he had spoken of how the merely 'trivial event' of some 'childish day' in the realm of personal history could be transformed by the power of emotion into 'tragedy', and then transformed once again into a Neoplatonic, transhistorical pattern through the mediation of story-telling.

By the opening of the final stanza of 'A Bronze Head', he can offer an alternative interpretation of Gonne which endows her explicitly with 'supernatural' power, because it is only in his memory of how he 'thought her' that she possesses it. Masochistic admiration for the 'stern' female makes her a captive of an historical teleology. She is a scourge of god, the carrier of some darker agency whose sterner eye looks through her eye, contemplating the massacre necessary to purge a modern world in decline and fall. No longer a free agent, her image (its metallic hardness part of the meaning) is recruited from the actual politics she espoused to a quite contrary cause, embodying that aristocratic disdain for democracy which in the 1930s Yeats sought in Fascism. If Yeats here thinks only massacre can save this world where heroic reverie is mocked by clown and knave, he in turn engages in mockery of the real historical subject whose memory is summoned up only to be misrepresented. He does not admit to such ruthlessness of motive, nor attribute it directly to Gonne. Instead, he envisages a power that works through and sometimes against the grain of the actual human intentions, rather like Hegel's 'cunning of Reason'. It is not Gonne but some supernatural power that looks through her eye and wonders what is left for massacre to save.

'Hound Voice', which comes shortly after 'A Bronze Head' in both arrangements of *Last Poems*, makes the connection explicit, not by dissociating the sweetness of the woman's voice from violence, but by linking it to the baying of the wild hunt of Irish and English legend. Its second stanza spills this out, evoking the concept of terror he associates with Gonne in 'A Bronze Head':

> The women that I picked spoke sweet and low
> And yet gave tongue. 'Hound Voices' were they all.
> We picked each other from afar and knew
> What hour of terror comes to test the soul,
> And in that terror's name obeyed the call,
> And understood, what none have understood,
> Those images that waken in the blood.

But these are not images out of the Great Memory. They rise up from a specifically modern source, a Nietzschean modern myth of a blood wisdom driving to tear up 'the settled ground' of civilisation. The poem itself summons the hound voices, a call to violence, 'Stumbling upon the blood-dark track once more', delighting in awakening from quotidian lethargy. After this poem 'High Talk' speaks contemptuously of those 'modern' people who lack high stilts, for some Promethean 'rogue of the world' stole them to 'patch up a fence or a fire'. The poem ends with a vision of the 'terrible novelty of light', a nightmare vision as 'night splits' of great sea-horses which bare their teeth and laugh at a dawn which heralds the really new: a postmodern era of ruthless predation. This new dawn is a Fascist one. 'Why Should not Old Men be Mad?' gives as reason for the poet's madness the degenerations of this filthy modern world which see:

> A girl that knew all Dante once
> Live to bear children to a dunce;
> A Helen of social welfare dream,
> Climb on a wagonette and scream.

Old men and old books alone possess a knowledge founded in and leading to madness. Women cannot keep their beautiful voices, once they venture into what for Yeats is a realm of male discourse, the order of politics and of history. Their scream then is not just demagogy but hysteria.

What these last poems of Yeats's speak of is the negation of all human agency. As in *A Vision*, human acts will fail or succeed insofar as they advance the intentions of some ferocious, transhistorical force, founded in wildness and terror with its own ideas of hierarchy and authority, foul and fair, gangling and great, ancestral pearls and modern sties. Yeats casts on to the universe a paradigm of ancient authority which has a brutally up-to-date aetiology. The supernatural is the site of a disturbance in the surface of Yeats's rhetoric, an attempt to contain within established forms historical forces which threaten to overwhelm and destroy them. But the poems repeatedly half admit that which they are repressing. 'The Statues', dated 9 April 1938, looks back in commemoration of the month in which the Easter Rising occurred to forge a direct link between the moment of modernity and the independence struggle. But it is a contradictory linkage, only redeemed by a supernatural intervention which transfigures squalid event into mythic archetype. The supernatural, itself a question dialogically awaiting an answer, enters history through the back door of the rhetorical question:

> When Pearse summoned Cuchulain to his side,
> What stalked through the Post Office? What intellect,
> What calculation, number, measurement, replied?
> We Irish, born into that ancient sect
> But thrown upon this filthy modern tide
> And by its formless spawning fury wrecked,
> Climb to our proper dark, that we may trace
> The lineaments of a plummet-measured face.

The origins of Modernism may be sought by enquiring into those ancient sects and sources, and everywhere in the poetry of Yeats as of Eliot and Pound we are encouraged to seek them there. But what we find, on enquiry, is an 'address not known' that returns us to the 'filthy modern tide' of contemporary history. If the posthumously published *Last Poems* address the historical emergency of the late 1930s, they repeatedly return us to those originary moments of the century in which this crisis of the Modern was forged. In its new-found modernity, *The Green Helmet* in 1910 was the first bitter revelation of what was to come.

Our Modern Preoccupation

'Reconciliation', the poem which follows 'No Second Troy' in *The Green Helmet*, is a particularly complex version of this crisis. Also of twelve lines and in the same measure, it begins like the preceding poem with the concept of blame, but statement rather than question projects the blaming on to others. 'Some may have blamed you', he says, for taking away the verses that could move them. One of Yeats's last rhetorical questions, in 'The Man and the Echo' in *Last Poems*, would remind us what that 'moving' involved: 'Did that play of mine send out / Certain men the English shot?' But Maud Gonne not only silences poetic discourse. She also magically imposes on the historical man a sensory blackout as extreme as Gerontion's, 'the ears being deafened, the sight of the eyes blind / With lightning', in a supernatural annunciation like that of Dionysus. The figure of the female ostensibly replaces that which in actuality she everywhere signifies. Gonne is supposed to represent Venus rather than Mars, but in reality she figures forth the violence of war and patriarchal power: 'kings, / Helmets and swords, and half-forgotten things / That were like memories of you'.

Anything that Yeats says about memory is full of contradictions, but this is a peculiarly convoluted utterance. He is deafened and blinded by her departure—but not dumb. Instead he sings about new topics which are actually old topics, topics she in her newness and modernity is supposed to have replaced. These 'half-forgotten things' of a time (his Celtic Twilight verse, the Keatsian inheritance) before he knew her seem also like memories of her. Before the full implications of this can be grasped, the poem shifts tack with an interruption which puts the world back in its irrelevant place and, calling up their shared hysteria, a laughing and weeping fit, hurls the imagery of war into the pit. She is 'gone', but the poem's final couplet appeals to her as if she were present, and speaks of a symbolic loss not of male potency but of female fecundity:

> But, dear, cling close to me; since you were gone,
> My barren thoughts have chilled me to the bone.

The final rhyme names her fullness ('gone' / 'Gonne') in contrast to his emptiness. Maud Gonne in her very name becomes the figure of lack, a gap in being who exercises power by virtue of her absence, opening a breach through which the ancestral voices prophesying war pass and repass. She is the site of that central contradiction indicated in the very title of the next poem of the sequence, 'King and No King':

> 'Would it were anything but merely voice!'
> The No King cried who after that was King,
> Because he had not heard of anything
> That balanced with a word is more than noise;
> Yet Old Romance being kind, let him prevail
> Somewhere or somehow that I have forgot,
> Though he'd but cannon—Whereas we that had thought
> To have lit upon as clean and sweet a tale
> Have been defeated by that pledge you gave
> In momentary anger long ago;
> And I that have not your faith, how shall I know
> That in the blinding light beyond the grave
> We'll find so good a thing as that we have lost?
> The hourly kindness, the day's common speech,
> The habitual content of each with each
> When neither soul nor body has been crossed.

The poem opens with the mysterious cry of the No King who afterwards was King, a lack which contains its fullness *in potentia*. But the cry suggests a discrepancy between the fulness of history and the emptiness of voice. Even the half-rhyme with 'noise' reinforces this sense, though the No King's lack arises in part from his inability to grasp that 'anything / That balanced with a word is more than noise'. He misses, that is, the speech as signification, reducing it to meaningless noise. It is precisely meaning that turns 'anything' into something, gives the potential body and fullness. Narrative gives context and body to event. But the language is strangely indeterminate here, as if taunting with the empty volatility of signifiers never fixed to time and place and significance. 'Old Romance', the cliché enacting the obsolescence to which it refers, allows the No King to prevail in his signifying void, and the poet's own forgetfulness leaves him dangling there, 'Somewhere or somehow that I have forgot'.

Out of this forgetfulness the armed man strides. Words are empty before the reality of power, the poet's tale defeated. But these words are defeated only by other words that suddenly take on a new and terrifying substance, in part because though spoken in momentary anger long ago they seem a pledge that cannot be broken. Cut short in an impotence figured as blindness, the speaker's rhetorical question rises to the full height of loss, which, at first unspecified, then emerges as the loss of a shared discourse in which solidarity also involves an invidious levelling, 'The hourly kindness, the day's common speech', where 'kindness' takes up the idea of Romance 'being kind', but also has resonances in that 'King and No King' Hamlet, another empty man . . . dispossessed by one 'a little more than kin and less than kind'.

'Common' is a word at a crossroads here. Yeats links it with insufficiency, 'mere' common speech, 'habitual content', mundane kindness, and the negation of the last line reinforces this. Yet this is also 'so good a thing . . . that we have lost'. The word focuses the central class contradiction in which the Modernist impulse originates. On the one hand, 'common speech' implies linguistic unification under the sign of power (King). On the other, it suggests the reduction of authority to the meanness of the mean (No King). The poem is strange in its refusal of specification. What it does however specify is linguistic insufficiency as the figure of an historical lack. Heir and usurper are simultaneously Kings and No Kings, the fullness of the referent and the emptiness of the signifier, self-negating in the play of mere voice, cry, word, noise, Old Romance, tale, pledge, common speech, conspiring to cancel each other out in a historical deadlock where only deeds and cannons can claim meanings unto themselves. Where words are deadlocked, that is, the discourse can be changed only by acts of violence.

Richard Ellmann has called our attention to the source of the poem's title in Beaumont and Fletcher's 1611 play, *A King and No King*.[4] Here, falling in love with the woman he believes to be his sister, Arbaces rages against the idea of kinship, whose bonds are mere linguistic fetters on behaviour. The speech that gives rise to Yeats's opening line questions the relation between words and swords. Systems of kinship are authorised it seems not by nature but by a consensus of common assumptions. But if the flesh rebels against these common values, where is the source of authority? How *can* discourse, mere voice, construct power?

> I have lived
> To conquer men, and now am overthrown
> Only by words, brother and sister. Where
> Have those words dwelling? I will find 'em out
> And utterly destroy 'em; but they are
> Not to be grasped: let 'em be men or beasts. . . .
> Let 'em be anything but merely voice.

If they were substantial things, Arbaces says, he could seize and destroy them. But they have ineluctable power precisely because they are 'merely voice'. Discourse is more irresistible than any physical force, because it cannot be fixed and extirpated. It is everywhere and nowhere, as Arbaces is King and No King, slipping from the grasp only to surround the troubled subject with bans and remonstrances.

The play finally reveals Arbaces to be an adopted child, and therefore not lineally king or brother. By marrying his supposed 'sister' he can become husband and king, entering into *real* relations not through inheritance but through contract. It is a profoundly significant myth for Yeats, combining the personal anguish, of a compulsory 'fraternal' relation with Gonne, with the whole question of legitimacy and succession, authority as both the signifier and the signified. Words are not to be grasped, yet they set the common limits and define the powers of authority, shaping the whole discourse within which acts become thinkable. Arbaces' normal solution would be violence, but this peculiar deadlock of words cannot be resolved by action because it is in the very nexus of ideological and material relations, of kinship and kingship, that the contradiction is most effectively transfixed.

The Green Helmet is obsessed with the relation between solitary individuals and crowds, from its very first poem, 'His Dream', which announces the painful transit from Celtic twilight at sea to the turbulent crowds of history on the shore. This baying crowd draws the poet into its agitation, so that he too takes up the song. But the mysterious figure in his boat is that of Death, the destiny to which poet and crowd alike are drawn. 'A Woman Homer Sung' tries to return Gonne to dream, detached from history, transformed into an image which 'shadowed in a glass / What thing her body was'. But 'thing', as elsewhere, dehistoricises and dehumanises. Similarly, in the image of her walking on a cloud, interpretation and event, history and story merge into a myth where 'life and letters seem / But an heroic dream'. 'Peace' likewise is about the wish that art might transform the historical 'storm' Gonne symbolises into a form of 'noble lines', combining delicacy, sternness and charm, sweetness and strength. The use of Homeric analogy as vehicle of reappropriation is exposed here in the wish that 'Time could touch a form / That could show what Homer's age / Bred to be a hero's wage'. The commodification of the woman as wage is the hidden agenda of all the romanticising, dreamy glorification. The troubadour motif of poetry as courtly tribute in 'Against Unworthy Praise' reveals its true face in the idea of a dreaming which 'Earned slander, ingratitude, / From self-same dolt and knave'. Gonne's life becomes a labyrinth 'That her own strangeness perplexed' because in part of the need to mystify her historical agency into strangeness, rhetorically transforming her into a mythical archetype combining the wildness of the lion and the vulnerability of the child, reinstating patriarchy as an act of loving kindness.

Three twelve-line poems linked together in this volume spell out the political undertones of this whole negotiation: 'Upon a House Shaken by the Land Agitation', 'At the Abbey Theatre', and 'These Are the Clouds'. The first speaks of Lady Gregory's house as one threatened by popular agitation. Its rhetorical question (How would the world benefit if this house were ruined, no longer a home for greatness?) answers itself negatively and in passing in a concessionary clause which dismisses the answer as trivial: 'Mean roof-trees' would be 'sturdier for its fall'. What is interesting, however, is the way this leads at once to the relation between language and power, between 'The gifts that govern men' and 'gradual time's last gift, a written speech / Wrought of high laughter, loveliness and ease'. That 'written/Wrought' combination relates to Gonne in 'A Woman Homer Sung', but is here applied to Lady Gregory, the disputed territory across which a debate is conducted with Gonne's politics. The argument assumes that the identification of traditional sanctity and loveliness with a life of leisured ease, that is, of culture with class privilege, cannot be refuted.

The oxymoron 'written speech', referring to Lady Gregory's transcriptions of Irish folk tales, attempts rhetorically to resolve a political division between a popular oral culture and the authoritative writing of those who govern men. In 'These Are the Clouds', also addressed to Gregory, the clouds are the crowds that mob a declining power, reducing all things to 'one common level'. But a syntactical Freudian slip confers 'The majesty that shuts his burning eye' (intended to be in apposition to the kingly 'sun') on the clouds (by implication the masses), complicating the poem's allegiances.

'At the Abbey Theatre' expands on the dilemma of this dual allegiance. The closeness of the imitation to its original in Ronsard, elegist of a declining aristocracy, adds a peculiar frisson to the up-to-dateness with which it speaks of contemporary Ireland. Ostensibly it addresses the idea of a new writing for a new nation, represented by the Gaelic verse of Douglas Hyde (under his Gaelic pseudonym). Yet in reverting to Ronsardian precedent Yeats undermines the very idea of originality: it is all a matter of fashion. He remarks that 'we' (it is not clear whether Hyde is included in the pronoun) have been attacked for being 'high and airy' and then contrarily mocked 'Because we have made our art of common things'. Hyde has dandled and fed his public from the book. Yeats asks for the secret, in an insulting request for 'a new trick to please'. But the way forward is not to trick or bridle this Proteus, the volatile, fickle crowd, as changeable as the sea, like the mob in Shakespeare's Roman plays. His two questions imply an excluded middle:

> Is there a bridle for this Proteus
> That turns and changes like his draughty seas?
> Or is there none, most popular of men,
> But when they mock us, that we mock again?

'Popular' is clearly, like 'common', at a semantic crossroads here, suggesting both 'of the people' (good) and 'demagogic' (bad). The ambivalent jeering tone speaks straight out of the vulnerable heart of Yeatsian ideology, and prepares the way for that carnivalesque counter-mocking which, in 'Easter 1916', 'Nineteen Hundred and Nineteen' and 'Meditations', contrasts the 'high laughter' of the genteel with the 'casual comedy', 'motley', 'jokes of civil war' of the low. Yeats's comments on Hyde, who became first president of the New Republic, as 'the cajoler of crowds'[5] are revealing. Of the charm of Hyde's Gaelic, 'all spontaneous, all joyous, every speech born out of itself', he wrote elsewhere in *Autobiographies*:

> Had he shared our modern preoccupation with the mystery of life, learnt our modern construction, he might have grown into another and happier Synge.... He had the folk mind as no modern man has had it, its qualities and its defects, and for a few days in the year Lady Gregory and I shared his absorption in that mind.... Nothing in that language of his was abstract, nothing worn-out; he need not, as must the writer of some language exhausted by modern civilisation, reject word after word, cadence after cadence; he had escaped our perpetual, painful, purification.[6]

The word 'modern' wears itself out by repetition here. By contrast with the complexity, exhaustion and self-subversion of the Modern, Hyde's Gaelic writings represent an impossible spontaneity and clarity associated with 'the folk mind' which cannot be depleted because it does not live in the temporal order of supersession which is the very site of the Modern. These poems seem to be about 'art' and its relations to society, to a public, a tradition. But they are actually about authority, about what discourse authorises action, whether in writing or politics. In a prose draft and comment to 'A House Shaken by the Land Agitation' Yeats argued explicitly that the traditional loveliness fostered by Coole Park was more important than the improvement to a hundred roof-trees for the poor, 'for here power has gone forth, or lingered giving energy, precision'. The poet cannot reconcile two allegiances of equal importance to his art and politics. He tries dialogically to impose a binary ordering on a disorderly world. But his antitheses spawn other antitheses, images beget fresh images in a sea which swamps all the dikes on which order struts.

Elsewhere in Yeats's verse it is precisely the violence of the independence struggle which overcomes the clash of allegiances in the word 'common' by specifying two parallel or convergent sources of linguistic power, a new legitimation of poetry and politics which reconciles the opposed forces of popular and elite traditions. One of his *Last Poems*, 'The Municipal Gallery Revisited', offers a retrospect on the images of thirty years of Irish history which, in the founding of a new order out of insurrection and terror, had raised the most fundamental questions about legitimacy in politics and culture alike. The intersection of the common and the elite determines the whole course of the poem, for its 'images of thirty years' record a struggle conducted not only by great men like Casement, 'Griffith staring in hysterical pride', O'Higgins's 'gentle questioning look' ('pride' and 'gentle' both carry class connotations), but also by the anonymous masses, represented by the nameless 'revolutionary soldier kneeling to be blest', with a humility that in the next stanza is cast as the complement of pride. Since both egregious individual and obedient masses are essential to the struggle, Yeats accommodates them in an image which has a similar dual authority, 'An image out of Spenser and the common tongue'. He has prepared the way for this metaphor by casting himself in the (unlikely) posture of humility, kneeling in imagination before the image of Augusta Gregory. Here too emptiness is transfigured to plenitude under her roof, in a strange incomplete sentence where noun and verb enter into problematic relationship—'all lacking found'. The verse sweeps on to another act of obeisance to the common people, speaking of the shared belief of Yeats, Lady Gregory and John Synge, 'our modern preoccupation' setting them apart from ordinary modernity, that—

All that we did, all that we said or sang
Must come from contact with the soil, from that
Contact everything Antaeus-like grew strong.
We three alone in modern times had brought

> Everything down to that sole test again,
> Dream of the noble and the beggar-man.

Mere historical accuracy is marred by a characteristic Romantic displacement. The final rhyme would more appropriately read 'working-man', since it was from the working classes radicalised by Connolly's and Larkin's near-general strike of 1913 and then by the Easter Rising and its aftermath that the revolutionary soldier will have been drawn, as his leaders came from the professional strata and from those lower-middle classes mobilised by the earlier national struggle. But Yeats cannot allow to that explicitly modern class, the proletariat, a proper role in Ireland's history, displacing onto the marginal beggar-man the linguistic vitality Joyce found in the Dublin pubs and work-places. Hence 'soil' and the classically distancing literary-mythological allusion to Antaeus deflect us from seeing where that struggle should have led, restoring us instead to the ordered hierarchical world to which Yeats's 'medieval knees' belong. Thus, we are not surprised to find that Synge's greatness arose in part from '"Forgetting human words"', despite his rootedness. Forgetfulness, we have seen, is always an *interested*, partisan act in Yeats's work, the repression of an otherwise insoluble dilemma.

The whole poem is cast in the light of retrospect. Its only future is that of unspecified consumers of the images to be found in the Gallery and in Yeats's verse. Those who come after will want to judge 'This book or that'. They will focus not on a future but on the traces of a past: 'Ireland's history in their lineaments trace'. Understanding history is a matter of seeking lineaments and lineages of the past in the present. Such an act seems to preclude an openness to any future beyond the moment of judging and tracing. History is all retrospect, even when it is still in prospect. Future seekers are urged to 'Think where man's glory most begins and ends'. It begins and ends here, in the timeless works of art. It is here, too, that Yeats seeks to place the origins of Modernism. A divisive, continuous, always incomplete history, the merely 'contemporary' in which the Modern is perpetually updated, is set against the finality of epitaphs: 'And say my glory was I had such friends'. Retrospection is the final horizon of Yeats's historical vision. This 'saying' is projected into the future only to round off the pastness of it all. The imagined epitaph preempts any other response, inscribing the refractory historical self in a unitary and 'common' textuality, the Book of the People, where the poet himself has, though dead, literally the last word, though he requires others to speak it. Yeats and his friends will thus be placed, not in the actual contingency and turmoil of their *histories*, '"The dead Ireland of my youth"', but in that imaginary tradition which mystifies discordant voices to a common significance, founded in a single principle of power, forging, from 'Approved patterns of women or of men', the phantasmagoria of "'An Ireland / The poets have imagined, terrible and gay'".

Nothing but a Book

The alternative titles of a 1916 poem called at different times 'The Phoenix' and 'The People' reveals Yeats's own vacillation between the personal (and exceptional) and the public (and common). Couched as a dialogue, the poem contrasts his own and Maud Gonne's responses to the national liberation struggle. Though he hankers after a life among 'The unperturbed and courtly images' of Renaissance Ferrara or Urbino, where (he alleges) artist, aristocrat and people shared common values, mixing 'courtesy and passion' as the Duchess and her people mingled on terms of respect, he himself inveighs against 'The daily spite of this unmannerly town' in an idiom which ironically links him to the despised, mercenary Paudeen—a language of buying and selling, profit and loss, 'earned', 'charge', 'trade'. Gonne's reply, consummately endorsing yet refuting all that the poet has said, is not that of a politician but of a dedicated revolutionary. She had driven away the dishonest crowds, but 'When my luck changed and they dared to meet my face' they crawled out to set upon her, even people she had served and fed: "'Yet never have I, now nor any time,/ Complained of the people'".

Her reply draws on Yeats's distinction (ultimately derived from Wordsworth) between a people and a mob—the one ideal and potential, the other actual. Stung, he responds with a distinction between his living in thought and hers in deed, and then (having spoken of her as 'my phoenix'), addresses her as one with 'the purity of a natural force'. He claims for himself what he despises elsewhere, 'the analytic mind'. The 'eye of the mind' cannot be closed to reality, nor the tongue kept from speaking truly by faith in a speculative renewal. But the final three lines, with their strategically placed repetition of 'abashed', speaking of nine years ago and of today, tell a different story. The poem is a powerful little drama of conflicting political interpretations, the more effective because although the poet has the last word in terms of the narrative, it is clear that that narrative does no more than concede defeat, acknowledging her rebuke because his heart, leaping at her words, rather than his head, tells him she was right. The very changes of title testify to this continuing struggle of interpretation, making the poem an unstable terrain. Maud Gonne is not here associated with traditional sanctity and loveliness. She implicitly rejects her identification with the Duchess of Urbino. Nor does she romanticise the people. As a revolutionary, rather than a fawning politician or foolish romantic, she has no illusions about their venality and reprobation. But complaint will change nothing.

Committed to completing a task, she has to find a way round, or a way of transforming, all these negatives. This poem casts as dramatic dialogue the conflict of elitism and populism, the eternal Book and the passing history, at the heart of Yeats's Modernism. That conflict is summed up likewise in the opening and closing poems of *Responsibilities* (1914), which define between them the conflicting responsibilities of the writer.

Introductory and envoi poems point in opposite directions. But this is not an antithesis of past and future, as one might assume at start and finish of a volume, but of two different pasts and two different futures. The opening poem addresses an actual patriarchy, begging pardon of those 'old fathers', his genealogical ancestors. The poem (and the volume) opens by speaking of them waiting already 'for the story's end'. The pardon he seeks is for reaching 49 without any heirs, because of 'a barren passion', an admission delayed in its enormity until the last two lines of a twenty-two line poem which is all one sentence:

> I have no child, I have nothing but a book,
> Nothing but that to prove your blood and mine.

Syntactically, it is a tour de force of delaying syntax, in which the poem enacts that deferral of significance of which it speaks, which has left his lineage incomplete, as here, his poetic lines are attenuated to the point of extinction.

The envoi of the volume by contrast turns from real to imagined fathers, the textual fathers of the literary tradition, for whom this book is a real child. The poem enacts the same delaying syntax, but it begins this time not in a vocative address to others, but in a foregrounding of the speaking subject, and its verb comes in three-and-a-half lines, surmising companions from the literary tradition, in particular naming and quoting Ben Jonson as a voice which authorises his contempt for the populace. The voice is newly confident here, having moved in the course of the volume from seeking pardon to venturing forgiveness. Even in its degraded and degrading final image the book asserts mastery. The very ability to speak thus suggesting calm defiance, the surety of 'a sterner conscience' which can overcome the 'undreamt accidents' that have made him 'Notorious'. 'Fame', 'Being but a part of ancient ceremony', has long perished, leaving his 'priceless things' as 'a post the passing dogs defile'. But the artist survives all this in solitary, tragic grandeur.

This is the mood of a poem such as 'Fallen Majesty', a product of 1912, a year in which the Third Irish Home Rule Bill was introduced in the House of Commons. Pound proposed various changes to the poem. One Yeats accepted involved dropping 'as it were' from the final lines:

A crowd
Will gather, and not know it walks the very street
Whereon a thing once walked that seemed, as it were, a burning cloud.

But he refused Pound's alternative 'A crowd / Will gather and not know that through its very street / Once walked a thing'. C.K. Stead says this was pride, refusing to get rid of the repetition and the awkward 'Whereon'.[7] Yeats, however, was right. The repetition emphasises the discrepancy of knowledge and power, knowing and doing. They walk now, she walked then; but, unlike him, they lack the magical knowledge of the connection, which transforms the mundane street. There is continuity between then and now, but also loss. The repetition is of a parcel with the others in the poem which juxtapose sameness and difference through time: 'Although crowds gathered once . . . A crowd will gather'. Stead is also wrong to object to the 'awkward' word 'thing' applied to Gonne, and to quibble about whether she was a 'burning cloud' or merely 'seemed' one. Yeats's language is quite clear: it specifies uncertainty. The poet doesn't know what status he attributes to Gonne. She is a 'thing' in the sense that in 'A Bronze Head' she seems both more and less than human. The strange, uncomfortable word relates her to the thing that climbs the stair and slouches towards Bethlehem, more historical agency than individual human being. As a 'burning cloud' she has the same determinate indeterminacy: like Jove visiting Io, she is a supernatural intervention in the material world; but like a cloud, she is also a vapid and vaporous natural process, lacking in contour and substance, with neither beginning nor end but a vague nebulous diffusiveness.

But this is not quite all, for there is another key repetition, which foregrounds the role of the poet as chronicler, and elucidates the title. The hand which writes, he says,

Like some last courtier at a gypsy camping-place
Babbling of fallen majesty, records what's gone.

Lineaments (external features) and a heart made sweet (internal effect) remain; but the poet repeats, 'I record what's gone', and rhyme and reiteration of that punning participle reinstate presence as it proclaims absence: 'I record what's Gonne'. Yeats's image is revealing. Its tenor is obvious: he survives to speak of a fallen majesty. But the vehicle—the metaphor itself—is as vague as the cloud to which Gonne is compared ('seemed', like the simile, a weaker device than metaphor, reinforces this sense of unsureness). His social status in this analogy is unclear. Is he a courtier surviving from the *ancien régime* now fallen, cast upon the gypsy camp to seek his bread by recalling a better world, playing on the nostalgia of the low for the greatness they have replaced? Or has he always been a 'courtier'—the term suffering terminal inflation—at the court of a gypsy 'king', rousing that 'king' to delusions of grandeur with tales of a fallen majesty he would like to think he shared? Yeats's own class-ambiguity as an artist is here defined. Does he survive from an older order of custom and ceremony, in which he had a small but valued place? Or did he always belong to this vile world in its decline and fall, to the raggle-taggle gypsies of the modern, democratic era, to be saved only by massacre?

There is then a further contradiction: his hand records, presumably by writing. Yet in the analogy the recorder is compared to one 'babbling of fallen majesty'. The contrast of script and voice (and incoherent voice) overthrows the usual hierarchy. The oral tradition is heroic, Homeric, goes back to the primal hierarchies of history. Writing belongs to the modern, democratic world of shared literacy. But here the simile confounds the whole contrast. Babbling is associated with the transiency of the gypsy camp, as opposed to the fixed order of majesty, yet it is a survivor of that era who is reduced to a babbling then redefined as writing. The metonymy 'this hand', depersonalising, distancing, becomes, by repetition, the focused subject of 'I record', almost as if the recorder had grown to fullness in his responsibility to link crowds in present and future, *without their knowing it*, to those in the past.

Crowds will gather now for an unspecified purpose which we might suspect to be a political meeting, in this year when Nationalist and Unionist forces grouped and regrouped at the prospect of Home Rule. But, though Yeats would wish us to believe that they once gathered simply to observe Gonne's beauty, wasn't the real reason, even then, the same? Didn't she draw crowds not because she was beautiful—though this may have contributed to her charismatic effect—but because she was a powerful orator arguing a sympathetic case? But to admit this would be to concede that there is some historical substance to that which Yeats regrets as merely loss and emptiness—a beautiful voice growing shrill with argument. The old men whose eyes grow dim are like those old men who looked on Helen at Troy. Yeats, that is, represses the whole historical dimension of Gonne's being-in-the-world, substituting an appropriating myth. Yet the poem registers the uncertainty of his interpretation in its use of the verb 'seemed' and in the way it reduces her to nebulousness, dissipating her actual concentrated agency into a diffuse and unstable presence. If the poem juxtaposes knowledge and ignorance, elite individual and raggedy crowd, it also in its confusion of script and voice opens up another schism in the text of history. It is one to which Yeats returned in his two Coole Park poems, in 1929 and 1931.

'Coole Park, 1929' was not published until 1931, and the date in the title implies a deliberate historical placing, calling our attention to this year of capitalist crisis and collapse. It centres its melancholy defiance of endings in the ambiguous image of 'a swallow's flight'. This flight is both that of the bird actually before his eyes, a figure of material presence, and the more abstract idea of the bird's migratory flight, a figure of loss and absence. In the fourth stanza, the writers associated with Lady Gregory are spoken as coming and going like swallows, but the sense of transience throughout is qualified by the consolation of return. The swallows are ambiguous figures in that they represent both the fleetingness of things and a constancy of repetition, returning to the same nest year after year. So the opening antithesis, between the stability of meditation, of the world of thought, and the transiency of the world of nature, is belied by the unfolding of the image.

This consolatory doubleness in the image of time is everywhere in the poem. The poet himself migrates in thought from swallow to 'an aged woman and her house', equally vulnerable to mutability. But in the human world, 'Great works constructed there in nature's spite' persist for new generations, 'For scholars and for poets after us'. Though history unravels, thought is knitted together into a unity and fullness. But this 'distaff' image—like the equally feminised images of dance and begetting—is then succeeded, in the second stanza, by a peculiar, complicating variation on a proverbial cliché. As scholars and poets will come after Yeats, so others preceded him. Foremost among these was Douglas Hyde, whose transcription of the old Irish legends did so much to prepare the ground for the cultural renaissance in which Yeats shared. But Hyde is seen as beating, not the sword into a ploughshare (or a pen), but rather as beating into (plebeian) prose 'That noble blade the Muses buckled on'.

As in 'The Gift of Harun al Rashid' and 'To Dorothy Wellesley', poetry is associated with the arts of war, not peace. The implicit class antithesis here reproduces itself in a series of other antitheses—Yeats's own 'manly pose' versus his 'timid heart', John Synge's 'slow' and 'meditative' nature contrasted with the impetuosity of Shawe-Taylor and Hugh Lane—before joining them all in a 'company' which reaffirms the corporate image of class collaboration between aristocratic and plebeian virtues encountered elsewhere, 'pride established in humility'. 'Established', like 'constructed' earlier, indicates how much effort is required to effect this combination. The linking of order and authorship in art with order and authority in society is the preoccupation of the next stanza.

Compared with the transient swallows, it is the constancy and continuity of 'a woman's powerful character' that maintains order. Lady Gregory's aristocratic power lies in her ability to 'keep a swallow to its first intent', to represent that primary fullness, that identity of purpose and act which makes half a dozen birds 'in formation . . . whirl upon a compass-point'. The air is dreaming, but 'certainty' can be found within it. As the birds can be held to their purpose across all the distractions of space, so a culture can be maintained, by resolution of purpose, in 'lines / That cut through time or cross it withershins'. The ambiguity of that word 'lines'—lines of verse, lines of genealogy—is continued in the last stanza, which speaks of a time 'When all those rooms and passages are gone'—'passages', as in Eliot's 'Gerontion', linking the material and verbal forms of the culture. But other elements in this last stanza suggest a third meaning to 'lines'—battle lines—which points back to the Muses' 'noble blade' as a figure of art founded in violence, gives a martial twist to the image of 'half a dozen in formation there', and suggests that 'cut through time' carries over the image of the sword.

The poem envisages a time when this stately house is no more than a shapeless mound and broken stone, topped by nettles and saplings. The image recalls, perhaps, the mound at Hissarlik which is all that remains of Troy—apart from Homer's lines. But the appeal to the itinerant traveller, scholar, poet who will view this inheritance of rubble adds other, more martial echoes. For he does not appeal to them to 'stand' here and view the desolation, but to 'take your stand'. The address recalls the epitaph of the Spartan three hundred at Thermopylae, 'Go stranger, tell the Spartans that we lie here, obedient to their command'. But 'take your stand' suggests that the future generation must also share in that last stand, not simply meditating upon but dedicating themselves to the idea of survival the image offers us. If the Spartans were the last defence of western 'civilisation' against Asiatic tyranny (and in 1929 this meant, of course, Bolshevism), that defence was founded not on democracy but on a slave-owning oligarchy. But so too was that other genteel order, the Confederate States of America, for which many a man in another era of civil war declared himself ready to 'take my stand for Dixie'.

It is unclear whether when writing this in September 1929 Yeats already knew of the projected manifesto of the 'Agrarian School' of Southern US writers, *I'll Take My Stand*, which was to appear in 1930.[8] But he was certainly aware of the Agrarians, who had transferred his organicist myth of rural Ireland, with its imaginary alliance of peasant, poet and aristocrat, to the antebellum South. There is here a similar battlecry of a rearguard action against an incursive modern barbarism, in the name of traditional sanctity and loveliness. When, then, Yeats calls on future visitors to this spot to 'dedicate . . . / A moment's memory to that laurelled head', the imagined bays combine martial and poetic honours. For Yeats, the lines of poetry, genealogy and battle belong to the same complex. Order in art is the same as order in society and in war. Authorship and authority, creative and political power, derive from the same source. It is in the stress that such an identification generates that the second of these two poems, 'Coole Park and Ballylee, 1931', finds its richness and its difficulties.

Yeats wrote in 'In Memory of Major Robert Gregory' that John Synge 'dying took the living world for text'. That, in a sense, is what Yeats is doing in 'Coole Park, 1929', reading off the significance of swallow, house, writers, aged woman, taking a stand in each case against the erosion of the meaningful into meaninglessness. Even as a pile of stones, he indicates, perhaps remembering Wordsworth's 'Michael' as much as Homer's Troy, that debris can be restored to significance by a mind able to meditate on the past. The 'luminous' western cloud in the first stanza recalls Coleridge's 'Dejection: An Ode', both in its opening scene-setting at evening and in its forced conviction that the imagination can recreate the dead world of material things like 'a fair luminous cloud'. Coleridge's poem too makes a distinction between the superior isolate mind and the dull dense crowd. 'Coole Park and Ballylee, 1931' makes explicit this Romantic lineage in the concluding stanza of the poem, at the very moment that it seems to admit its insufficiency. But before that, much has been prepared for. The poem takes the living world for text, but it moves conspicuously from the book of nature to 'what poets name / The book of the people'. The text that Yeats reads here defines the trajectory of Modernism in the 1930s.

The poem opens in the living world, with an item by item delineation of the material reality under his window. But, as in Coleridge's 'Kubla Khan', with its river that also rises from and returns to measureless underground caverns, the landscape is transformed into a symbolic terrain. By the end of the first stanza, the real river of otters and moor-hens and Raftery's cellar has become, if only in a rhetorical question, a figure for the 'generated soul' out of Porphyry's essay on the Cave of the Nymphs. Yet this racing, running, rising, dropping and spreading does not cease to be a tangible process, the sense of reality enforced by that unpoetic 'hole' which prepares the final couplet.

The lake and woods, depicted in mid-winter banality, are also transfigured by a sense of nature's histrionics: 'For Nature's pulled her tragic buskin on / And all the rant's a mirror for my mood'. This theatricality may not simply mirror but may in Coleridgean fashion be created by the poet's mood, which projects onto the book of nature a text that is only there to his interpreting gaze. The thunder of the swans' wings compounds this ambivalence. It is something out there which actually interrupts his internal reverie, making him turn about and look. But it is also immediately incorporated into discourse, acclaimed as 'Another emblem there!' The third stanza unfolds the full complexity of such an intuition.

We know from other poems some of the emblematic significances Yeats attributes to the swan. In 'Nineteen Hundred and Nineteen', with his usual deliberate insouciance about sources, he remarks that 'Some moralist or mythological poet / Compares the solitary soul to a swan'. But though he says 'I am satisfied with that', the amplification of the image goes beyond mere comparison, to a point at which the actual creature overwhelms its emblematic significance. His description of its flight makes the image stand before us as 'a living thing', flesh and blood and muscle in action, so that the soul takes second place to that which is supposed to signify ('cygnify') it. Soul and swan fuse, so that the syntax acquires a double subject, 'it' ambiguously referring to either, making each the mirror of the other:

> Satisfied if a troubled mirror show it,
> Before that brief gleam of its life gone,
> An image of its state.

The soul is then considered in a formula ('Some Platonist affirms') which repeats the construction of the opening analogy before returning to the physical, embodied image of the swan. The return totally transforms the argument, cutting it short with a powerful, corporeal rebuke to all this abstraction. The 'image' takes on a life of its own, a real creature out there in the wind and water, not a mere emblem of something else. In its very substantiality it bursts into the argument, refuting the 'desolate heaven' of thought with the display of a force that interrupts discourse, threatening to cut short the acts of writing and imagining themselves:

> The swan has leaped into the desolate heaven:
> That image can bring wildness, bring a rage
> To end all things, to end
> What my laborious life imagined, even
> The half-imagined, the half-written page.

The wildness here, interrupting discourse, is like that wildness he detected in Maud Gonne or the bestially divine Zeus invading the body of history in 'Leda and the Swan', a supernatural irruption into the ordered language of philosophy, writing, society itself. In 'Coole Park and Ballylee, 1931' the same dramatic reversal occurs:

> Another emblem there! That stormy white
> But seems a concentration of the sky;
> And, like the soul, it sails into the sight
> And in the morning's gone, no man knows why;
> And is so lovely that it sets to right

What knowledge or its lack had set awry,
So arrogantly pure, a child might think
It can be murdered with a spot of ink.

The bird is first of all constituted in discourse, a signifying emblem. But, though it still functions as a signifier of the signified 'soul', its signification disrupts that discourse, appearing and disappearing beyond knowledge. Knowledge and its lack are curiously fused in unity as sources of disorder, compared with what the loveliness sets right. The bird seems merely 'a concentration of the sky'; but that abstract noun hovers between mental and physical—between thinking concentratedly and making denser, more concentrated. The bird remains as if a written sign in that sky, concentrated white on white, so that a child, uninitiated into the difference between mind and world, imagination and reality, might think of it as no more than a sign, a mark on paper, easily overwritten. The word 'murdered', however, establishes the distance between erasing a sign and killing a living thing. The whole stanza insists on the discrepancy between discourse and reality in a world in which, nevertheless, the real can be apprehended only through discourse.

When in the fourth and fifth stanzas Yeats turns to the human scene, the same interplay occurs between what people and places *are* and what they *signify*—between the sound of a stick on the floor and the old woman who wields it, between that old woman and the Ascendancy tradition she metonymically embodies. The poem works through a series of expanding metonymies, in which each item indicates a set which then becomes the metonymy for another set. The sound of the stick suggests an undefined 'somebody that toils from chair to chair'; but the chair becomes part of the furniture of rooms in which age does not diminish but enhances value; the rooms become the haunts of the generations who found content or joy here; and then, in the final concentration of the tradition, like the swan in the sky, Lady Gregory emerges as the 'last inheritor' of all that richness, a richness set against 'lack' and 'folly'.

That the parallel between woman and swan is not fortuitous is suggested by the recurrence of the words 'lack' and 'spot' (again associated with survival and extinction) immediately after. This house is 'A spot whereon the founders lived and died', and the place becomes a metonymy for a succession of marriages, alliances, families. The whole living world, that is, is constructed like a text the meaning of which can be read off by the initiated eye from each instance and particular. For the interpreting imagination, it is impossible to distinguish the trees from the 'ancestral' lineage they evoke, the gardens from the memories in which they are rich, the inheritance they 'glorified'. But this spot only 'Seemed once more dear than memory', as the swan only seems a concentration of the sky, and only in a child's thought can be murdered with a spot of ink. The discourse can be expunged, the poem suggests, and indeed is in process of being expunged. Coole Park and all it stands for can be erased as easily as a sentence on the page. A spot of ink can do it all, the signing of a will, or a builder's contract.

What animates Yeats here, then, is the memory of an emptiness. This is the repository of all that has been evacuated of meaning, lost to history. We know that there is much that has been forgotten. We know that whole civilisations have disappeared from the historical record. For millennia, we thought that Troy was just a story, but Schliemann revealed it to be history. Before this could be assimilated, however, we had seen the fictive certainties of Homer disappear, leaving us with a mound of rubbish. Archaeology, which seemed to vindicate Homer as history, then problematised him, by offering us a different, more parochial and local Troy, just as textual scholarship dissolved the unitary patriarch 'Homer' into several generations of anonymous bards handing on tales collected belatedly in the age of Pisistratus. As Yeats noted dispassionately in 'Lapis Lazuli', whole civilisations are put to the sword, their wisdom vanishes, 'No handiwork of Callimachus ... stands' (that word again), and no one remembers. Why, then, should this little local phenomenon, the Ascendancy culture, be privileged? The memory of an absence generates the expectation of an absence—a future in which this so substantial present has vanished without trace, translated into debris for the archaeologist to reconstruct.

It is here, then, that Yeats forges a link with earlier poems, with that 1910 image of himself as the recorder of fallen majesty, the last courtier in a gypsy camp, and with the 1923 'Gift of Harun al Rashid', with its idea of a knowledge partially recovered by patient reconstruction, putting together from scattered and surviving fragments a story that is always in danger of being misattributed, misinterpreted, turned into fantasy. This story may be discovered in one surviving parchment, hidden in another book from a library long dispersed, or it may be culled from its many variants in the oral tradition, with 'no chronicler / But the wild Bedouin'. In *Per Amica Silentia Lunae*[9] Yeats had set up an antithesis very similar to that expounded here, between high tradition and folk memory, speaking of the Arab boy become Vizier, whose wisdom has '"taken stock in the desert sand of the sayings of antiquity"'. In 'The Gift of Harun al Rashid', the young bride and her aged scholar husband pursue 'old crabbed mysteries', 'old dry writing in a learned tongue', in a perpetual recession and recension of interpretings, straining 'to look beyond our life'. What speaks at the end of all this labour is a Djinn, voicing truths beyond the written tradition:

> Truths without father came, truths that no book
> Of all the uncounted books that I have read,
> Nor thought out of her mind or mine begot,
> Self-born, high-born, and solitary truths,
> Those terrible implacable straight lines
> Drawn through the wandering vegetative dream,
> Even those truths that when my bones are dust
> Must drive the Arabian host.

Yeats's simile in the closing lines of 'Coole Park and Ballylee, 1931' compounds intertextual references to his own past writing. It may be that, losing this rich inheritance, the modern imagination too is dispossessed, shifting about 'Where fashion or mere fantasy decrees . . . / Like some poor Arab tribesman and his tent'. Neither fashion nor fantasy recognises any integral relation between the sign and what it signifies, perpetually and lightly fashioning transient correspondences between a shifting succession of objects, as Yeats himself successively offers water and then the swan that swims on it as emblems of the soul. The synecdochic 'emblem', suggesting a transitory succession of one-for-one correspondences between sign and signified, sunders that unity of thing and meaning contained in the metonymic symbol, where 'Old marble heads, old pictures everywhere' both symbolise and are the inheritance, the 'great glory' they figure forth.

The modern world is one in which the chronicler shifts like an Arab nomad about a desert stripped of meanings, packing up his purely personal and arbitrary symbols every dawn. But we know from 'The Gift of Harun al Rashid' that it is among just such that the truth has been preserved, in an oral, not a written tradition. The final stanza of 'Coole Park and Ballylee, 1931' makes a stand against desolation by reaffirming 'Traditional sanctity and loveliness' at the very moment that it laments their passing, indeed, concedes that they have passed. The ambivalence is focused in an uncertain shifting between song and writing. The elegiac voice concedes its own supersession, concedes that 'all is changed, that high horse riderless'. But at the very moment that the lost order is mourned, the dead theme is resurrected as the new theme of a poem whose very date proclaims its modernity as the latest thing, even more up-to-date than 'Coole Park, 1929':

> We were the last romantics—chose for theme
> Traditional sanctity and loveliness;
> Whatever's written in what poets name
> The book of the people; whatever most can bless
> The mind of man or elevate a rhyme;

But all is changed, that high horse riderless,
Though mounted in that saddle Homer rode
Where the swan drifts upon a darkening flood.

Yeats achieves his effect by insisting on the interdependence of interpreting mind and interpreted world. That world is not simply a thing in itself: it is also a 'theme' for poetry, an already written compendium of narratives, and a source for other, yet to be written texts. The reflections on literary history are less important than the poem's strange condensations of perspective. These last romantics, at the end of things, were not like their Romantic predecessors, impelled by some irresistible urgency of utterance. They could *choose* their themes, and what they chose was a past already 'traditional'. Yet they also chose whatever is written, a past act of *writing* now become, in the present, an always-already *written*. The shift into the present tense is extended in that rebellious auxiliary 'can'. This 'book of the people' is not simply the oral tradition. Rather it is 'what poets name / The book of the people': it has to be constructed, called into being by writers who choose whatever most can bless and elevate. The book of the people looks not backwards but towards a future, both blessing the mind of man and 'elevating', in the sense of both ennobling and building, a *new* rhyme, a newness not undercut by the archaisms which echo first Wordsworth ('elevated thoughts', 'in the mind of man') and then Milton ('build the lofty rhyme'). And these unnamed poets of epic, Neoplatonic and Romantic voices, one chronicling the loss of paradise, the other of glad animal movements, lead back to the origin of things as they lead forward to the poem's conclusion, to that first voice of the European tradition, named in the very moment that his absence is acknowledged, Homer.

The 'rode'/'drifts' antithesis suggests a history without direction, yet moving inexorably on a darkening flood. The impersonal terse 'But all is changed' reinforces this sense of the loss of human control. But there is an odd contrary current in the phrase 'that high horse riderless'. This is Pegasus, certainly, crossed with an Arab stallion, and we should not stop to ask too many questions about a blind man riding a horse, or about taking a horse to water. But a 'high horse' is something presumptuous, a false pride. Is Yeats saying that it was right to get down from that high horse, right to abandon the pretensions of 'traditional sanctity and loveliness'? Is there more than a hint of dismissal in that opening proposition: we were hopelessly romantic, like Pound's E.P., out of key with our time?

In the very moment that he writes an elegy for a lost tradition, Yeats defiantly recreates and continues it, making of his poem a new embodiment and emblem of what it mourns, itself cast upon the darkening flood. At the beginning of the 1930s, as Modernism entered the decade in which all its projects foundered, Yeats's intertextual echoes call up, not a dead history, but a living one, which is neither progress nor decline but a series of successive shocks and confrontations in which changing social forces clash upon a darkling plain. As part of that continuing history, Wordsworth and Coleridge in the 1790s had sought to open up the book of the people in *Lyrical Ballads*, as an act, as Eliot recognised in *The Use of Poetry* of political as well as cultural revolution. A century-and-a-half earlier, Milton had written as a participant in a popular revolution aimed at rewriting the book of the people. Yeats's allusions, far from returning us to the origins, bring us back to the very world where Homer is no longer in the saddle. The solitary soul, which has been compared to a swan, finds itself drifting rather than riding upon the darkening flood of what has always been a collective history.

The last stanza, that is, sets up but then effaces a contradiction which is at the centre of Yeats's work and at the heart of Modernism itself: between 'traditional sanctity' and 'the book of the people', between the leisured culture of the Gregories and the Hydes, genteel collectors of folk tales, and the polyphony of a 'people' that refuses the monological authority of tradition. The poem records the dilemma of Modernism at its most endangered and desperate extreme, adrift on the filthy modern tide of a history no longer, if it ever was, in capable hands, a riderless horse. 'At the Abbey Theatre' in 1910 had asked what seemed like mocking rhetorical questions of a new century:

> Is there a bridle for this Proteus
> That turns and changes like his draughty seas?
>
> Or is there none, most popular of men,
> But when they mock us, that we mock again?

Already by 'Nineteen Hundred and Nineteen' that century had given hard and mocking answers, telling those who had 'planned to bring the world under a rule' that they were 'but weasels fighting in a hole', its 'levelling wind' mocking an age where 'we / But traffic in mockery'. In 1919, there is 'Violence upon the roads: violence of horses' but at least 'Some few have handsome riders'. By 1931, it is clear that there is neither bridle nor rider.

Notes

1. Margaret Ward, *Maud Gonne: Ireland's Joan of Arc*, London: Pandora Press, 1990, provides a full biography and some measure of the extent to which Maud Gonne has become a figure of myth. On the *fin-de-siècle* stereotypes within which Gonne was configured, see Jennifer Birkett, *The Sins of the Fathers: Decadence in France 1870–1914*, London: Quartet, 1986, particularly pp. 19–34.

2. To his credit, Pound did not himself subscribe to this reading. Reviewing *Responsibilities* in 1914, he dismissed the fashion-following question 'Is Yeats in the movement?' with the riposte that 'Mr Yeats is so assuredly an immortal that there is no need for him to recast his style to suit our winds of doctrine' but added 'there is nevertheless a manifestly new note in his later work', a 'new note' which, he says, 'was apparent four years ago in his *No Second Troy*'. With the appearance of *The Green Helmet*, he continues, 'one felt that the minor note . . . had gone or was going out of his poetry' (Ezra Pound, 'The Later Yeats', *Poetry*, vol. 4, no. 2, May 1914; reprinted in *Literary Essays of Ezra Pound*, T.S. Eliot (ed.), London: Faber and Faber, 1954, pp. 378–81). For Eliot's assessment, see T.S. Eliot, *To Criticize the Critic*, New York: Farrar, Straus and Giroux, 1965, p. 58.

The volumes discussed in the present chapter are as follows: W.B. Yeats, *The Green Helmet and Other Poems*, Dundrum: Cuala Press, 1910 (New York, 1911; London: Macmillan, 1912); *Responsibilities: Poems and a Play*, Dundrum: Cuala Press, 1914 (London: Macmillan, 1916); *The Wild Swans at Coole*, Dundrum: Cuala Press, 1917 (London: Macmillan, 1919); *The Tower*, London: Macmillan, 1928; *The Winding Stair and Other Poems*, London: Macmillan, 1933; *Last Poems and Two Plays*, Dublin: Cuala Press, 1939; *Last Poems and Plays*, London: Macmillan, 1940.

Richard J. Finneran (ed.), W.B. Yeats, *The Poems: A New Edition*, London: Macmillan, 1984, proposes a radically different sequence for *Last Poems* from that in the standard *Collected Poems of W.B. Yeats*, London: Macmillan; 1950. The order of the latter is followed by Peter Allt and Russell K. Alspach (eds), *The Variorum Edition of the Poems of W.B. Yeats*, New York: Macmillan, 1977. On this, see Richard J. Finneran, *Editing Yeats's Poetry: A Reconsideration*, Basingstoke: Macmillan, 1990. This chapter extends some of the arguments initiated in Stan Smith, *W.B. Yeats: A Critical Introduction*, Basingstoke: Macmillan, 1990.

3. See Maud Gonne MacBride, *A Servant of the Queen*, London: Victor Gollancz, 1938; Rosemary Cullen Owens, *Smashing Times: A History of the Irish Women's Suffrage Movement 1889–1922*, Dublin: The Attic Press, 1984. For an account of the Transport Workers' Strike, see Austen Morgan, *James Connolly: A Political Biography*, Manchester: Manchester University Press, 1988, chapter 6, pp. 111–35.

4. Richard Ellmann, *The Identity of Yeats*, London: Macmillan, 1954, p. 252.

5. W.B. Yeats, *Autobiographies*, London: Macmillan, 1955, p. 219. Book 2 of *The Trembling of the Veil* (first published separately in 1922), offers a shrewd thumbnail sketch of Hyde and of his contribution to the Irish cultural renaissance (pp. 216–19).

6. *ibid.*, pp. 439–40. This section, *Dramatis Personae*, was originally published separately in 1935.

7. C.K. Stead, *Pound, Yeats, Eliot and the Modernist Movement*, Basingstoke: Macmillan, 1986.

8. 'Twelve Southerners', *I'll Take My Stand: The South and the Agrarian Tradition*, New York: Harper, 1930. The Agrarians sought explicit precedent for their vision of the South in Yeats's fantasy of an organicist, quasi-feudal, corporatist Ireland where aristocrat, poet and peasant scorned the class-based politics of the modern world. Leading figures of the movement such as Allen Tate were clearly influenced by Yeats stylistically as well as ideologically. In the 1930s, the Agrarians seemed to offer a politics and a poetics which took a third way between capitalism and 'Bolshevism' appealing to many modern writers. At the beginning of *After*

Strange Gods (1934), p. 15, Eliot, for example, speaking in Virginia, reveals that he had been 'much interested' in the Agrarians 'since the publication a few years ago' of *I'll Take My Stand*, relates this specifically to the concerns of 'Tradition and the Individual Talent', and imagines that in the South there is still 'at least some recollection of a "tradition", such as the influx of foreign populations has almost effaced in some parts of the North'. See Paul K. Conkin, *The Southern Agrarians*, Knoxville: University of Tennessee Press, 1988.

9. W.B. Yeats, *Per Amica Silentia Lunae*, London: Macmillan, 1918.

ANDREW SWARBRICK

Philip Larkin High Windows

Of *High Windows*, Andrew Motion has written: 'The book changed Larkin's life more decisively than any of his previous collections. *The Less Deceived* made his name; *The Whitsun Weddings* made him famous; *High Windows* turned him into a national monument'.[1] But in order to construct that monument, Larkin's eager public had to overlook or explain away the most disturbing aspects of *High Windows*. Where *The Less Deceived* was tormented by questions of love and *The Whitsun Weddings* by loneliness and death, *High Windows* is charged with anger. Forces which in *The Whitsun Weddings* were held delicately in tension can be seen disintegrating in *High Windows*. Poems celebrating continuity and communal ritual remain, and there is a tender regard for futile human gestures of compassion (the 'wasteful, weak, propitiatory flowers' of 'The Building'). But the collection also lays bare feelings of fury and rancour which show Larkin's lyrical impulse being threatened by its twin: a mocking philistinism. This is most obviously apparent in the taunting coarseness of Larkin's language in many poems. It seems that at times *High Windows* wants to say again, with the fury of disappointment, that 'books' and all they represent really are 'a load of crap'.

In *The Whitsun Weddings*, a poetry-reading public found its representative voice. The first 4000 copies were sold in two months[2] and Larkin found himself, only a little unwillingly, something of a celebrity. 'You wouldn't see the frenzy of activity on Northern broadcasting services, I expect: today I had a Guardian feature writer for nearly 4 hours. I long to be anonymous again', he wrote to Barbara Pym.[3] Critical attention was not universally flattering, but even less enthusiastic reviewers such as Al Alvarez recognised Larkin's importance as representing a particular culture. 'Perhaps his special achievement is to have created a special voice for that special, localised moment: post-war provincial England in all its dreariness, with the boredom of shortages no longer justified, the cheap, plastic surface of things which nobody wants and everybody buys.'[4] Emerging a decade after *The Whitsun Weddings*, *High Windows* was awaited and consumed by an expectant public: the first 6000 copies were sold in three months and 13,500 copies reprinted in the following few months.[5] Reviewers argued about Larkin's 'development' ('Only mediocrities develop', Larkin had already tartly observed, quoting Oscar Wilde[6]) but could not then know the bleakest significance of *High Windows*: that by its publication in 1974 Larkin had largely written himself into silence. Only half-jokingly, Larkin wrote to Barbara Pym in 1975: 'the notion of expressing sentiments in short lines having similar sounds at their ends seems as remote as mangoes on the moon'.[7] Larkin had always been anxious about the meagreness of his output but the remark he made in a radio broadcast in 1972 expresses this anxiety in a different way:

> There is great pressure on a writer to 'develop' these days: I think the idea began with Yeats, and personally I'm rather sceptical of it. What I should like to do is write different kinds of poems that might be by different people. Someone said once that the great thing is not to be different from other people, but to be different from yourself.[8]

This replaces the notion of 'development' with an altogether more radical aspiration and reflects the pressure of imminent poetic silence Larkin felt. Although these sentences have been applied to the more adventurous poems in *High Windows* (by Simon Petch, for example), their importance is central to the whole of Larkin's work. *High Windows* can be read as the sometimes despairing conclusion to Larkin's lifelong quarrel with himself about his own identity and the value of art.

In 'Toads Revisited', Larkin once again settled for the world of work, duty and responsibility, but not without first taking the measure of himself against 'the men / You meet of an afternoon . . . All dodging the toad work / By being stupid or weak. / Think of being them!' Beneath its gruff surface, the poem does indeed 'Think of being them',

> Turning over their failures
> By some bed of lobelias,
> Nowhere to go but indoors,
> No friends but empty chairs

Indeed, *The Whitsun Weddings* repeatedly thinks of 'being them': Mr Bleaney, the widow, the women in 'Faith Healing', all of them in some way damaged, or failures, or casualties. The willingness to feel compassion in the poems expresses a shared sense of fear and deprivation. The poems' integration is not only of a social kind, but of meaning, whereby the contingencies of circumstances are assembled into a more enduring significance. David Trotter has pointed out how meaning emerges differently in *The Less Deceived* and *The Whitsun Weddings* poems. Citing 'Church Going' and 'I Remember, I Remember', he writes:

> Both poems complete their description of a particular event before paying attention to the feelings it has aroused . . . Only then, in the ebbing of event, does the significance of either occasion become apparent. Meaning occurs after the event . . . Larkin relates individual experience to shared significance by organising them into temporal succession: first event, then meaning.[9]

But later poems such as 'Here' and 'The Whitsun Weddings' work differently: ' . . . meaning does not occur in the aftermath of event. It is produced by the final act of the journey, the moment when the tightened brakes take hold . . . Event and meaning, so distinct in "Church Going" and "I Remember, I Remember", have begun to merge'.[10] This marks another stage in the process of 'self-forgetting' and asserts a faith in implicit meaning, in a shared understanding between writer and reader.

But it is possible to read in *High Windows* a loss of faith in this consensus.[11] The rancorous tone, the general sense of desperation, whilst they can obviously be linked to the increasingly horrified contemplations of old age and death, suggest also a deepening anxiety about the relationship between self and community. There are still poems in which Larkin thinks of 'being them' and they remain amongst his most moving achievements. But other poems wilfully resist integration. The voice of 'The Old Fools', for example, is patently egocentric, with the focus on *me* being them. Other poems in *High Windows* are more daringly lyrical because they can no longer lose themselves in the lyrical moment, but jeopardise it by making their moralising more explicit. Trotter concludes that

> The glancing agnosticism of poems like 'Here' and 'The Whitsun Weddings' was no longer sufficient . . . And Larkin responded . . . by shifting to a far more militant and assertive stance than he had ever adopted before . . . between *The Whitsun Weddings* and *High Windows* Larkin began to affirm a connection between individual experience and shared meaning which he might once have left to chance. The shaming pragmatism of the sixties drove him to speak his mind, to give his poems the authority of conscious and unequivocal dissent.[12]

Stan Smith has argued in much the same way, suggesting that in *The Whitsun Weddings* Larkin's attitude to 'welfare-state social democracy, where mass values prevail' was usually 'to maintain an equivocal balance in his responses to such a world, poised between annoyance and deference. In more recent work, such as the poems . . . in *High Windows* (1974), this balance has gone, and the mood is a more tight-lipped one, of disdain sharpening to odium'.[13]

So in *High Windows* the attempt 'to be different from yourself' is more strenuous, and sometimes more strenuously defeated. The impulse to celebrate is now more defensive and cornered. Where in *The Less Deceived* and *The Whitsun Weddings* the poetic personality modulated and mediated itself by way of slightly shifting ventriloquisms, in *High Windows* it is more declarative and dogmatic, or else absents itself within the manifestly fictitious creations of 'Livings'. It is as if in *High Windows* the need 'to be different from yourself' is both more desperate and more difficult to fulfil. The lyricism is more risk-taking because it emerges side by side with its opposite: the philistine.

As Janice Rossen has observed, 'Larkin's habitual melancholy is so clearly driven by intense fury'.[14] During the period when the *High Windows* poems were written, there was much to fuel Larkin's fury. His personal life grew increasingly complicated, unsatisfactory and guilt-inducing. To Monica Jones he wrote in 1966: 'it's my own unwillingness to give myself to anyone else that's at fault—like promising to stand on one leg for the rest of one's life. And yet I never think I am doing anything but ruin your life & mine'.[15] A little later, he expanded:

> I feel rather scared these days, of time passing & us getting older. Our lives are so different from other people's, or have been,—I feel I am landed on my 45th year as if washed up on a rock, not knowing how I got here or ever having had a chance of being anywhere else . . . Of course my external surroundings have changed, but inside I've been the same, trying to hold everything off in order to 'write'. Anyone wd think I was Tolstoy, the value I

> put on it. It hasn't amounted to much. I mean, I know I've been successful in that I've made a name & got a medal & so on, but it's a very small achievement to set against all the rest. This is *Dockery & Son* again—I shall spend the rest of my life trying to get away from that poem.[16]

As he sank further into unhappiness and apathy, so his sense of general worthlessness intensified. Writing to his old college friend Norman Iles in 1972, Larkin confessed:

> For the last 16 years I've lived in the same small flat, washing in the sink, & not having central heating or double glazing or fitted carpets or the other things everyone has, & of course I haven't any biblical things such as wife, children, house, land, cattle, sheep etc. To me I seem very much an outsider, yet I suppose 99% of people wd say I'm very establishment & conventional. Funny, isn't it? Of course I cant say I'm satisfied with it. Terrible waste of time.[17]

The continuing stream of honours towards the end of his life only served to increase Larkin's sense of fraudulence as a national poet who had all but stopped writing. Responding to a request for a poem in 1983, Larkin wrote: 'poetry gave me up about six years ago, and I have no expectation of being revisited'.[18] Indeed, Larkin wrote very little between the appearance of *High Windows* in 1974 and his death in 1985. Thus, one central significance of *High Windows* is that it represents the period when Larkin wrote himself into silence. We can now read these poems in the full recognition that on their margins, and sometimes at their centre, is the battle to get them written.

Amongst the competing forces in that battle are contradictions seen before in Larkin's work, fundamentally between the aesthete and the philistine. The aesthete earlier revered Lawrence, preserved in lyrics moments of heightened perception, combined Yeatsian vision with Hardyesque pathos. The philistine was iconoclastic, recognised itself as a failed writer who never won 'the fame and the girl and the money / All at one sitting', and satirically mocked romantic illusions. Larkin found a way of expressing this argument with himself as one between 'Beauty' and 'Truth': 'When I say beautiful, I mean the original idea seemed beautiful. When I say true, I mean something was grinding its knuckles in my neck and I thought: God, I've got to say this somehow, I have to find words and I'll make them as beautiful as possible'.[19] The experience of beauty is in Larkin's poetry always in peril and his most lyrically thrilling moments contemplate negation: 'One longs for infinity and absence, the beauty of somewhere you're not'.[20] In *High Windows* it is possible to see the lyrical, beauty-creating Larkin now much more obviously threatened by the mocking philistine. Trotter and others read the poems as belligerent reactions to the changing social and political circumstances of the 1960s and early 1970s and they are right to emphasise the tension in the poems between consensus and conflict. Nevertheless, the fury in these poems is the fury of disillusionment not only in life but in art. Yet that philistinism, that refusal to take 'Art' as a theology, is what guarantees Larkin's poetic integrity. 'The whole poetic career', writes Barbara Everett, 'in so many ways so prudently managed, is also a drive to extinguish the false artistic ego'.[21]

In *The Less Deceived* and *The Whitsun Weddings*, it was possible to distinguish between the various speakers of the poems who were subject to varying degrees of irony. In that way, the poems could be read as complex projections of attitudes which were actually self-scrutinising. But in a significant number of the *High Windows* poems, the degree of critical distance between author and speaker is much harder to determine. This might simply be a way of saying that in *High Windows* Larkin speaks much more unambiguously *in propria persona*, sacrificing the earlier masks (often ironically self-revealing) for a bluntly declarative directness. This instability of tone can be read in 'The Old Fools'. Is this a poem in which Larkin expresses his fear and disgust with unmediated frankness? Or are we to see it as the projection of an attitude which is subverted by its own language and then corrected into compassion? This latter view is taken by R. P. Draper, for whom the poem's progress 'is one of deepening attention, moving from a seemingly detached, jeering stance . . . to an increasingly sympathetic identification with the subject of senile decay'.[22]

Certainly, 'fury' drives the language at the opening:

> What do they think has happened, the old fools,
> To make them like this? Do they somehow suppose
> It's more grown-up when your mouth hangs open and drools,
> And you keep on pissing yourself, and can't remember
> Who called this morning?

Clearly, there is a mock ingenuousness about the rhetorical questions and the venom they direct at senility. This loud aggression is self-defensive: it loathes old people because they remind the speaker of his own old age and death. Booth calls these lines an 'embarrassingly obvious' displaced terror of death.[23] But that is their point. There are no strategies of refinement in the language, no rhetorical deviousness which places this voice within a structure of ironies. The terror, like the language, is naked and has gone beyond embarrassment. Just as other poems in *High Windows* flaunt their certainty, this flaunts its outrage: 'Why aren't they screaming?'

The poem shifts ground to consider death and to imagine what it feels like to be old before curving back in horror to 'The whole hideous inverted childhood'. But although there is fascination, there is no compassion. The language refuses throughout to modulate into pathos. Despite the amplitude of the stanzas, there is no real development of attitude or disguised self-scrutiny. The effect of the abrupt half-lines is to bring up short both the stanza and any possible sympathy. Terry Whalen wants to rescue a 'tough compassion and bewildered reverence', arguing that '"the million-petalled flower / Of being here", coming as it does from Larkin's more open and romantic impulse as a poet, highly qualifies the terror of the uglier images and feelings which the poem seeks to transcend'.[24] But the image Whalen isolates cannot stand up to the brute force of description surrounding it: 'Ash hair, toad hands, prune face dried into lines . . . '. Larkin's 'million-petalled flower' is rawly sentimental. Against the forces of age and death, it desperately wants to assert the preciousness of life. But its sweetness, its own 'bloom', its rhythmical lilt, look fragile compared with the simple, terrifying, anatomising plainness of

> At death, you break up: the bits that were you
> Start speeding away from each other for ever
> With no one to see.

This is truth rather than beauty. Even when in the third stanza the poem imagines what it feels like to be old, the picture of solitariness 'describes something so purely "over" it seems asphyxiated'.[25] The language remains inert, a trudging sequence of clauses in a tiring sentence. So when towards the end of the poem the phrase 'the old fools' recurs, its tone has not been altered. The ending of the poem, 'Well, / We shall find out', is brutally laconic. In earlier poems, 'well' was a conversational gesture or a shrug of the shoulders; 'now it is properly vicious, full of menace'.[26] Of course the poem is cruel and implicates us in its cruelty. It does not expect fair-mindedness and its bad-mannered language signals the rejection of rhetorical niceties. It desperately fends off old age and silence. 'The Old Fools' illustrates one of the 'developments' in *High Windows*. Rather than integration and reconciliation, it represents a disturbing intensity and urgent directness.

'The Building' approaches the subject of death more indirectly, but the stealth knows that it is evasive. The tone is more subtle and glancing than 'The Old Fools' and the poem manages to affirm human value in the face of death, though it is hardly consolatory. The strategy is different: rather than head-on confrontation, the poem adopts a *faux-naïf* periphrasis, pretending not to know that it is describing a hospital (the draft title was 'The Meeting House'[27]). This allows Larkin eventually to unveil the truth as if it were a new discovery. Like 'The Old Fools', the poem wants to convey renewed shock in the face of familiar horror. But where 'The Old Fools' was essentially personal (despite its 'you' and 'we'), 'The Building' assumes consensus. The hospital is portrayed as the place where we discover our essential sameness; at a rhetorical level, the poem relies on the reader's complicity in the pretence of not knowing that a hospital is being described. This also gives the hospital the force of a gradually emerging symbol.

As a symbol, the building allows Larkin to develop the familiar insider/outsider antithesis, this time to intensify the contrast between routine life, and life when it faces death. Inside the building is a dislocating familiarity. We recognise scruffy 'porters', vehicles which 'are not taxis', a room 'Like an airport lounge', though its inhabitants suggest it is 'More like a local bus': the building assembles fragments of the familiar which will not cohere. This is 'ground curiously neutral' which erodes difference and individual identity in a situation representing 'The end of choice'. Awareness dawns of 'more rooms yet, each one further off' in increasing isolation, before attention turns outside. Suddenly, the ordinariness outside takes on a new preciousness, and freedom is walking out of the car-park. As the affectionately demotic language indicates, the humdrum world of 'kids' and 'girls with hair-dos' fetching 'Their separates from the cleaners' represents a miracle from which those imprisoned inside the building and its final realities are excluded. Larkin clarified this for himself in a manuscript note:

> 'Once removed from the outside world we see it as a touching dream to wch [*Larkin's abbreviation*] everyone is lulled, but from wch we awake when we get into hospital. In there is the only reality. There you see how transient and pointless everything in the world is. Out there conceits and wishful thinking'.[28]

Where in 'The Old Fools' Larkin tried to convey a 'miracle' by a lift in the language ('the million-petalled flower / Of being here'), in this poem the commonplace is suddenly numinous because of the way Larkin has situated the speaker. There, he looked at death from life; now, he looks at life from death. The ordinary can no longer be taken for granted:

> O world,
> Your loves, your chances, are beyond the stretch
> Of any hand from here!

The 'conceits / And self-protecting ignorance' which constitute life outside the building have collapsed: what 'Ambulances' called 'the unique random blend of families and fashions' is reduced to undiscriminating categories: 'women, men; / Old, young'. Again, the approach of death is conceived in terms of a levelling anonymity in a language drained of rhetoric: 'All know they are going to die. / Not yet, perhaps not here, but in the end, / And somewhere like this'.

But where 'The Old Fools' was unremittingly harsh, 'The Building', although it rejects religious consolation, offers an affirmation of social routine. Outside the new hospital 'close-ribbed streets rise and fall / Like a great sigh out of the last century', representing an enduring community where in 'short terraced streets' kids and young girls will compose from 'loves' and 'chances' their universally unique lives. They are amongst the 'crowds' who 'each evening' try to disperse 'The coming dark . . . With wasteful, weak, propitiatory flowers'. As so often before, Larkin asserts the value of human life in terms which recognise its ultimate futility. That final hanging line, superfluous to the syntax and metrically stumbling, nevertheless welcomes life, however attenuated. Thus, 'The Building' recalls the integrating movements of *The Whitsun Weddings*. This time, though, its voice speaks as an insider looking jealously outside, rather than as the outsider looking suspiciously in.

The building isolates those suddenly 'picked out' of the 'working day' from their ordinary lives and confers new value on the humdrum routines that are now imperilled. 'I don't want to transcend the commonplace, I love the commonplace, I lead a very commonplace life. Everyday things are lovely to me', Larkin told an interviewer.[29] His remark illustrates that resistance in Larkin to the transcendent and helps explain the impetus behind a group of poems in *High Windows* which, severed from any defining context, render in miniature the very stuff of ordinary life. 'Friday Night in the Royal Station Hotel' and the sequence called 'Livings' represent what we might call, following Barbara Everett, a 'philistine' aesthetic in Larkin. This is to be distinguished from the 'philistinism' hitherto identified in Larkin: the hatred of 'abroad' and foreign poetry (though even these should not be taken at face value), the dogmatic attitudes and political bigotry. But the aesthetic which loves the commonplace and which risks expressing itself with an air of artlessness, and which most of all escapes 'personality', is a 'philistine' one in a more positive sense. Everett has suggested how 'the factuality' of these poems (there in 'The Building' as the welcome perception of 'Red brick, lagged pipes') 'is something other than *just* a sense of place: it is, rather, a sense of life . . . The "philistine" conditions, sufficiently loved, offer up an unused, fresh symbol of life in its workaday transience and in its moments, like the poem itself, of fugitive, wasted, inexplicable glory . . . '.[30] This 'philistine' Larkin puts at the centre of these poems a kind of modesty. He manages to be different from himself by finding fictional identities which absorb his own, and preserves in these poems fragments of ordinariness. The escape from personality means that, in Everett's words, 'The artist as such has no standing, but sets his goods among the "lambing-sticks, rugs, / Needlework, knitted caps, baskets, all worthy, all well done, / But less than the honeycombs": a bee could do better'.[31] The silence surrounding these poems is the silence of modesty, convinced of its own unimportance, become mute.

These poems run counter to the declamatory tendency in *High Windows*. They signally fail to disclose their contexts. In this way, they resemble the most absorbing of *The Whitsun Weddings* poems such as 'Here' and 'The Whitsun Weddings' ('Friday Night in the Royal Station Hotel' was written in 1966) by merging, in Trotter's terms, 'event' and 'meaning'. In fact, by dispensing with 'event' altogether, they go one stage further. 'Friday Night in the Royal Station Hotel' describes the emptiness of a hotel and the three poems in 'Livings' are monologues spoken by three anonymous individuals imagined in entirely different circumstances. These are quite 'causeless' poems, quite without narrative structure or moralising purpose. Larkin's 'symbolist' tendency here finds its most extreme expression in these most 'philistine' of poems. Their beauty lies in the simple truth of the things they name.

'Friday Night in the Royal Station Hotel' is absorbed in emptiness, silence, and self-protective isolation. But it thrills to residual presences: the 'full ashtrays' of the salesmen now returned to Leeds, the dining-room of 'knives and glass', the lights still on in 'shoeless corridors'. This 'fort' protects dormancy, lull, a between-times; this hotel represents a strange 'exile' from 'home', event, purpose. From here, in the suspension of activity, 'letters of exile' might be written, letters which communicate solitariness and a rapt attentiveness to elemental presences: '*Now / Night comes on. Waves fold behind villages*', where the metaphor transforms the actual into an image of calming comfort. But of course this letter is not written. The ending of the poem retreats into abeyance, the might-have-been-written which finds itself written. It is like the poem itself. 'Friday Night in the Royal Station Hotel' is a love poem, a sonnet addressed to the merely contemplative imagination which broods on empty chairs and passing hours simply because they are there. It is a poem in which nothing comes into being except the experience of imagining. 'Philistine' in Barbara Everett's sense, its wilful modesty means that the poem offers nothing except its own contrivance. In that way, the poem refuses to be 'symbolist' in the conventional sense:

> ... his poetic objects—the empty chairs, the corridors, the ashtrays—which could hardly be perceived with more intensity if they *were* symbols, have a complex burden to bear: that of not even being capable of symbolizing the absence which they happen to remind one of. For Symbolism necessitates and is arrogant ... [32]

This 'philistinism' is an art which refuses to be Art and, in conjuring it, Larkin is purely anonymous. In this way, he manages to be different from himself.

The triptych of poems entitled 'Livings', written separately over three successive months at the end of 1971, can be read as further attempts to escape from personality, what Everett describes as 'the concentration of personal feeling ... accompanied by an extreme circumscription of any merely personal expression of the self'.[33] Larkin himself described them as 'miniature derivatives of Browning's dramatic lyrics' which were not intended to have a unified meaning.[34] ' ... I thought I was going to write a sequence of lives, or livings, little vignettes, but it petered out after three.'[35] Although Larkin cites for 'Livings' the example of Browning's dramatic monologues, they merely extend that strategy of projecting different 'voices' which has been central to all Larkin's work; this time, the voices are fictionalised as monologues (recalling 'Wedding-Wind' written twenty five years earlier). In that very obvious sense, then, they are 'impersonal'. The first is spoken by a grain merchant. He has inherited his father's business and is passing the time in a rural hotel he uses every three months to conduct business. The year is 1929. The second is spoken by a lighthouse-keeper and the third by a seventeenth-century Cambridge scholar. The poems are dense evocations not so much of people or places as circumstances, of the particularities of three different sensibilities. They are interested in minutiae, in the currency of ordinary living. Like 'Friday Night in the Royal Station Hotel', they are 'philistine' in their modesty, wanting only to render the everyday, the glory and pathos of the usual.

For the speaker of 'Livings I', the usual is this three-monthly hotel stay, the single beer, the soup and stewed pears, the Smoke Room chatter. The poem is stocked with lists, the apotheosis of routine: 'Births, deaths. For sale. Police court. Motor spares', and 'Who makes ends meet, who's taking the knock, / Government tariffs, wages, price of stock'. These routines fill a life, however grudgingly accepted: 'I drowse ... wondering why / I think it's worth while coming ... It's time for change, in nineteen twenty-nine'. Suddenly, the historical perspective opened up by the poem fills it with melancholy. The factuality of its details, the comic pictures on the walls—'hunting, the trenches, stuff / Nobody minds or notices'—take on, from this remote distance, the pathos of the 'Red brick, lagged pipes' seen from inside 'The

Building'. Somebody has noticed, and minded. '"Things like dips and feed": the phrase itself half-ironically half-salutes that densely actual commonplace existence that all Larkin's poems "invent" as their subject'.[36]

'Livings III' is even more historically remote and as a result a little more mannered, an effect pointed up by the strict iambic tetrameters and self-conscious diction. But the poem follows the same movement as the first, from 'inside' to 'outside' and with it comes an intensification of emotional pressure. The 'big sky' (of 'Livings I') and 'Chaldean constellations' which 'Sparkle over crowded roofs' situate these poems simultaneously in their imagined historical time and our own. Thus, as in many of Larkin's most affirmative poems, they merge difference and unity, individuality and timelessness, contingency and continuity.

In the two side-panels of the triptych, two speakers betray some anxiety about their isolation and constricting routines. In the central poem, however, isolation and routine are embraced joyously. 'Keep it all off!' it shouts. Cut off in a storm, the solitary lighthouse-keeper listens to the radio 'Telling me of elsewhere' and exults in his self-sufficiency. In terms of 'The Importance of Elsewhere', the 'elsewhere' of everywhere else underwrites his existence here in a lighthouse which is thrillingly exposed but 'Guarded by brilliance'. The adventurous imagery, taut lines and exclamatory tone convey the intense excitement of living so far beyond the social. As before, it is the simple presence of elemental forces which charges the affirmative gesture, when human presence is dwarfed and chastened by vastness. Taken together, 'Livings' express the contrarieties in Larkin: the yearning for difference, self-sufficiency and remoteness; and the grateful acceptance of sameness, community and mutual reliance.

It is worth stressing how *High Windows* represents a more risk-taking Larkin, not just in the didactic and hectoring tones of its most disenchanted poems, but in their obverse: the purer, symbolist, freely imaginative poems. 'Money' is an instructive case. It starts in typically curmudgeonly fashion. Then, after three stanzas of sour resentfulness, the poem suddenly lifts:

> I listen to money singing. It's like looking down
> From long french windows at a provincial town,
> The slums, the canal, the churches ornate and mad
> In the evening sun. It is intensely sad.

Whilst this does not alter the saturnine mood of the poem, the vertiginous shift from aggressive colloquialism to this mysterious simile transfers us from the worldly to the imaginative, from a kind of truth to a kind of beauty. The poem risks incongruity, sentimentality, affectation: all the 'artiness' that the 'philistine' Larkin avoided. 'Money' persuades because, for all its sudden extravagance, it remains exact to feelings of anger, self-reproach and finally an impersonal dismay. It shows in miniature how in his later poems Larkin is more willing to juxtapose contrary modes of expression rather than integrate them and, sometimes, to leave meaning tantalisingly implicit. It is in such self-reflexive poems as 'Friday Night in the Royal Station Hotel', 'Livings' and 'Money' that we find the adventurously post-modernist Larkin.

The title-poem, 'High Windows', is risk-taking in these and other ways. The most obvious is its frank language, designed partly to shock (' . . . these words are part of the palette. You use them when you want to shock. I don't think I've ever shocked for the sake of shocking'[37]). The candid vernacular, so visible in a number of *High Windows* poems, is part of the idiom of bluff, plain-speaking to which many of these poems are drawn. Even more startlingly than 'Money', 'High Windows' juxtaposes contrasting idioms and states of feeling. 'As with much of the later verse, this starts out looking like a poem about sex, and becomes a poem about religion.'[38] The feelings of contempt and jealousy expressed in the speaker's attitude to sex are, without warning, suddenly overtaken by the awed sublimity of the end of the poem. This kind of development is reminiscent of 'Here', but the lyricism of 'High Windows' is more daring in its vulnerability, in its having to overturn language and attitudes so vehemently anti-lyrical.

The 'bad language' of 'High Windows' works to define its speaker. The brutality of 'couple of kids . . . he's fucking her and she's / Taking pills or wearing a diaphragm', the 'paradise' with its teasing run-on which modifies ironically its meaning, serve as attempts to mask feelings much more ambiguous and troubling. For this is the paradise 'Everyone old has dreamed of all their lives'. Of course, it need not be 'paradise' for the 'couple of kids', but it seems so in the eyes of an older man jealous of youth's sexual freedom. The unfolding first sentence which surges across stanza breaks and grabs at slightly off-key images (the 'outdated combine harvester' and 'the long slide') suggests feelings that are only just kept under control. The superficial disgust for sex made mechanical expresses something else. This is envy, and not a little rage. So the speaker's conjecture about an older generation having envied his own ('*No God any more, or sweating in the dark // About hell and that*') is a way of distancing his own feelings of unfulfilled desire. In each case, it is a version of freedom—'the long slide'—that is envied, but a freedom the logic of the poem suggests is illusory. For the speaker plainly feels that '*He and his lot*' never in truth went down the long slide to happiness, and by extension the 'couple of kids' he now envies are not in 'paradise'. Part of the poem's anger lies in the implicit recognition that freedom is only ever relative, a recognition felt in the absurd simile of going '*down the long slide/ Like free bloody birds*'. Hence, the poem's sudden lift represents an imagined escape into pure freedom, a freedom from all desire and language, an escape from identity and expression. This is 'that padlocked cube of light' of 'Dry-Point':

> Rather than words comes the thought of high windows:
> The sun-comprehending glass,
> And beyond it, the deep blue air, that shows
> Nothing, and is nowhere, and is endless.

This is an authentic paradise (and the 'high windows' have religious associations). But as the effortful repetitiousness of the last line indicates, it is a vision which must remain even beyond words. Unlike 'Here', the poem confesses its own inadequacy: it is the glass which is 'sun-comprehending', not the speaker who can 'know' only the illusory 'paradise' of mortal longings. The poem is often seen as the expression of a transcendent Larkin, with its 'sublime emotional elevation out of negatives'.[39] But the poem knows it is thwarted. The ultimate freedom it posits is a wordless 'thought': the 'air' shows 'nothing' which is imagined as boundlessly 'nowhere'. Characteristically, these negatives function as teasing positives, but ultimately they are not reassuring. The sky shows 'nothing'. It is an endless 'nowhere'. Whilst it is true that 'Once again it is the contemplation of his own absence which most thrills him',[40] the poet of 'High Windows' finally admits that in poetry the ultimate freedom of absence can only ever be a rhetorical contrivance. Outside the poem true absence beckons: silence.

So there are complex cross-currents of affirmation and denial in the poem: that the freedom others seem to enjoy is denied us; that such freedom is actually an illusion; that true freedom, an escape from the self and all desire, is inaccessible to language. This helps to explain why there is an undertow of anger in the poem, an anger and movement towards silence which characterise *High Windows* as a whole. Andrew Motion's biography describes Larkin's first drafts of the poem, where the conclusion was:

> Rather than words comes the thought of high windows
> The sun pouring through plain glass
> And beyond them deep blue air that shows
> Nothing, and nowhere, and is endless
>
> and fucking piss.

Motion comments: 'The poem grows out of rage: the rage of unsatisfied desire, the rage of "shame", the rage of having to persuade everyone that "the thought of high windows" guarantees happiness. The poem's beautifully achieved shift from the empirical to the symbolic cannot disguise or subdue Larkin's appetite for what he has never had'.[41] Nor, it seems, for what he will never have: not just sexual fulfilment, but the fulfilment of desirelessness and the poetic expression of the inexpressible. Written in 1967, the poem is the natural successor to 'Here' but also suggests why, to use Larkin's formula, poetry was beginning to leave him.

The poem also reflects the philistine iconoclast in Larkin which constantly threatens the aesthete. The 'fucking piss' of the draft is a comment on the poem's transcendental yearnings, 'and yet the way it sabotages the high hopes of the preceding lines forms an important part of the poem's meaning'.[42] 'Sabotage' is a useful way of describing a significant number of poems in *High Windows*, poems which relish their rancour, their saturnine irony, their intolerant political dogmatism. The most obvious example is 'This Be The Verse'. It returns to familiar preoccupations with parenthood and childlessness. But where 'Dockery and Son', for example, gave the appearance of arguing its way to its bleak conclusion and framed its 'philosophy' within narrative devices, 'This Be The Verse' bullies us into assent. It is a deliberately 'bad mannered' poem in its direct language and monosyllabic bluntness. As so often in Larkin, the problem is to know how seriously to take the speaker, how to judge the critical distance between author and persona. Much depends, in Larkin's poems, on pronouns which assume the reader's involvement and consent so as to speak on behalf of the reader, and on strategies which ironise the 'I' of the poem. But in these more outspoken poems, Larkin seems less concerned to develop rhetorical strategies and so they are more defiantly dogmatic. Constructing personae in Larkin's poems can lead to debatable conclusions. Simon Petch, for example, wants to argue that the speaker of 'This Be The Verse' 'uses sardonic humour to mask the bitterness of his attitude to experience . . . and the poem uses its speaker to take a swipe at the very fatalism of which Larkin has been accused'.[43] But this depends on emphasising the 'humour' at the expense of the 'bitterness'. It is true that the nursery-rhyme lilt is comical, but the comedy does not necessarily make the sentiments ironic. The comic jingle seems rather to reinforce the dogmatic conclusiveness of the poem: 'the truth is as simple as this', is what the epigrammatic terseness suggests.

Certainly, the poem is ironic, but not about its fatalistic attitude. As Thomas Hood's 'I Remember' stands behind Larkin's 'I Remember, I Remember', so Robert Louis Stevenson's 'Requiem' stands behind 'This Be The Verse':[44]

> Under the wide and starry sky,
> Dig the grave and let me lie.

Glad did I live and gladly die,
    And I laid me down with a will.

This be the verse you grave for me:
Here he lies where he longed to be;
Home is the sailor, home from sea,
    And the hunter home from the hill.

Stevenson's epitaph gives Larkin the epigrammatic model and the object of his irony: that stoical acceptance of life and death. Larkin's equivalent epitaph is anti-death by being anti-life:

Man hands on misery to man.
    It deepens like a coastal shelf.
Get out as early as you can,
    And don't have any kids yourself.

'It's perfectly serious as well', said Larkin when commenting on the poem's humour (its opening, for example, which punningly suggests the literal conception of children as well as how parents 'bugger you up once you are born'). The poem teases us by not quite telling us how seriously to take it. In that way, it gets away with being viciously cynical and uncompassionate. As Larkin said of the *High Windows* collection: 'There are some quite nasty ones in it'.[45]

Shortly after' completing 'This Be The Verse', Larkin wrote 'Vers de Société' (an ironically pretentious title), another satirically saturnine poem. It again argues about society and solitude and its dramatised structure means that, unlike in 'This Be The Verse', a conclusion appears to evolve and its satire works more explicitly. Even so, its opening, to use Motion's word again, is another example of 'sabotage'. Warlock-Williams (a sinisterly comical name) does not actually write '*My wife and I have asked a crowd of craps / To come and waste their time and ours*'; the speaker's voice has already sabotaged the language of decorum with its own brute cynicism. (Janice Rossen takes the opening literally, 'an attempt to appear sophisticated by being off-hand and at ease',[46] but if Warlock-Williams is himself being ironical, it rather ruins the irony of the rest of the poem.) The invitation triggers a familiar debate between the claims of community and solitariness. Being sociable requires an effort of politeness 'to catch the drivel of some bitch / Who's read nothing but *Which*', and is a waste of 'spare time that has flown // Straight into nothingness by being filled/ With forks and faces'. The tone modulates to something more reasonable—being sociable is idealistic, 'It shows us what should be'—before quickly collapsing into rancour: 'Too subtle, that. Too decent, too. Oh hell, // Only the young can be alone freely'. On the other hand, solitariness is associated with lyrical attentiveness: 'Day comes to an end. / The gas fire breathes, the trees are darkly swayed . . .' and 'spare time' is

> repaid
> Under a lamp, hearing the noise of wind,
> And looking out to see the moon thinned
> To an air-sharpened blade.

'*Virtue is social*', but the poem's rhetoric wants to argue that solitariness is fulfilling. As so often in Larkin, the poem asserts that it is in states of isolation that receptive communion is found with intensely perceived external presences: the light, the wind, the moon. But what 'High Windows', and *High Windows*, recognises is that this kind of raptness entails silence. And in the end, 'Vers de Société' settles for sociability because

> sitting by a lamp more often brings
> Not peace, but other things.
> Beyond the light stand failure and remorse
> Whispering *Dear Warlock-Williams: Why, of course—*

The poem rehearses familiar tensions in Larkin: between the compassion of community ('we should be careful // Of each other, we should be kind / While there is still time': 'The Mower'[47]) and society's erosion of individual freedom; between the lyrical pleasures of solitariness and the fear of loneliness. Each stanza has a short three-stress line (the third in the opening and closing stanzas, the penultimate elsewhere); the first and last stanzas are written in rhyming couplets whilst the other stanzas variously deploy three rhymes. Technically, the poem represents a kind of loose symmetry equivalent to its process of reasoning. Its conclusion represents not the reconciliation of contraries but a grudging acceptance of the lesser evil, for in the end 'how hard it is to be alone'.

Though 'Vers de Société' partly counterbalances the nihilism of 'This Be The Verse', poems such as 'Homage to a Government' and 'Going, Going' confirm the impression of dogmatism in *High Windows*, an intemperate philistinism which is the obverse of Barbara Everett's 'sense of life' in the mundane. It is in such poems of social comment that Larkin seems to abandon the rhetorical finessing of his best poems in favour of coercion. Where there was a perhaps confusing level of irony in 'Naturally the Foundation will Bear Your Expenses', the irony of these poems is plainly directed at their objects of scorn rather than emerging from a more sophisticated rhetoric. 'Homage to a Government'—heavy-handed irony—is the most explicit response in *High Windows* to the growing political, industrial and economic difficulties of Britain in the late 1960s, and its sociopolitical context explains much of the rancorous tone and some of the characteristic imagery of *High Windows*.[48] It laments the closure of a British colonial base in Aden (now in the Republic of Yemen) for economic reasons and condemns the decision as an index of Britain's imperial decline and moral corruption. The lame irony of the repeated 'it is alright' betokens the general naivety of a poem which expresses only a single attitude of political dissent. The conclusion—'Our children will not know it's a different country. / All we can hope to leave them now is money'—attempts an unearned plangency. Whereas the best of Larkin's poems work towards emotional honesty, this is a mess of inchoate feelings which wants to blame the masses for the shameful loss of colonial power: 'We want the money for ourselves at home / Instead of working'. Clearly, 'ourselves' does not include the speaker. Whilst the poem tentatively opposes the values of 'money', it fails to construct a genuine dialectic or to engage with real feelings. Instead, it relies on appeasing the reader's predisposition.

These social satires reveal the most damaging aspects of Larkin's philistinism. In them, Larkin's political prejudices are all too vulnerably exposed. Quizzed about the poem, Larkin said:

> Well, that's really history rather than politics. That poem has been quoted in several books as a kind of symbol of the British withdrawal from a world role. I don't mind troops being brought home if we'd decided this was the best thing all round, but to bring them home simply because we couldn't afford to keep them there seemed a dreadful humiliation. I've always been right-wing. It's difficult to say why, but not being a political thinker I suppose I identify the Right with certain virtues and the Left with certain vices. All very unfair, no doubt.[49]

Written in 1969, 'Homage to a Government' is in truth no more substantial than the reactionary political squibs which begin to appear in Larkin's private correspondence at this time. Together, they represent an increasing belligerence which in *High Windows* is allowed to threaten the poetry.

Larkin should have resisted more strongly the temptation to versify his political prejudices. When in 1972 he was asked by an acquaintance sitting on a government working party to produce a poem about the environment, he wrote 'Going, Going'. The poem represents the predicament in which Larkin's fame had now trapped him: the poet whose earlier work had been 'nothing if not personal' now had a public persona to project, one designed to protect his privacy. And the public poet was all too ready to offer his readership hand-me-down opinions and prejudices designed to flatter expectations about himself. In 'Going, Going', stereotyped attitudes and sentimental cliché are deployed unquestioningly. 'I have actually finished a poem, and thin ranting conventional gruel it is', he confessed in a letter.[50]

At first, the elegiac tone holds back the polemic, but then impatience breaks through. The lament for a pastoral England threatened by commercial greed turns into an intolerant attack on caricatures: 'The crowd / Is young in the M1 café; / Their kids are screaming for more', and 'On the Business Page, a score // Of spectacled grins approve / Some takeover bid'. As in 'Homage to a Government', rancour hardens into attitudes of disdain which seek easy targets, in this case the 'cast of crooks and tarts'. Against this dystopia, the poem tries to measure an ideal England: 'The shadows, the meadows, the lanes, / The guildhalls, the carved choirs'. Significantly, all it can manage is this tourist-brochure list of clichés. It is worth comparing this with the England of 'MCMXIV':

> And the countryside not caring:
> The place-names all hazed over
> With flowering grasses, and fields
> Shadowing Domesday lines
> Under wheat's restless silence . . .

The difference lies not just in the more intense visualisation of the latter, but in its apprehension of a real relationship between the speaker and the landscape. In 'Going, Going', the list is expected to trigger a predictable response; in 'MCMXIV' the language 'cares' in despite of 'the countryside not caring'. 'MCMXIV' constructs a particular historical moment as its context, but 'Going, Going' only manages to suggest 'the landscape of a nebulous golden age'. The poem is 'a little smaller than life where it means to grow larger',[51] a failure generally true of the weakest poems in *High Windows*.

In poems like 'Homage to a Government' and 'Going, Going', Larkin signally fails to be different from himself. They are philistine in the sense that they are content to mock, that their 'opinions' are not mediated by self-interrogative rhetoric, that they offer no antithesis to their resignation. The aesthetic impulse of 'Friday Night in the Royal Station Hotel' and 'Livings', Barbara Everett's positive 'philistinism', honours the commonplace and the empirical, and preserves fragments of ordinary human experience without wanting to transcend them. But elsewhere, that impulse capitulates to a philistinism which wants to mock all artistic enterprise and which develops into the reactionary boorishness apparent in some aspects of Larkin's later life.

These tensions between the aesthete and the philistine which underlie so much of Larkin's work are dramatised in 'The Card-Players'. Posing as 'a verbal *tableau vivant* from a former century, an enactment of an interior scene painted by a Dutch Old Master',[52] the poem (a sonnet) subverts its artistic frame by revelling in the base, the primitive, the disgusting. Whilst the extravagant language might suggest an element of parody, it is not clear what is being mocked, and long before its end any satire has been overwhelmed by excited complicity. The scatalogical language ('Jan van Hogspeuw . . . pisses at the dark . . . Jan turns back and farts') and the grossly vulgarised names are part of the poem's wild uninhibitedness. It is a picture of animal comfort—the pissing, belching, farting and gobbing, the smoking, drinking and singing. 'This is a world without families, an exclusively and gloatingly male world where mothers, wives and mistresses are not admitted'.[53] More than that, it is a world without pretentiousness or artiness. Someone 'croaks scraps of songs . . . about love', but only as an accompaniment to the ale, the mussels and 'the ham-hung rafters'. 'This lamplit cave' is a vision not of Platonic essence, but of its opposite: ripe, self-sufficient earthiness. The dislocated last line, reminiscent of the ecstatic conclusion of 'Absences' and the urgent 'Bestial, intent, real' of 'Dry-Point', welcomes retreat into gross, elemental sensuousness. Although at first sight the poem suggests a way of Larkin being different from himself (the manuscript draft bears the note '*Unlived lives*'[54]), it in fact releases that deeply-felt vulgarian in Larkin. Buried under 'Wet century-wide trees', this is a low life which is the natural antithesis of the aspiring, wordless transcendence of 'High Windows'. In effect, it picks up where 'High Windows' left off—'and fucking piss'—before that poem found its edited equilibrium. *High Windows* makes more explicit than any earlier collection the collision in Larkin between the aesthete and the philistine and the relative silence following its publication in 1974 tells its own story.

As Andrew Motion has shown, that story involves amongst other things the death of Larkin's mother and increasingly complicated and guilt-inducing relationships with women. Larkin's love poems are more usually poems about lovelessness, but in *High Windows* there is a deafening silence about love (though the subject returns vividly in a few poems written after 1974). In fact, a long, unfinished love poem called 'The Dance' was in progress as *The Whitsun Weddings* was published. Although it combines incident and reflection in the self-interrogative manner of 'Dockery and Son' and 'Reasons for Attendance' (which it resembles in other ways too), 'The Dance' is more startlingly intimate and 'confessional' than either. It describes the emotional turmoil of attending a dance with a woman to whom the poet is disturbingly attracted. Its feelings are a familiar mixture of scorn and self-loathing, of desire and fear. The dance is '*Alien territory*'; when in front of the woman, the speaker yearns 'desperately for qualities // Moments like these demand, and which I lack'. When he senses sexual responsiveness, desire merges with panic at 'something acutely transitory / The slightest impulse could deflect to how / We act eternally'. Shame confirms 'How useless to invite / The sickened breathlessness of being young // Into my life again!' But when he dances with the woman again

I feel once more
That silent beckoning from you verify
All I remember—weaker, but
Something in me starts toppling. I can sense
By staring at your eyes (hazel, half-shut)
Endless receding Saturdays, their dense
And spot-light-fingered glut
Of never-resting hair-dos . . . [55]

'Its five printed pages in the *Collected Poems* are a fascinating ruin, their fragmentariness powerfully reinforcing the poem's theme of incompletion'.[56] A poem so nakedly exposed to the moment-by-moment intensities of recollected feelings looks therapeutic, and it is no surprise that Larkin could not finish it.

Written some ten years later, 'The Life with a Hole in it' (a bitter allusion to a famous advert) returns to the illusions and disillusionments of choice, the 'something acutely transitory' which deflects 'To how / We act eternally'. The contrast with 'The Dance' is instructive. There, choice is fully acknowledged and recognised as frightening and perilous. Now, an attitude of self-pitying belligerence opts for the comforts of resignation and fatalism. The life he might have had ('the shit in the shuttered château') and the life he is glad to have avoided ('that spectacled schoolteaching sod') are 'far off as ever'. Life is not a matter of free choice, but of being imprisoned:

Life is an immobile, locked,
Three-handed struggle between
Your wants, the world's for you, and (worse)
The unbeatable slow machine
That brings what you'll get. Blocked,
They strain round a hollow stasis
Of havings-to, fear, faces.
Days sift down it constantly. Years.[57]

This is another fine 'performance on the Larkin'. But where the similar 'Send No Money' dramatised its resentments so as to leave room for self-parody, 'The Life with a Hole in it' offers no such critical distance. Only the final line shifts the poem to a more impersonal register, an echo of the faith in lyricism which in Larkin's earlier work transformed rawly personal feeling into a larger awareness. 'This is brilliantly effective "bad" writing. The poet presents himself as flailing about, unhappily aware that his exasperation is out of proportion to its apparent occasion.'[58] But it also confirms the impression that in his later poems Larkin is boxed in by apathy, resignation and a sense of futility. Where earlier the clash of contrary impulses reverberated in complex ironies, now 'bad language' carries the force of simple odium.

Nevertheless, a significant number of poems in *High Windows* do affirm their faith in the lyrical moment, although even here are undercurrents of darker feeling. 'The Trees', for example, with its simple rhymes and soothingly end-stopped lines, wants to welcome renewal: 'Begin afresh, afresh, afresh'. Still, 'Their greenness is a kind of grief' because they mark the passing of the old, just as 'Their yearly trick of looking new' is a reminder of our own mortality. So it comes as no real surprise to learn that in the privacy of his manuscript notebook Larkin wrote beneath the poem, 'Bloody awful tripe'."[59] Larkin's lyricism knows it is wishful thinking. As Donald Davie reminds us, 'The pristine and definitive form of lyric is the song; and the singer is not on oath. The sentiment and the opinion expressed ... are to be understood as true only for as long as the singing lasts. They are true only to that occasion and that mood ...'.[60]

Larkin's deflating comment is a kind of retaliation, a self-protective acknowledgement that lyricism can only ever be transitory and thereby delusory. A different sort of acknowledgement is made in 'Cut Grass', which focuses on an image of transitoriness. The simultaneity of life (the 'young-leafed June ... With hedges snowlike strewn') and death ('Brief is the breath / Mown stalks exhale. / Long, long the death // It dies ...') is captured in the poem's final image of weightlessness and slowness: 'that high builded cloud / Moving at summer's pace'. In effect, the poem works by an accumulation of images, all intensifying a lyrical moment but incapable of adding to it. Instead, they emphasise the fragility not only of the cut grass, but of the lyrical moment it comes to symbolise. As Larkin wrote more intemperately of the poem: 'Its trouble is that it's "music", i.e. pointless crap'.[61]

Written in 1964, 'Solar' was the first poem completed after *The Whitsun Weddings* and is amongst the most purely symbolic of Larkin's poems. It represents one of his most extravagantly romantic and Lawrentian gestures, a prayer to the sun more unembarrassedly devotional than 'Water'. Seamus Heaney has commented: 'The poem is most unexpected and daring, close to the pulse of primitive poetry . . . The poet is bold to stand uncovered in the main of light, far from the hatless one who took off his cycle-clips in awkward reverence'.[62] It reverently addresses a personified sun as an idealised image of self-sufficiency which yet pours 'unrecompensed' and gives 'for ever'. It rises above the emotional entanglements of its predecessor, 'The Dance', to escape into a sublime impersonality, an overwhelming 'You'. There is nothing else quite like it in Larkin's work and it is hard to resist the conclusion that Larkin was making an ironic comment on the poem by printing next to it 'Sad Steps' in *High Windows*. Together, they represent once again the conflicting impulses of celebration and mockery, 'the two halves of his poetic personality in dialogue'.[63]

As before, the literary allusion in Larkin's title functions ironically. The thirty-first of the Elizabethan poet Philip Sidney's sequence of love poems, *Astrophel and Stella*, begins 'With how sad steps, O moon, thou climb'st the skies, / How silently, and with how wan a face', wherein the moon is made to stand in the poem as a symbol of disappointed love. Larkin's poem wants to assert, on the contrary, that the moon is just the moon, although in fact the moon ends the poem as an anti-romantic symbol. Nevertheless, although 'Sad Steps' challenges 'Solar' by debunking the stereotypes of literary symbolism, its witty inventiveness and play of linguistic registers develop strategies whereby Larkin is able to rise above mere mockery.

The poem begins with defiantly idiomatic language. Sidney's moon climbed with sad steps; the poem's speaker gropes his way back to bed 'after a piss'. Parting the curtains, he is 'startled' by the moon's brightness and unsure of his response. 'There's something laughable about this', and the off-key imagery catches the confusion of emotions: the clouds 'blow / Loosely as cannon-smoke' and the moon is tamely apostrophised as 'High and preposterous and separate'. Then the poem tries comically for an elevated rhetoric, before collapsing gratefully into conversation and literalness:

> Lozenge of love! Medallion of art!
> O wolves of memory! Immensements! No,
>
> One shivers slightly, looking up there.

But it is from the reductive, earth-bound 'shivering' that the poem curves towards its real emotional centre. It does so by deploying a language that looks unembarrassingly empirical but catches the fullness of impressions and experience, and which in its plainness honours the moon's plainness:

> The hardness and the brightness and the plain
> Far-reaching singleness of that wide stare

> Is a reminder of the strength and pain
> Of being young; that it can't come again,
> But is for others undiminished somewhere.

The poem makes it appropriate that the painfully affirmative symbolic resonance of the moon should be expressed in a negative prefix: 'undiminished' (like the 'strong // Unhindered moon' of 'Dockery and Son'). The rhetorical control of the poem resists, predictably, the urge to grandeur and, more importantly, the plunge into the self-pitying brashness seen elsewhere in *High Windows*. Indeed, it achieves a more impersonal elegy by arguing its way (unlike, for example, 'Cut Grass') to an emotional centre. Like the moon, the language has a 'hardness' and 'brightness' which fend off easy sentiments either of exaltedness or of mockery. The envy of youth expressed in the conclusion carries with it 'a sense of shared endeavour'.[64] 'Sad Steps' shows ('Dublinesque' is another example) that there remain moments of integration in *High Windows*.

It is in the three central set-piece poems—'To the Sea', 'Show Saturday' and 'The Explosion'—that these moments of integration are most fully realised. Each of them is set within a community: a seaside crowd; a country fête and a mining village. The first of them to be written, 'To the Sea', is a tribute to habit and duty. There are no metaphysical yearnings here, just a contented contemplation of ritual. The opening infinitive noun-phrase ('To step over . . . Brings . . .') establishes a sense of suspension in time which the poem celebrates in its enumeration of repeated ritual. So, the waves' 'repeated fresh collapse' and the 'white steamer stuck in the afternoon' are instances of sustained continuity, of change become stasis, just as for the poet this visit 'Brings sharply back something known long before'. Stepping over the dividing 'low wall' is to step into a realm where time seems to stand still: 'Still going on, all of it, still going on!' Even when the day begins to fade, it does so with almost unnoticeable gentleness: 'The white steamer has gone. Like breathed-on glass / The sunlight has turned milky'. The continuity the poet feels with his own past and with his parents' past (who 'first became known' here) is extended in the observation of other families who are 'teaching their children' and 'helping the old'. So, 'through habit these do best'. The continuity of these annual visits to the seaside, of the mutuality of the generations, of the shared recognition of duty as a way of countering 'our falling short': these constitute the affirmative values of the poem. At the heart of this affirmation lies an acceptance of time's passage perceived not as division but as continuity.

'Show Saturday' expresses the same solace in communal ritual. It is a symphony of details, a gradual orchestration of difference into a wonderful harmony. Starting with the country show, it spreads outwards to absorb the rhythms of numberless individual lives. In this, the poet resembles the observer of 'The Whitsun Weddings' who memorialised what 'none / Thought'; but now, rather than placing himself at the centre of the web, the poet is just another point of interconnection in this 'recession of skills'. For five long, elaborately constructed stanzas the poem simply lists: it is a cornucopia of makings and showings, even if they are all 'less than the honeycombs'. Then, as the crowd disperses, the poem tracks its participants

> to their local lives:
> To names on vans, and business calendars
> Hung up in kitchens; back to loud occasions
> In the Corn Exchange, to market days in bars,
>
> To winter coming, as the dismantled Show
> Itself dies back into the area of work.

As in the most celebratory of Larkin's poems, there is a recognition of the miraculousness of the ordinary. The integration of the individual and the universal is achieved in the poem's return

> to private addresses, gates and lamps
> In high stone one-street villages, empty at dusk,
> And side roads of small towns (sports finals stuck
> In front doors, allotments reaching down to the railway) . . .

The list insists on the singular become plural, and the parenthesis, far from mocking welfare-state sameness as some of Larkin's poems do, modestly honours shared uniqueness. So the annual Show becomes, like everything else in the poem, part of an organic rhythm, 'something people do' to disperse 'time's rolling smithy-smoke'. The poem's conclusion swells into a prayer and a command:

> something they share
> That breaks ancestrally each year into
> Regenerate union. Let it always be there.

This time, the poet is not figured as an excluded observer or unwilling participant, but as an intermediary who negotiates with the reader for 'them'. Still, the ending 'is as much a plea as an assertion'[65] and the poem's vision of a shared, common culture is willed into being by its eager accumulation of separateness. In that sense, like all Larkin's lyrics, it refuses to delude itself. Nevertheless, the poem expresses its faith in the power of lyrical perception to hold in significant order experiences that are otherwise random and arbitrary. It is as much a contrivance as the other objects on show. As Barbara Everett writes:

> The virtue of the poem is its impassive, interested, packed inventiveness ... Within a world void of any reassuring concept, the world of sense takes on the semblance of innocence, an extraordinary steady gravity, a weighty floating-free in time and space: as the 'folk' endlessly poise on their random straw dice, and the wrestling match shines for ever against the empty sky ... The very *un*reality of this poetic world, its beautiful hollowness and the severe limits to the kind of reassurance it can give, are really the solid terms which give poet and readers a meeting-place, like the 'great straw dice' on which 'folk sit'.[66]

When Larkin said in a radio broadcast that he wanted to write 'different kinds of poems that might be by different people', he went on by way of illustration to read 'The Explosion'. Various features of the poem are notably untypical, but its central affirmations are absolutely characteristic of the lyrical Larkin. As Peter Hollindale has shown, the poem is uncharacteristic in its 'two contrasting lines of ancestry',[67] the use of Longfellow's *Hiawatha* rhythm, and the working-class ballad of industrial disaster (and, more vaguely, the influence of Lawrence for the description of mining villages).

The trigger for the poem was a television documentary about the mining industry that Larkin watched during Christmas 1969, though the poem's values are enduring ones in Larkin's work.[68] The importance of the *Hiawatha* metre in a poem which merges death with a vision of after-life is that it is 'a verbal and experiential rhythm of continuity ... The power of the *Hiawatha* metre is that it causes nothing to stop: condition merges with condition, like season with season, by almost imperceptible gradations'.[69] Reinforcing the effect of the metre is the alteration between verbs in the past tense and present participles. Moreover, Larkin's unrhymed triplets, though they modify Longfellow's metrics, propel the poem forward even as they frame the poem's ballad-like narrative stages. And in necessitating 'an isolated and resolving final line', Larkin's structure 'provides imaginative space for the poem's two great images of affirmation to be completed'.[70]

The narrative structure is designed to suggest circularity: we know at the opening of the explosion to follow in the middle, and the nest of lark's eggs will become the final affirmative symbol. The image of the sun recurs to mark the poem's three stages. In the morning sun 'the slagheap slept' as the men, 'Shouldering off the freshened silence', walk to work. At noon, 'there came a tremor' and as the masculine endings of the lines take hold, the 'dimmed' sun marks a pause. Then the narrative seems to cut forward, with the pastor's italicised words, to the funeral service. But the manipulation of tenses (from the continuous present of the pastor's quoted words, to the past 'It was said' and 'Wives saw men', and forward to the present participles of the momentary vision) creates the syntactical logic by which men walk 'Somehow from the sun' at the very moment it has 'dimmed' for the underground explosion. The effect of this, quite miraculously, is to annihilate the moment of death, not by meekly editing it out of the poem, but by silently building it in to what survives that moment of death. The men are unbroken, like the eggs. They have simply passed 'Through the tall gates standing open'.

In 'The Explosion', Larkin manages to modify his fear of death by making the moment of death continuous with life, so that like the closing of the day in 'To the Sea' there is an imperceptible change of state. Equally, the poem is careful not to be seduced by the wives' understandable need to see an after-life. They see only 'for a second', and it is their vision, not the poem's. The emphatic 'Somehow', typical of Larkin's indefiniteness at his most intensely lyrical moments, preserves 'the protective uncertainty which keeps a margin of reservation between the poet's needs and the risk of deceptive fulfilments'.[71] The ending is not a religious consolation. Its beauty resides in an ordering of human experience which asserts the fragile preciousness of compassion. A single line silently conjures up a network of human relationships: 'Fathers, brothers, nicknames, laughter'. These miners, 'Coughing oath-edged talk and pipe-smoke', shoulder their way into the poem's opening silence. Anonymously,

> One chased after rabbits; lost them;
> Came back with a nest of lark's eggs;
> Showed them; lodged them in the grasses.

As the man took care of these eggs, so the poem with the men. It shows them, and lodges them in their community, amongst their nameless wives and families. The poem makes them 'Larger than in life they managed'.

In choosing to conclude *High Windows* with 'The Explosion', Larkin continued the pattern of *The Less Deceived* and *The Whitsun Weddings*. He ends with poems of qualified affirmation: the enviable anonymity of the horses in 'At Grass'; the 'almost true' proof of our 'almost-instinct' about love in 'Arundel Tomb', and now the visionary intensity of 'The Explosion'. Though Larkin cited this last as a 'different kind of poem', its central concerns are ubiquitous in Larkin's work, so much of which is taken up with being 'different from yourself'. The poems he wrote after the publication of *High Windows* continue to show his obsession with questions of love, identity and death. For all their emotional power, 'The Explosion', 'To the Sea' and 'Show Saturday' represent only moments of relative serenity. For the rest, perhaps the most significant feature of the poems written in the final fifteen years or so of Larkin's life is their infrequency. The lifelong quarrel with himself about the value of art, about the circumstances of his own life, about the rival claims of the aesthete and the philistine, seem to have yielded to a silence occasionally punctuated by a few poems of 'required writing' (amongst them birthday tributes and some 'official' verses) and a few agonised meditations on death and love.

In 'Aubade', which Larkin published in 1977, the traditional dawn which separates the lovers is now a horrifying reminder of mortality. It is a poem which brings 'the solving emptiness / That lies just under all we do' to the surface and stares at it, 'blank and true' ('Ambulances'). The confrontation is sustained in language 'resolutely declarative, unwavering in its intent, with none of the hesitation of discovery imitated in "Dockery and Son"—none of the self-doubt of the earlier poetry'.[72] As the poem broods on 'nothing more terrible, nothing more true', it can only find ways of saying the same thing in negatives drained of sublimity: 'Not to be here, / Not to be anywhere, / And soon'. Religion is dismissed as a pretence and 'Courage is no good: / It means not scaring others'. Only in the final stanza, added some time after the others had been written,[73] does the poem shift its gaze.

> Meanwhile telephones crouch, getting ready to ring
> In locked-up offices, and all the uncaring
> Intricate rented world begins to rouse.
> The sky is white as clay, with no sun.
> Work has to be done.
> Postmen like doctors go from house to house.[74]

The ordinary, workaday world is 'uncaring' and 'rented'. But as always in Larkin, that world also secures his deepest affections. Tucked between the two dismissive adjectives but prominent at the beginning of the line, 'Intricate' pays tribute to whatever resists, however temporarily, the encroachments of death. It is the 'Intricacy' of 'smells of different dinners' ('Ambulances'), of 'sports finals stuck / In front doors' ('Show Saturday'), of 'Fathers, brothers, nicknames, laughter' ('The Explosion'). A draft ending of 'Aubade' made a sense of survival more explicit:

Postmen go
From house to house like doctors to persuade
Life to resume.[75]

The final 'Postmen like doctors' are emblems of that workaday world which sustains itself by individuals' mutual reliance. They contribute to that 'Intricacy', representing every tender preservation in Larkin's poems of an empirical, stubbornly material reality.

Honour that world as Larkin's poems do, it is a world from which he feels himself ultimately excluded. 'Love Again' rehearses with shocking intensity all the resentments and despair which finally overwhelmed Larkin as a poet. It remained unpublished in his lifetime.

Love again: wanking at ten past three
(Surely he's taken her home by now?),
The bedroom hot as a bakery,
The drink gone dead, without showing how
To meet tomorrow, and afterwards,
And the usual pain, like dysentery.

Someone else feeling her breasts and cunt,
Someone else drowned in that lash-wide stare,
And me supposed to be ignorant,
Or find it funny, or not to care,
Even . . . but why put it into words?
Isolate rather this element

That spreads through other lives like a tree
And sways them on in a sort of sense
And say why it never worked for me.
Something to do with violence
A long way back, and wrong rewards,
And arrogant eternity.[76]

Andrew Motion shows how the poem 'summarizes the conflicts between "life" and "art" that had shaped Larkin's whole existence'.[77] The need to 'say why it never worked for me' is why even the most triumphant of Larkin's poems are about failure, and why the poems ultimately prefer silence to words:

Then there will be nothing I know.
My mind will fold into itself, like fields, like snow.
('The Winter Palace'[78])

Notes

1. Motion, *A Writer's Life*, p. 446.
2. Ibid., p. 342.
3. Postcard to Barbara Pym, postmarked 12 May 1965. See MS Pym 151/36 in the Bodleian Library.
4. Al Alvarez, review of *The Whitsun Weddings*, *Observer*, 1 March 1964, p. 27.
5. Motion, *A Writer's Life*, p. 445.
6. Interview with Ian Hamilton, *London Magazine*, vol. 4, no. 8 (November 1964) p. 77.
7. *Selected Letters*, p. 521. Clive James, in his review of *High Windows*, emphasised its note of desperation: 'The total impression of *High Windows* is of despair made beautiful . . . Apart from an outright cry for help, he has sent every distress signal a shy man can'. *At the Pillar of Hercules* (London: Faber and Faber, 1979) pp. 51 and 57.
8. 'Not Like Larkin', *Listener*, 17 August 1972, p. 209.
9. David Trotter, *The Making of the Reader* (London and Basingstoke: Macmillan, 1984) p. 179.
10. Ibid., p. 181.
11. See, for example, Regan, *Philip Larkin*, pp. 123–42.
12. Trotter, *The Making of the Reader*, pp. 184 and 186.
13. Stan Smith, *Inviolable Voice: History and Twentieth-Century Poetry* (Dublin: Gill and Macmillan, 1982) p. 176.
14. Rossen, *Philip Larkin: His Life's Work*, p. 131.
15. *Selected Letters*, p. 386.
16. Ibid., p. 387.
17. Ibid., p. 460.
18. Ibid., p. 696.
19. Haffenden, *Viewpoints*, p. 116.
20. Ibid., p. 127.
21. Barbara Everett, 'Art and Larkin', in *Philip Larkin: The Man and His Work*, p. 131.
22. R. P. Draper, *Lyric Tragedy* (Basingstoke: Macmillan, 1985), p. 205.
23. Booth, *Philip Larkin: Writer*, p. 157.
24. Whalen, *Philip Larkin and English Poetry*, p. 24.
25. Motion, *A Writer's Life*, p. 427.
26. Trotter, *The Making of the Reader*, p. 186.
27. DPL 11 (in BJL).
28. Ibid.
29. Haffenden, *Viewpoints*, p. 124.
30. Everett, 'Art and Larkin', in *Philip Larkin: The Man and His Work*, p. 134.
31. Ibid., p. 132.
32. Barbara Everett, *Poets in Their Time* (London: Faber and Faber, 1986) p. 243.
33. Everett, 'Art and Larkin', in *Philip Larkin: The Man and His Work*, p. 131.
34. *Selected Letters*, p. 453.
35. Ibid., p. 653.
36. Everett, 'Art and Larkin', in *Philip Larkin: The Man and His Work*, p. 135.
37. Haffenden, *Viewpoints*, p. 128.

38. Steven Clark, 'Get Out As Early As You Can: Larkin's Sexual Politics', in *Philip Larkin 1922–1985: A Tribute*, p. 241.
39. Booth, *Philip Larkin: Writer*, p. 168.
40. Ibid.
41. Motion, *A Writer's Life*, p. 355.
42. Ibid.
43. Petch, *The Art of Philip Larkin*, p. 101.
44. In fact, the relationship between Hood's poem and Larkin's is rather less ironic. Hood's poem, for all its sentimental drooping, is essentially as fatalistic as anything in Larkin.
45. Haffenden, *Viewpoints*, pp. 128–9.
46. Rossen, *Philip Larkin: His Life's Work*, p. 126.
47. Larkin, *Collected Poems*, p. 214.
48. See Regan, *Philip Larkin*, pp. 123–42.
49. *Required Writing*, p. 52.
50. *Selected Letters*, p. 452.
51. Motion, *A Writer's Life*, pp. 419 and 418.
52. Roger Day, *Larkin* (Milton Keynes: Open University Press, 1987) p. 66.
53. Motion, *A Writer's Life*, p. 395.
54. DPL 9 (in BJL).
55. Larkin, *Collected Poems*, pp. 154–8.
56. Motion, *A Writer's Life*, p. 338.
57. Larkin, *Collected Poems*, p. 202.
58. Booth, *Philip Larkin: Writer*, p. 101.
59. Motion, *A Writer's Life*, p. 372.
60. Donald Davie, *Czeslaw Milosz and the Insufficiency of Lyric* (Cambridge: Cambridge University Press, 1986) p. 42.
61. Motion, *A Writer's Life*, p. 411.
62. Seamus Heaney, 'The Main of Light', in *Larkin at Sixty*, p. 133.
63. Ibid.
64. Regan, *Philip Larkin*, p. 129.
65. Ibid., p. 127.
66. Everett, *Poets in Their Time*, pp. 254–5.
67. Peter Hollindale, 'Philip Larkin's "The Explosion"', *Critical Survey*, vol. 1, no. 2 (1989) p. 139.
68. Motion, *A Writer's Life*, p. 394.
69. Hollindale, 'Philip Larkin's "The Explosion"', p. 141.
70. Ibid, p. 144.
71. Ibid.
72. Tolley, *My Proper Ground*, p. 135.
73. See Motion, *A Writer's Life*, p. 468.
74. Larkin, *Collected Poems*, p. 209.
75. DPL 11 (in BJL).
76. Larkin, *Collected Poems*, p. 215.
77. Motion, *A Writer's Life*, p. 477.
78. Larkin, *Collected Poems*, p. 211.

RAINER EMIG

From Eros to Agape: The Philosophy of Auden's Later Works

Premature Extrapolations

The previous chapter [of *W. H. Auden: Towards a Postmodern Poetics*] began to challenge the notion entertained by some critics that there is a proper conversion to Christianity in Auden's biography that finds unequivocal expression in his writings. Auden himself mentions the incisive event of a sudden feeling of agape he experienced as early as 1933. Agape means 'brotherly love' without any sexual elements, and refers to the early Christian practice of a love-feast commemorating the Last Supper. The experience is described in the poem 'A Summer Night'.

Yet far from giving the impression of an overtly religious text, 'A Summer Night' in fact blends in remarkably well with the rest of Auden's poetry of the 1930s, in that it is an assessment of the status of the self in relation to others.[1] It moves from 'I' to 'we', and in the process from the viewpoint of an individual position to that of a privileged group that is exempt from the threats that the European situation has in store. The poem also contains a further shift, that from the 'tyrannies of love' (*CP* 103), which creates a hierarchy of desire and power, to a feeling of equality in the company of colleagues.

The poem, indeed, employs some vaguely religious terms, such as 'congregated' (which is applied to leaves, however), 'chosen' (a reference to the workplace of the speaker), and 'dove-like' (describing the light), an arrangement that culminates in the rather hyperbolic 'And Death put down his book'.

Yet from Stanza 5 onwards, we are firmly in the familiar terrain of Auden's early poetry, when the text mentions 'healers', 'brilliant talkers', 'eccentrics' and 'silent walkers', in order to move on towards England's position in the alarming political uncertainty of the time, and then once again towards fairy-tale monsters and issues of parental authority.

If there are first glimpses of religious motives here, then they are those that are already evident in Auden's earliest writings. They are ambiguous and only ever appear in deflated form, reduced to materialistic insights or obvious hyperbole. Not even the shift that Auden himself saw in the poem, that from erotic love with its inevitable undertones of egotism and potential failure to a brotherly love embodied in agape, is completely evident. The 'good atmosphere' of the text (in itself a rather transient form of the good place that Auden's poetry constantly yearns for) is indeed described as composed of 'the sexy airs of summer and the bare arms'. Rather than saying farewell to eros and embracing caritas, the text shows the two as intermingled. Critics who follow Auden's own wilful appropriation of this poem as the starting-point of a personal 'conversion' are, indeed, required not to read the text, and must merely take its author's biased reading for granted.

Yet despite the continual deflation of positions, there is an ongoing debate about the status of love and sexuality versus society in Auden's writings. There is also a clear interest in questions of religion—an interest surfaces not only in Auden's biography, but also in his admission of uneasy feelings when he noticed the closed churches in Spain during the Civil War or the fact that he started going to church again, on an experimental basis, as he claimed, usually leaving before the sermon.[2] What is easily mistaken as a conversion narrative in his writings, however, is more likely a reworking of personal and existential concerns into a new framework, one that no longer aspires to universal significance or complete fulfilment. It is more likely a pragmatic reduction of the anxieties of his early phase into a form that proved personally manageable—and therefore artistically honest. This chapter will try to outline the development of this framework in Auden's writings. It will also show that, far from integrating his thought into established religious patterns, be they Protestant or otherwise, Auden retains an openness and polyvalence that has more in common with postmodern thinking than established religiosity.

The conflict of eros and caritas, or sexuality and a love that is more than idealistic, egotistic (and perhaps even narcissistic) is, as I have claimed above, present from Auden's earliest writings. Yet the solution of the problem must not be sought in a rejection of one for the other. This would merely support a binarism of right and wrong, good and evil, that creates the tensions between the two concepts in the first place. Auden himself wrote that 'Agape is the fulfilment and correction of eros, not its contradiction'.[3] His much anthologised love poem 'Lullaby' should consequently be read as a reconciliation of eros and caritas—or at least as an acknowledgement of the force of interested, sexual desire together with its relativising and integration into a more mundane daily practice that actually accepts the desire of the Other in more than narcissistic, ego-supporting ways. What starts out like a traditional, perhaps even Metaphysical love poem is already undermined by its second line. It adds two great levelling terms to the love it describes, 'human' and 'faithless' (*CP* 131–2). The two seem to be intimately related.

The poem continues by undermining another staple of love poetry, beauty. It sets individual beauty—which is reified and objectified, and therefore temporal—against the beauty that lies, traditionally, in the eye of the beholder. Here, however, the text goes beyond another cliché by amalgamating the beauty that the loved one embodies for the speaker with mortality and guilt. Together they add up to 'the living creature' that is the love object in this poem, a love object very different from idealistic metaphysical elevations. The notion of boundless body and soul is then satirised as part of the 'ordinary swoon' that love produces. It is as much a delusion as 'supernatural sympathy' and 'universal love and hope', but is also 'abstract insight'. Once again, there is no simple construction of hierarchies and binaries in which one element is elevated over another. There is, on the contrary, a continual undermining of these metaphysical concepts, concepts that are outside the realm of daily practice, beyond 'the living creature', and therefore either useless or even potentially harmful for it.

The poem's third stanza then evokes classical modernist images, the stroke of midnight from Yeats's 'Byzantium', the madman from Eliot's 'Rhapsody on a Windy Night' and the 'dreaded cards' from *The Waste Land*'s 'Burial of the Dead' as examples of attempts at transcending daily life and practice. It sets them against its own universe, which is a much reduced one that knows only 'this night' and its whispers, thoughts, and kisses. Rather than transcending these mundane elements in the direction of a 'truth' about love, the poem merely wants to cherish them for themselves.[4] It distrusts metaphysics and is happy with existence. This is corroborated in its fourth and final stanza, which prays for the possibility of finding 'our mortal world enough' and emphatically places its love not with a universal one, but simply with 'human love'. And it goes even further by adding to the inconspicuous and yet so challenging term the adjective 'every'. This human love is not merely available to the isolated individual alone, which would simply make it the equal of egotistical passion, but is accessible to every one. In this anti-metaphysical love that is none the less far from anti-erotic and asexual lies a key towards the bridging of the abyss between individuals. Here self and society can join forces, but only when eros and caritas merge rather than cancel each other out.

The German theologian Martin Buber calls this attitude 'the hallowing of the everyday'. Edward Callan's perceptive study *Auden: A Carnival of Intellect* adds two more modern thinkers to those who provided the concepts for Auden's new perspective: Dag Hammarskjöld and Karl Jaspers. Jaspers, Callan summarises, defines an authentic response to life 'as the determination to affirm life again and again; the willingness to persist in creative activity in spite of seeming futility'.[5] Hammarskjöld put this philosophy into practice as Secretary General of the United Nations during the difficult years of the Cold War, until his death in a plane crash in 1961.

Multiple Codes

In *New Year Letter*, dated 1 January 1940, Auden not only says farewell to the 'low dishonest decade' which 'September 1, 1939' had labelled the 1930s, but also attempts a first full-scale assessment of what the beginning of the long poem calls 'A common meditative norm' (*CP* 161). This places its point of departure between the three options of 'Retrenchment, Sacrifice, Reform'. Although undoubtedly echoing wartime rhetoric (Roosevelt's, for example), retrenchment also reiterates the narcissistic regression into the Oedipal triangle of father, mother, and child which characterised so many of Auden's early poems. The term 'retrenchment' encompasses the dilemma produced by this attitude, for it leads both to aggression and to paralysis, since there is no escape from the entanglement with one's personal as well as social, cultural, and political past other than its rejection (and thereby its implicit acknowledgement) or its wholesale adoption. In the same way, sacrifice is no option either. As self-sacrifice it would be the denial of personal fulfilment, be it sexual, materialist, even spiritual. It can also function on a social scale, where it produces heroic, but deeply problematic leader figures, whose detachment from the masses and failure to become 'truly strong men.' . . .

Reform stands for a more productive attitude, since it involves compromise and negotiation. None the less, its practicality and viability must have seemed doubtful at a time when the Second World War had just started to be a real war rather than a phoney one. *New Year Letter* is aware of the precariousness of its speculation, since it posits itself in the rift between the pre-war era ('Twelve months ago in Brussels', *CP* 161) and the martial reality of its present. None the less, it manages to use its anchoring in a problematic 'now', the existence so cherished in 'Lullaby', for a productive assessment that is neither reduced to immediate responses nor escapist in its attempt to remove itself from the immediacy of the threats it describes. It places a variety of limited positions next to one another, the position of 'a man alone', the seemingly unmotivated and uncontrollable events of a ship changing its course and a train making an unwonted stop, the not-so-unmotivated crowd that smashes up a shop, and eventually the totally planned patterns of generals (*CP* 161). Coincidence, subtle manipulation, and obvious strategy are shown as linked in the complexity that is daily practice. And even though time might moderate its tone and seemingly have different messages in store for the singular individual, perhaps a thinker trying to make sense of historic events, the poem still insists that all are part of the same messy reality that finds its most drastic expression in the generals' 'sharp crude patterns'.

Linked, too, are those that reside in an apparently cosy exile, in America or, more specifically, a cottage in Long Island, where culture is so safe that listening to Buxtehude can affirm the belief in a *civitas* composed of assent (an anticipation of Habermas's concept of the communicative action).[6] The third stanza of *New Year Letter* presents the Enlightenment credo of the true, the beautiful, and the good: 'For art had set in order sense / And feeling and intelligence, / And from its ideal order grew / Our local understanding too' (*CP* 162). Yet the shift from an ideal order to a local understanding is far from convincing in a text that has just exposed its own setting as a privileged and, in many ways, an escapist one. That the poem does not trust those idealist formulas becomes clear when it takes up the problem of order immediately in its subsequent stanza. There it shows order as equally desired by Eros and Apollo, by life and art, even though their concepts of order are vastly different.

The poem itself runs into trouble when it then tries to define order both as synthesis and process, or even struggle, only ever leading to partial fulfilment—and simultaneously as an end in itself. This is where Auden's poetics of openness, dialogue, and development clash with the Enlightenment and modernism's yearning for absolutes. *New Year Letter* tries, in a typically dialogic, Audenesque way, to reconcile the irreconcilable, to merge life with order. But synthesis itself can turn into closure, thus undermining the very openness and dialogue from which it emerges. That the poem realises this danger is evident when—after having gone through a rather fruitless discussion of the conflict of will and fulfilment—it finds itself forced to sever art from society: 'Art is not life and cannot be / A midwife to society, / For art is a *fait accompli*' (*CP* 162). This is a premature move that denies any social influence to art and also leaves very little space for new artistic production after the pronouncement of art's finite status. The poem makes this more than evident when its discussion continues—which would make no sense if the claim was to be taken seriously. Only a few lines later the text indeed speculates about 'Great masters who have shown mankind / An order it has yet to find' (*CP* 163). This is very much in line with the complicated message of 'Musée des Beaux Arts', where it was also an old master, Breughel, who depicted an order, yet an order only to be found in actual existence, not in metaphysical or theological premises or the promise of an ordered existence yet to come.

This is the crux of *New Year Letter*, a crux that is slyly realised in its very title. It announces something new through the very medium of the letter, but this news is always also an already-realised one, in the same way that a New Year requires the year as an established category in order to be one. It can therefore only ever be partially new, and must carry with it the incompleteness and possible mess of the old. The problem that Auden's early writings debate under the label of tradition resurfaces in his middle phase in the search for a balance of will and order, or singular artistic statement and the society of which it unwillingly forms part. The message that art therefore has in store for the mankind addressed earlier is consoling and unsettling at the same time. After rousing the dreamer by presenting itself as deed, encouraging the striving through the success of its very existence and comforting the mourner by displaying its lasting value, its message culminates in the combined statement and order 'I am. Live' (*CP* 163).

This doubling of art and existence is also implied in the American title of *New Year Letter*, *The Double Man*, a reference to Montaigne.[7] It contains in its own shape another doubling, that into text and notes. Some of these notes, partly written in prose, partly poetry themselves, ended up as individual poems in Auden's *Collected Poems* ('Diaspora' is one example). They have a very different status from the notes to Eliot's *The Waste Land*, for example, which are afterthoughts and addenda rather than intrinsic parts of the text. Auden's *New Year Letter* uses its original notes to set up another internal doubling, another dialogue of distinct voices and positions. This is the reason why some of the notes are themselves poems. Out of the existence of art as dialogue, at least a minimal dialogue between artefact and existence involves the obligation of the individual to take this existence seriously, similar to the way 'Lullaby' argues in connection with love.

Yet a causal relationship between art's factual existence and the individual's responsibility for his or her own can hardly be found in this statement. Indeed, it must not be found, for otherwise the perfect inescapable order would already have materialised. Its establishment would leave no room for individual existence and, indeed, would take the responsibility for it out of the hands of the individual. *New Year Letter* must remain flawed as an argument in order to make its point—a point that also insists that art can have an impact on society, but not in the form of teaching its truths in a straightforward way. One of the reasons why art cannot speak with one voice is indeed that it is made up of a multitude of voices, as the self-reflexive section towards the end of the first part of *New Year Letter* demonstrates. In it Auden goes through a list of capitalised authors ranging from Catullus via Voltaire and

Blake to Tennyson, Hardy, Baudelaire, Kipling and Rilke—only to conclude that he himself has adopted what he would disown, other inauthentic voices. But rather than branding this his own particular fault, he goes on to call it 'the sin / Particular to his discipline' (*CP* 165).

The polyphony and intertextuality that produces inauthenticity in poetic and all literary language is, however, also the one that connects it with history and society and, indeed, prevents it from ever becoming a *fait accompli*. With this in mind, it becomes clear that it is not only too restrictive but indeed counterproductive to squeeze *New Year Letter* into a closed philosophical model, as Edward Callan attempts when he simply equates the three sections of Auden's poem with Kierkegaard's triad of the aesthetic, the ethical, and the religious sphere.[8] Although Callan also recognises that *New Year Letter* is a discussion of order, he sacrifices Auden's poetic insights into the problematic of this order by subjecting them to a philosophical model that he tellingly characterises as 'an all-embracing, notional scheme'.[9] Moreover, his interpretation misses the important insistence of Auden's poem on the 'now', an emphasis repeated at the start of each of its sections.

Rather than modelling his poem on an established philosophy, Auden in *New Year Letter* assumes a position that resembles Adorno's views on art. Adorno, too, sees the relationship between art and society in a complex light and refuses to accept it as a simple one. He rejects both the mimetic premise according to which art mirrors society and the simplistic didactic one according to which art holds some straightforward lessons for society in store. Instead he argues concerning the relation of art and its context:

> Context, viewed as the life that inheres in works of art, is an after-image of empirical life. Meaningfulness emanates from the former and illuminates the empirical world. The concept of a context of meaning is dialectical, for the art work is not oriented to a fixed concept but instead unfolds its concept internally, on its inside. What is more, this process does not lend itself to theoretical understanding until after the context of meaning itself, along with its traditional conceptualization, begins to lose its footing.[10]

This also becomes evident in the second and third part of *New Year Letter*. Part Two of the poem stresses the mismatch of human intellect and imagination—which are capable of and eager to show unlimited possibilities and potentials to the human self—and the human situation as an infinitely small and insignificant element inside the universe and even inside human concepts, such as world history. Nietzsche's parable of humankind as intelligent animals who take themselves very seriously until their planet freezes and they are completely forgotten comes to mind, when the poem reminds its reader of the status of humans as 'children of a modest star' (*CP* 167).[11] The problem is not the unlimited potential of imagination, but the adapting of this imagination to the requirements of existence and daily practice. Once again Auden's poem declares its anti-idealism, and once again it couples it with an insistence on change and plurality: 'each great I / Is but a process in a process / Within a field that never closes' (*CP* 167).

The poem moves on by depicting side by side extreme acts of imagination and egomania. The Dutch astronomer Sitter (1872–1934) who claimed that the universe is expanding, and calculated its size and contents, is placed side by side with eccentrics such as Labellière (who insisted on being buried upside down) and Sarah Whitehead, the infamous 'Bank Nun', all of whom are immortalised in Edith Sitwell's *English Eccentrics*.[12] The power to differentiate between imagination and delusion is then strikingly enough linked with the devil, the 'Prince of Lies' (*CP* 168). Yet, once again, rather than simply adopting an established religious stance, Auden's text constructs its own notion of the devil, a devil that comes extremely close to the very premises that spawn human freedom, will, and imagination in the first place. In fact, if the devil in the second part of *New Year Letter* has an ancestry, it is not so much a religious as a literary one. While common critical agreement locates Auden's attitude towards the problem of free will in his readings of the theological works of Charles Williams and Reinhold Niebuhr,[13] his devil is amazingly similar to a literary rather than a theological one. His model is Mephistopheles in Goethe's *Faust* (with whom he also shares his name). Like Goethe's devil, he is more of an insistent sceptic and experimenter than the traditional embodiment of evil.

Rather than merely representing the stable opposite of God and salvation, in Auden's processual universe this devil is actually necessary to push along human will on its search for salvation. He is part of the inquiry that characterises human existence—even though his presence is also experienced as 'paralysing' (*CP* 169), because it is a constant one and one that steers human inquiry towards mere binary oppositions.[14] None the less, the poem refuses a simple victory of mechanistic thinking—embodied in 'The formal logic of the clock' (*CP* 169)—and reminds its reader that in the same way that concepts are continually shifting, so perception itself 'has shifting contours like a dream' (*CP* 169). The bottom line of the argument is therefore that both a monistic idealism and a simplistic dualism are unproductive—as illustrated in the examples of Descartes and Berkeley, who are both accused of having been unable to practise what they preached. The great point of orientation that the poem sets up against monism and dualism is once again 'Experience', or human practice. Thinking in binary oppositions 'must falsify experience'

(*CP* 170). It is eventually held responsible for separating the individual from the community and thereby engendering human isolation and alienation ('O cruel intellect that chills / His natural warmth until it kills / The roots of all togetherness' (*CP* 170).

Yet the poem is on far less stable ground when it tries to come up with an alternative to intellect and its reliance on binary hierarchies and oppositions. Its advocation of 'instinct' and '*Beischlaf* of the blood' (*CP* 171) smacks of D. H. Lawrence, if not of the blood-based ideology of fascism. It hardly goes together with an equally clichéd '*ordre du coeur*' either—whose link with *moeurs* (morals) is also a mere desideratum. In many ways, though, the text must once again miss its ideal to uphold its overall argument about order as process rather than certainty. In fact, it wraps its ideal formula into a question—and reduces its authenticity by clothing it in foreign languages and thereby turning certainty into quotation. The voice of truth is replaced by the multiple voices of biased positions. Flaubert, Baudelaire, Aristotle, and Rilke form an uneasy debating team, one that does not come up with conclusive statements but decides to turn on the radio instead, not in order to listen to the news, but rather to Wagner's Isolde and her desire. The emphasis is again on deferral and absence of fulfilment rather than the establishment of securities and truths. Once again, Auden's poetics proves to be a poetics of desire and dialogue rather than of monological truth.

In a characteristically devious move, the poem then scrutinises its own logical set-up in order to expose it as similar to that of the dialectic devil. In structural terms, the text performs the modernist act of self-reflection, but not in order to ascertain its closure and simultaneous universalism or to assert its 'intolerance of all externality'.[15] Rather, it performs what it advocates by becoming a process itself. It also spots the devil of dialectic in historical processes: Washington crossing the Delaware or Wordsworth mistaking the fall of the Bastille for the Second Coming (albeit of liberty instead of Christ) are placed in an analogous position to visionaries and eccentrics. They, too, are taken in by their own imagination, and in the case of Wordsworth this delusion actually leads to a politics that is in obvious contradiction to the original ideal. Another worldly advent listed in the second part of the poem is the Russian Revolution. It is seen to prefigure 'the potential Man' (*CP* 173), an ideal of Auden's middle phase that is very different from the 'truly strong man' of the early poetry, and has less in common with Nietzsche's detached superman than with the self-relativising and sceptical practitioner first encountered in poems such as 'Brussels in Winter' and 'Musée des Beaux Arts'.

This potential man is seen through a Marxian lens, yet it is also made clear that while Marx's writings produce mere complacent intellectual response, the Russian Revolution set into motion something very different:

less thought than action. Its underlying Marxist ideas are questioned in a manner that would resurface after the collapse of the Soviet Union in the 1980s: 'What if his hate distorted?' and 'What if he erred?' (*CP* 174). At the same time Marx is partly excused, since he is still portrayed as entangled in his own Oedipal struggle against a 'father-shadow' and the victim of psychosomatic effects of suppressed love. In short, Marx is turned into an Audenesque hero—or rather, into the now-obsolete 'strong man' of his earlier writings. He is both treated with sympathy and eventually discarded: and his mistake is his attachment to pure ideas. Theory, the poem makes clear, is detached from action and reality: 'Expecting the Millennium / That theory promised us would come: It didn't' (*CP* 175). But pure thought is difficult to leave behind. Consequently it is now specialists who 'must try / To detail all the reasons why'. Once again, not a monolithic reason determines events, but its dialogic and messy entanglement with another force, that of Eros. The poem uses a genetic paradigm to make its point:

> The rays of Logos take effect,
> But not as theory would expect,
> For, sterile and diseased by doubt,
> The dwarf mutations are thrown out
> From Eros' weaving centrosome. (*CP* 176)

The products of the dialogue are dubious. It is not clear whether they, the dwarf mutations, are the sterile and diseased ones, or if theory is so afflicted. The end of the second part of *New Year Letter* continues to elaborate this insecurity. It denounces those entangled in a narcissistic enjoyment of their own dialectic split as 'moral asymmetric souls', 'either-ors' and 'mongrel halves', implicitly holding them responsible for the state of affairs and the far-from-realised freedom. At the same time it points out that 'half-truths' also contain the gift of a 'double focus'. Incompleteness, bias, and the need to complement oneself and one's position can lead to a different kind of enlightenment. The explanation that the poem offers for this hidden potential, however, is 'hocus-pocus'. By having recourse to images of Aladdin's magic lamp that must only be used correctly, the logic of the poem is not much more convincing than the fairytale solution of a poem as early as '1929'. The focus is now obviously broader, but the means of achieving and securing a stable philosophical perspective on the interaction of reason and libido—or truth and love—are not yet in sight.

Not surprisingly, then, the final, third part of *New Year Letter* shifts music back into the focus of the poem. In the same way as in 'The Composer', music is seen as miraculously detached from the conflicts outlined in the poem's earlier sections. Music is in fact in the same privileged position as the speaker and his community in the poem. It is of course this very detachment that would have provoked a severe criticism from Adorno, had he engaged with Auden. Adorno's simple claim is: 'While art opposes society, it is incapable of taking up a vantage point beyond it. Art's opposition is thus in part identification with what it opposes.'[16] This claim has much more in common with the dialectic entanglement of art and society in Auden's poems that the idealistic attempt to find a loophole in the medium of music.

The memories of a wedding that took place in the same location as the music, Elizabeth Mayer's house (to whom *New Year Letter* is dedicated), are used to develop a utopian image of the perfect harmonious linking of 'the erotic and the logical'. In a move that reintroduces a Renaissance ideal easily visible in the happy marriages that serve as conclusions to Shakespeare's comedies, 'food and friendship', a 'privileged community', and 'that real republic' are merged. Not content with its own fiction of miraculous harmony, the poem then goes on to find it everywhere and at all times: 'O but it happens everyday / To someone' (*CP* 177). That may be the case, but equally certainly injustice, brutality, and suffering happen to someone every day. *New Year Letter* becomes infatuated with its own imagination, in a manner eerily prefigured by the eccentrics of its second part. Interestingly enough, it is exactly this infatuation that eventually leads to the critical blindness of the text towards itself that has enchanted many of its critics, because it seemingly supports the establishment of belief in Auden that they are so eagerly looking for.

The poem unsurprisingly employs traditional allegories to celebrate the discovery of its ideal. A 'well of life' appears, as does the tree of knowledge, in thinly disguised form as 'the tree / And fruit of human destiny' (*CP* 178), after God has made a guest appearance as 'perfect Being'. The third part of this third and last part is as bland as can be imagined, and one is almost relieved when the poem returns to its speculations of will, truth, and lie in Stanzas 4 and 5, even if one feels that the discussion is not a new one. The rest of this long third part of *New Year Letter* now engages in a number of attempts to condense faith out of the conflicts of freedom of will, doubt, and desire. But one cannot help but feel that the section is at its best when it actually takes recourse to the mundane position of the fictional writer of the section rather than to the illustrious assembly of European philosophers that it recruits as witnesses of its philosophical miracle. This miracle turns out to be nothing but poetry, when the text rather uneasily but very revealingly holds its newly achieved ideal against the well-known concerns and images of Auden's poetry. Limestone and Roman walls, mines and tramways meet the mythical Über-Mother, and all is well because all is Auden and not a second-hand philosophy or a proper religious conversion.

The argument of the poem's finale is a mess, but it is a productive one, productive in a poetic sense rather than a logical one, as the text itself readily admits: 'Our road / Gets worse and we seem altogether / Lost as our theories, like the weather / Veer round completely every day'. *New Year Letter* veers around fairytale images like the unicorn, doves that represent science as well as faith, the fish as the symbol of Christ, but playfully hidden rather than revealed, Audenesque allegories like the clock and the keeper of the years, hell, the hill of Venus, and the stairs of the will. If it presents an image of faith, it is a faith in assemblages. What goes on in the conclusion of *New Year Letter* is not a succumbing to established faith, but a *bricolage* of images, out of which emerges a *jouissance* that may be divine, but not an orthodox belief.[17] If its penultimate stanza concludes by addressing God with 'O da quod jubes, Domine' (*CP* 193), its final one closes inconclusively with 'The world's great rage, the travel of young men'. It focuses not on reconciliation, but once again on conflict and process, on the particular and personal rather than the universal and impersonal.

Dialogue and Its Dissidents

The Sea and the Mirror, written between 1942 and 1944, takes the theme of dialogue and polyphony even further. It is subtitled 'A Commentary on Shakespeare's *The Tempest*', and thus assumes a similar position to the classical play as the notes in Auden's *New Year Letter*. It further frames itself by starting off with an address by the stage manager to the critics, another form of dialogue. Moreover, by not only commenting on the play but having the protagonists of Shakespeare's play comment on it and on their own positions in it, *The Sea and the Mirror* achieves a careful exposition of philosophical positions as well as a multifaceted debate on the relation of art to existence. *The Tempest*, as John Fuller points out, used to be regarded as a dramatic treatise on art, philosophy, sensuality, and religion in the nineteenth century.[18] Even if this allegorical reading has become unfashionable, it is none the less clear that the play uses its plot and island setting to explore some consequences of the emerging rational philosophies in connection with issues of magic, as well as learning and power.

The main protagonists of its implicit debate are Prospero, the puller of strings, whose island kingdom merges knowledge, magic, and power; Ariel, his servant spirit; Antonio, Prospero's brother, who has usurped Prospero's Dukedom in his absence; Ferdinand, son of Alonso, King of Naples, with whom Prospero's daughter Miranda falls in love, securing the harmonious ending of the play; Sebastian, the king's brother; plus an assortment of sailors, a cook, and so on. But there is also a character in the play who does not fit in: Caliban, a native of the island, the son of a witch whom Prospero overcame when he took possession of the island. That the dissident voice of Caliban takes up the largest part of *The Sea and the Mirror* will be of importance below.

The Preface that starts off Auden's poem is already much more than an appeal for a sympathetic review that traditional epilogues tend to be. Here, the stage manager addresses the critics not so much in a mercenary vein as in an existentialist one: he talks about terror and lack, and concludes with a metaphor of the relation of art to existence that shows that art can only comment (as does Auden's poem on Shakespeare). Its commentary must be concerned with its own insubstantiality, but not in order to set against it the fullness of life: rather, that which art sets itself up against is the silence of existence. It has no obvious and tangible substance (this is Auden's rejection of empiricism and actionism), but is rather like the other side of a wall that one cannot see and from which no sound reaches the desperate ear. Yet this silence of existence, independent of what it represents (if it stands for anything), still ripens in the poem, until this ripeness becomes all.

The poem cleverly avoids a clear position on existence. It neither assumes a nihilistic stance (there is nothing to be found in it) nor a mystical or theological one (the silence clearly stands for something). Instead it points out that the effect of the absence of certainties shapes human existence, and it can do so in very productive ways, even though its effect may be ambivalent, as the poem continues to demonstrate. Auden's existentialism is once again not one of certainties, not even of the nihilistic certainty of absence and nothingness *à la* Sartre. It is, instead, an existentialism of productive questioning and of listening: in short, once again one of openness and dialogue, even if it cannot be certain of the Other in the equation.

Prospero supplies the first voice in the text's chorus. He is about to abandon his island as well as his power, and that includes the knowledge and learning contained in his books. He wishes to get rid of them by throwing them into the sea 'which misuses nothing because it values nothing' (*CP* 312). Value and related sense-making operations characterise human existence, as he continues to elaborate when he describes his own intellectual growth from dependent child to tormenting despot. He yearns to be free from these traps of the intellect—which in their final analysis helped him to erect a kingdom in which he was all-powerful, but at the price of not being able to escape from it. Prospero becomes an allegory of rationality which, in tandem with imagination, is capable of building complete realities of its own in which it reigns supreme. Yet these embodiments of uncontrolled and uncontrollable logocentrism are also monadic and closed to any external reality. What Prospero also yearns for, strikingly enough, is death, something that an all-powerful intellect can never imagine for itself. He labels Ariel, the spirit, his tool in these operations of logocentric power, and tells this agent of his own rationality how difficult it is to part with it.

After this second philosophical introduction, the second part of the poem then sees the rest of the cast add their particular perspectives to the debate. Antonio is shown to be another outsider in the seemingly harmonious finale. He sees through the conventions, as he points out when alluding to the traditional literary examples of setting things right, the transformation of pigs back into men from the *Odyssey*, and the happy union of the loving couple that restores harmony on earth and in the universe. Antonio is convinced that these emblems of harmony only disguise the fact that a stable harmony can never be achieved. Human will, he is convinced, must soon raise its ugly head again and restore Prospero's broken wand. The books of knowledge that he wants to cast into the sea will reappear undamaged, because human agency by its very nature stands outside—and thereby creates the inside–outside dichotomy underlying binary oppositions and hierarchies. What the doubting and denying devil stood for in *New Year Letter* Antonio represents in *The Sea and the Mirror*. He is a constant reminder that the mirror wins, because it can even turn the sea into one. That the chthonian chaos of the sea is itself merely an escapist fiction of rationality will later become evident in Caliban's long speech.

Ferdinand, the sailors, Alonso, Sebastian, and Miranda then discuss their individual motivations and beliefs. In the case of Ferdinand, it is his romantically naive conception of love that he both experiences as sensual (and therefore transient) and wishes to elevate into metaphysical dimensions. He represents a traditional concept of love which is quite opposed to Auden's non-metaphysical one, as expressed in 'Lullaby'. Stephano is enclosed in another form of sensuality that threatens to become universalist: he is a worshipper of his stomach, but wonders whether he is the master of his desires or mastered by them. Alonso, the pessimistic doubter with a strong dislike of the supernatural, also has to acquiesce in the seemingly restored harmony, even though he does so without rejoicing. Alonso worries about his son who will rule after their return to Milan. He fears that the trappings of power will distort his view on the realities of power, which is forever threatened by resistance and betrayal, but also by its own blindness, an echo of Prospero's absolute and exclusive rule. Sebastian, the usurper, then discusses the thirst for power as the natural consequence of the trust in will and imagination: 'What sadness signalled to our children's day / Where each believed all wished wear a crown' (*CP* 323).

Trinculo, the clown, is the one who recognises most clearly that the various complications of will, existence, and power are inextricably linked with language as the means of expressing imagination and desire: 'My history, my love, / Is but a choice of speech' (*CP* 324). He is closest to the traditional image of the poet who recognises the potential terror and danger in his capacity to manipulate language and therefore the imagination, the mundane equivalent of Prospero, the magician: 'A terror shakes my tree, / A flock of words fly out' (*CP* 324).

Miranda eventually complements the chorus of voices with her song. Rejoicing in her newly found love, she uses its positive images to dispell a number of childhood fears, such as the Black Man and the Witch. However, the refrains of her little ditty are themselves ambiguous: 'And the high green hill sits always by the sea' and 'My Dear One is mine as mirrors are lonely'. While the first refrain might simply contain an emblem of eternity and therefore a sign of her trust in her love, the second one brings in the mirror of the poem's title as well as the idea of loneliness—which is obviously antagonistic to the ideal of a happy union. It is also seemingly nonsensical, since mirrors double. It makes sense, however, if one sees it as a further echo of Antonio's insistence that there is no way of overcoming binary oppositions. Harmony and union are only possible as concepts that are set against their opposite, disharmony and loneliness. Even inside happiness lurks the awareness that it is only conceivable in connection with unhappiness and suffering. As Antonio's ominous claims hover over the section, so his words intersperse it. After each statement of individual will there follows his ghostly refrain, which relativises what has just been said by its insistence on his dissident position.

Your all is partial, Prospero;
My will is all my own:
Your need to love shall never know
Me: I am I, Antonio,
By choice myself alone. (CP 318)

This is his first assertion of the egotistical separation of his voice as well as his indomitable will. Still, this separation and dissidence do not spoil the argument of *The Sea and the Mirror*, even though they undercut its pretended harmony. They are necessary to affirm the very insistence of Auden's text on plurality. This plurality must not find its embodiment in the harmonised voices of a group in which the individual positions fade into a unified whole, something which would merely reproduce mythical forms of unity and deny the very separateness of the individual and its will that is the prerequisite of its painful freedom. Dissidence goes hand in hand with harmony in the same way that resistance is inseparable from power. Its denial would undercut the argument by setting up holistic utopian solutions. The presence of dissidence is a positive reminder of the implications of dialogue and plurality as much as a negative reminder of the continuation of hierarchies, injustice, and oppression.[19]

Caliban, of course, is the most poignant reminder that there is something left over and, indeed, left behind in all the ostensibly achieved harmony of *The Tempest*'s finale. He lived on the island long before the arrival of Prospero and Miranda and the establishment of their logocentric realm, and, indeed, is both the anagrammatised cannibal and Caribbean of the emerging rational project of Imperialism of which Shakespeare's play is an early indication. At the same time he is not essential either: he is neither nature, body, desire, nor sexuality. He is himself already separated from an earlier wholeness. While Caliban has to be taught language by Prospero in Shakespeare's play and thanks his teacher by cursing him, Auden's Caliban speaks in the elaborate style of Henry James, the author who takes rationality to its logical extreme in his style and thereby paves the way for the tumbling of this rationality into the abyss of modernism, modernity turning in on, or indeed against, itself. Caliban has a lot to say. His speech, the only prose section of the text, takes up at least as much space as all other sections taken together. The dissident voice is shown to be not marginal but central, central to the establishment of a real dialogue, but also as incapable of really becoming independent from what it stands against.

Surprisingly enough, rather than singling out his voice as the deviant and unrepresentative, Caliban assumes the position of authority in his very first statements. This authority goes beyond that of a mere individual voice, but claims to represent, if not the author of *The Tempest*, Shakespeare himself ('our so good, so great, so dead author', *CP* 325), then at least the 'very echo' of the audience's demand to be made privy to the author's intentions. Once again, the text argues in favour of seeing existence as the desire and yearning for answers, and of regarding these answers as nothing but the echoes of insistent questions. The answer Caliban gives to the questions once again emphasises plurality. His defence of the theatrical muse as at least apparently non-exclusive culminates in the image of the 'mixed perfect brew' (*CP* 326). Yet if the Muse of theatre is the perfect symbiosis of existence and art, if she is capable of suspending the limitations of history, geography, and sense through her charm, as Caliban argues, she must still exclude and oppose one thing. (And which of the three theatrical muses does he have in mind anyway? Melpomene, the muse of tragedy, Thalia, the muse of comedy, or Terpsichore, the muse of choral poetry?) The harmony of art must remain the enemy of 'unrectored chaos'.

> Just because of all she is and all she means to be she cannot conceivably tolerate in her presence the represented principle of

> *not* sympathising, *not* associating, *not* amusing, the only child of her Awful Enemy, the rival whose real name she will never sully her lips with—'that envious witch' is sign sufficient. (*CP* 327)

It is of course Caliban himself who is the only child of the witch Setebos, who has been deprived of her rule over the island by Prospero. But he is not chaos himself—which would turn him into an essence or nature. Rather, he is a 'represented principle' and thus already partly entangled in the logocentric systems that he opposes. His aim is therefore suspiciously close to that of reason. He does not wish to be in direct contact with chaos ('We most emphatically do not ask that she should speak to us, or try to understand us; on the contrary, our one desire has always been that she should preserve forever her old high strangeness'; *CP* 327–8). Reason requires chaos as its Other—and the strangeness is needed as a label to differentiate it from the familiar. All the same, the reasonable dissident against reason, Caliban, speaks with reason's voice when he requests 'that for a few hours the curtain should be left undrawn, so as to allow our humble ragged selves the privilege of craning and gaping at the splendid goings-on inside'. Reason is infatuated with its Other, but this Other is already a construction. Behind the curtain, the beginning of *The Sea and the Mirror* has informed us, is silence. Yet even the marginalised, constructed Other of reason cannot help but think in logocentric terms and speak in a logocentric voice.[20]

Art and chaos are not mere opposites; they are indeed linked. Yet while the principle of reason prefers to remain without obvious representation, it represents itself negatively by giving a discrete outline and limiting shape to its opposite: Ariel is a spirit, but Caliban is a brute animal. None the less, they are entangled in their mutual constitution, as becomes evident when Caliban worries about the permeation of their two realms: 'For if the intrusion of the real has disconcerted and incommoded the poetic, that is a mere bagatelle compared to the damage which the poetic would inflict if it ever succeeded in intruding upon the real' (*CP* 331). But this is, of course, what has happened from the very start, when the imaginary (and therefore poetic) distinction divided chaos and art, instinct and reason, existence and will. The effect of the damage is the continual desire of reason for the opposite it has created but can now no longer reach, because its very existence depends on the separation of the two.

This becomes evident in Ariel's love song to Caliban, which forms the surprising conclusion of *The Sea and the Mirror*. There Ariel, the spirit of logocentrism, calls itself a mere shadow of the mortality embodied by Caliban. The refrain of his love song mirrors Caliban's self-characterisation as the echo of the desire of the questioning audience. The 'I' that ends each stanza of Ariel's song is the echo of its penultimate lines. It is at the same time the fragmented echo of three forms of utterance, the reply (the effect of dialogue), the cry (the reduced monologue), and the sigh (the sad remainder and reminder of lacking communication as well as self-confidence). In language, the Siamese opponents, art and existence, meet, yet their encounter is as unsatisfactory as that between Narcissus and the nymph Echo.

Allegories of Anxiety

In the title of his Christmas oratorio, *For the Time Being*, Auden had already expressed man's anxieties in time. His next major work, another long poem which used verse forms going back to the beginnings of English verse, to *Beowulf*, *Deor* and *Piers Ploughman*, displays its concerns in its very title, *The Age of Anxiety*. It describes the meeting of four strangers in a bar on 3rd Avenue in New York during the Second World War, and indicates that Auden had transformed the approach of his works rather than changed its orientation in that these strangers are symbolic representations of the four psychic faculties according to the psychoanalytic theories of Freud's rival, Carl Gustav Jung. They stand for thought, feeling, intuition, and sensation. *The Age of Anxiety* exercises the very opposite of the explosive dissolution of identity in *The Orators* or the unresolved entangling of voice and dissident echo as exemplified in the finale of *The Sea and the Mirror*.

The 'Baroque Eclogue' describes the attempted 'integration' of a group of strangers to something resembling the agape of Auden's experience of 1933. The text, indeed, takes up the theme of agape explicitly when it describes the gathering and *rapprochement* of its characters in the following terms: 'For it can happen, if circumstances are otherwise propitious, that members of a group in this condition can establish a rapport in which communication of thoughts and feelings is so accurate and instantaneous, that they appear to function as a single organism' (*CP* 371). The prerequisite of this miraculous merger is described by the text as 'semi-intoxication', drunkenness, which can enhance 'our faith in the existence of other selves'. Once again, the text is concerned with the awareness of others, with the link between self and community. However, its attempt is rather different from the earlier ones encountered above. What *The Age of Anxiety* attempts is not a display of polyphony but a miraculous merger. The text is set on All Souls' Night, and thus signals both a spiritual universalism and a Christian approach.

But does the text deliver what it promises? Some early reviewers of *The Age of Anxiety* seemed to think so, like M. L. Rosenthal, who discussed the poem in the *New York Herald Tribune* in 1947. He claimed that the reader's 'attention will be absorbed by the various centers of concentration along which the "plot" is strung, each of them one aspect of a continuous, straining effort to get at the heart of the human condition and trace the lines of possible (or impossible) salvation'.[21] Yet if it attempts to represent the anxiety of an age, or, vice versa, a special period of anxiety in human history, it chooses for it a framework and protagonists that counteract a possible universalism from the very start. The text is framed in multiple ironies. Its subtitle, 'A Baroque Eclogue', is the first indication that its message must be taken with a pinch of salt. 'Baroque', as Rosenthal grudgingly acknowledges, might indeed be a rather cheap pun on the poem's setting. The bar that made a first, important appearance in 'September 1, 1939' is a particularly dubious setting for an experience of agape, since it commonly stands for alienation, anonymity, and commerce. The 'Baroque' of the poem's subtitle further hints at the length of *The Age of Anxiety*, which rather contradicts the conventional meaning of an eclogue—a usually short, often dialogic poem, which employs a pastoral setting. Dialogic the poem certainly is, even polylogic, yet it is neither pastoral nor short—and it also has little in common with the idylls of Virgil, the poetic prototypes of eclogues.

Rather than an eclogue, *The Age of Anxiety* is an allegory. It tries to mirror its message in its shape and represent an abstract idea, the anxiety of its title, in its structure. It corresponds to an earlier technique of Auden's *oeuvre*, the parable, used, for example in '1929'. Yet while the didacticism of the parable is clothed in an underlying narrative—and therefore functions through metonymic fragmentation and recurrence—the allegory attempts a metaphorical fusion, which in *The Age of Anxiety* merges place (the New York bar), time (All Souls' Night), and its protagonists. Since its aim is holistic rather than procedural, it is also more manipulative, as Rosenthal's uncritical projection of 'the heart of the human condition' into the text aptly demonstrates.

The protagonists of the poem are themselves allegorical representatives of particular types: Quant, Malin, Rosetta, and Emble. Critics have rarely overlooked the obvious symbolism of their names and tend to associate Quant with quantum physics, Malin with the French word for ill will, Rosetta with the undecipherable Rosetta Stone, and Emble with the concept of the emblem itself. Yet a closer look at their monologues (for even after they start talking to one other in the poem, they rarely respond to one another) reveals that their characterisation—as the arbiter of rationality who seeks the explanations science cannot provide in mythology; the (self-)destructive cynic; the embodiment of sensuality and the need to please and be loved; and the naive young man whose only thirst is for a life he hardly understands—is neither thorough nor entirely convincing. Indeed, what the characters have to say and how they say it seems very similar. Their cases differ, but their anxieties are the same.

One could take this to signal that the poem is indeed on the right track, that the age it depicts shares common problems and the feeling of crisis. However, the fact that the characters are mere facets of a common problem rather undermines the need for a merger that the text pretends to achieve and illustrate. Another indication of a short circuit that prevents the rather grandiose project of a poem for the age from succeeding is therefore the absence of real dialogue—something that *The Sea and the Mirror* and even *For the Time Being* achieved. Another case in point is the clumsy framing of the monologues in explanatory prose. When Caliban speaks in the style of Henry James in *The Sea and the Mirror* there is a structural reason for his stylistic dissidence. In *The Age of Anxiety*, the prose explains that which the poetry is meant to deliver. The very first section, indeed, outlines what the whole text is meant to stand for. The framing is not dialogic, as in *The Sea and the Mirror*, but reinforces the attempted didactic monologue of the text. Needless to say, the poem does not live up to the generalisations outlined in its prose prologue. It is still too poetic, too open, and full of contradictions for this. It is also too playful, and never manages to maintain its earnest proselytising tone for very long before it lapses into favourite Audenesque images, such as the illicit glance through keyholes or the unmotivated introduction of 'limestone heights' (*CP* 347).

A further structural feature that is designed to homogenise positions and integrate them into a larger pattern (rather than accepting difference and separateness) is the reference to the Renaissance concept of the seven ages of man, from infancy via adolescence, maturity, to old age, in Part 2 of the poem. It is then echoed in 'The Seven Stages' of the poem's third part. These stages stand for an allegorical journey that the protagonists undertake, through a mountainous region via a valley and a pass to a tavern, from the tavern to two ports, over the sea, inland again by air and rail to a city and eventually a big country house, to a graveyard, to hermetic gardens, and eventually into a mysterious forest. Their paths separate and unite several times during this journey, and eventually, when they expect to be completely lost in the forest, they are again reunited. But their quest is not over yet. Wondering whether they can ever succeed in finding what they cannot know, because they are carrying it inside themselves, they are eventually reunited with the world. From this world their quest has led them away on an escapist journey. Facing the world is their ultimate challenge, and it is quite clear that being reunited with it is far from pleasant.

Eventually the quest is unveiled as a vision when the four characters find themselves in the same bar in which the story began. Yet again the mirroring of the issues of restlessness, lack of orientation, and simultaneous yearning for directions and certainties in the various parables of *The Age of Anxiety* does not add nuances and facets to the story. It merely repeats a monolithic message, even if this message speaks of fragmentation and absence of meaning. The poetic equivalent of this quest that leads nowhere because it is never seriously undertaken would not be *The Waste Land* so much as Eliot's seemingly most desperate poem, 'The Hollow Men'. It, too, manages to achieve a remarkable stability in its absences, and also does this mainly through repetition.

The next steps in *The Age of Anxiety* use rituals as their foil. Part 4 employs the religious ritual of the dirge; Part 5 the secular one of the masque. Part 4 sees the voices united in a chorus of bleakest pessimism and denial. It is the closest Auden's poetry comes to nihilism, and it is a nihilism based on the Nietzschean postulate of the death of God. In 'Dirge', the protagonists mourn 'Our lost dad, / Our colossal father' (*CP* 394), even though there is still a trace of irony in the familiar term. Without Him truth is no longer linked with time, the 'world-engine' that is 'creaking and cracking' in a metaphysical metamorphosis of the engines of Auden's early poems, because it no longer has an appropriate engineer. Yet as was already implied in the term 'colossal father', here the reference to the absent force as 'watchman' makes it abundantly clear that the presence of a metaphysical ordering principle introduces not only security, but also the other aspect of authority, domination, and potentially terror. Even in its most metaphysical sections, *The Age of Anxiety* retains an element of ambivalence concerning its losses and desires.

'The Masque' contrasts the nihilistic existentialism of 'The Dirge' with an emphasis on appearance and its elevation over essences. Sincerity, the section claims, is the preserve of animals and angels, but not available to human beings. Being human means being an actor. Consequently the characters enact little rituals, all of which are connected to their individual desires. Rosetta and Emble express their mutual physical attraction by dancing. Malin builds an altar out of sandwiches! Yet rather than pure blasphemy, this altar is once again an allegory of Auden's aim to reconcile the mundane and the metaphysical. Its sacrifice is an olive, and the god that it means to invoke is Venus. Venus is indeed conjured up, both in the sense of eros and agape. Emble and Rosetta break into a surreal duet of love vows, first to allegorical structures ranging from the 'Four Faces Feeling can make' via the three 'Grim Spinning Sisters', the fates, the 'Heavenly Twins' (Castor and Pollux, rather misplaced), to 'that Oldest One whom / This world is with'. But instantly the metaphysical is replaced by the mundane again: 'If you blush, I'll build breakwaters. / When you're tired, I'll tidy your table' (*CP* 396).

In the same way that the bar proved a rather unsuitable setting for a feeling of agape, now Rosetta's flat becomes the scene of the mutual feeling of communion. And since agape was traditionally a love meal, their sharing of loves of various kind and quickly prepared sandwiches and drinks is indeed its contemporary equivalent. Quant, the empiricist, consequently directs his prayers for the couple not towards God or mythical figures, but towards the bugs and viruses of the household. Malin, the cynic, invokes the restrictions of love when he reminds Rosetta of the child that shapes the man (an echo of the old Oedipal entanglement in Auden's verse). Eventually they all become overwhelmed by their feeling of communion and their hope that it could be projected onto the entire world. When they declare in turn their faith, their declaration is not a re-enactment of the liturgic ritual, and the list of their beliefs and hopes remains a solidly mundane one that is even childish in places. Emble, for example, declares, 'Nor money, magic, nor martial law, / Hardness of heart nor hocus-pocus / Are needed now on the novel earth' (*CP* 400), at the same time as asking for 'Barns and shrubberies for game-playing gangs' (*CP* 401).

When Malin and Quant eventually leave the happy couple, the idea of communion is further challenged. After exchanging addresses in the Epilogue of the poem and immediately forgetting each other's existence, they head home to their own places. Allegorical again, the poem asserts that communion is transient, a feeling rather than reality. Living one's life is a task left to the individual alone. None the less, both Malin and Quant have gained something from the experience. Malin finds that, contrary to what the managers of the mirror claim, we don't learn from the past, there is something worth learning, and that is that one must not 'refuse the tasks of our time' (*CP* 407). Despite the pressures of arbitrary authority and the terror of contingency, it is action rather than narcissistic despair that is called for. Quant, too, learns to balance scientific knowledge and unscientific yearnings, such as that for security, and interpret them as related ways of dealing with existence.

Even Rosetta, whose sexual union with Emble is prevented when Emble passes out drunkenly on her bed, is not betrayed and deprived of fulfilment, but sees the event in a positive light. Sexuality would have been merely another mask that the following morning would have destroyed. As Auden claimed in an early journal entry, it would merely stand for something else: intimacy.[22] This intimacy was already achieved in *The Age of Anxiety* when Rosetta gained an insight into Emble's existence and into her own, even when this moment of communion convinces her of their separateness. The strangers of the poem have undergone a psychic journey together which brings them insights into their respective personalities as well as their common anxieties, but afterwards they go their separate ways. The world has not been changed—as it certainly would have been had one of the modernists, Eliot, for instance, worked the same plot into a poem. (The cosmic overtones of *Four Quartets* once more come to mind in this respect.) Despite the multiple allegories, beginning with the title, integration is only approached, and it remains temporary. *The Age of*

Anxiety earned Auden a Pulitzer Prize in 1948. Leonard Bernstein used it as the basis of one of his symphonies. The poem attests that Auden did not give up the great themes, neither did he say farewell to his analytic and even scientific approach. But he worked themes and approach into relative frameworks that he linked with the actuality of existence, with everyday practice.

In Praise of the Limit

One of the most striking changes during the shift from idealistic concepts to practice in Auden's writing is the changing role of the limit. In the early quest poems, the limit (often allegorised, as in 'The Quest') stood for restrictions that were beyond the control of the individual. Together with the Oedipal attachments to the past, limits of various kinds were the reason for the failure of the 'truly strong man'. Yet even in Auden's early writings there is an element of ambivalence in the limit. In the shape of the frontier, for example, the limit also generates adventure and excitement. It enables those who risk an encounter with the limit to be on two sides simultaneously, to gain insights into self and Other, even if this knowledge proves costly.

In the poem 'In Transit' of 1950, there is already evidence that the frontier will become a positive force in Auden's later works. Rather than seeing the transit across cultural and political barriers as a displacement that leads to loss—and must therefore be countered with an emphasis on identity, Englishness, the past—the poem discovers in the no-man's-land that is the transitional abode of its speaker a place for reflection. 'Somewhere there are places where we have been' (*CP* 413), he remarks, signalling that the transit, the crossing of borders, does not lead to a simple abandoning of the past. At the same time it refrains from seeing the new as an area of unlimited opportunity, even though it invests it with typical Audenesque imagery: 'I admire a limestone hill I have no permission to climb.' What is even more important than this balanced view is that the speaker of 'In Transit' realises that his condition is not particular to him. He manages to envisage another person on the other side in exactly the same state of reflection: 'maybe an ambitious lad stares back, / Dreaming of elsewhere and our godlike freedom'. The godlike freedom is also that of Auden, the American citizen, in a postwar Europe.[23] Yet the term 'godlike' is clearly over-determined; the speaker is sceptical towards his position, while he simultaneously enjoys the encounter with his cultural Other, the lad, and with 'Italian sunshine, Italian flesh'.

The poem is set in an explicit 'nowhere', but it is not the nowhere of pessimistic absences, as in *The Age of Anxiety*. Even though the speaker abstains from considering the effects of his visit on this nowhere and does not even attempt to connect with it ('unrelated to day or to Mother / Earth in love or in hate; our occupation / Leaves no trace on this place') and in fact sees his presence as potential aggression, there is still a possible consequence of the encounter. It affects both speaker and environment: when he is taking off by plane, the nowhere is transformed from a 'congested surface' into a 'world'. Only from the outsider perspective can reality achieve its full significance. At the same time, the surface that the speaker leaves behind, a reality in which 'wrongs and graves grow greenly', the slaves of this reality feel the urge to live, even against their will. Existence is stronger than will, and this existence is affirmed by 'a loose bird', the plane of the speaker as well as his song, the poem itself. In the disconnected and possibly unconcerned or even hostile experience of otherness, existence affirms itself, even though this affirmation does not automatically lead to happiness. There is no promise inherent in the contingencies of existence. It can spare cities through prayer—or it may open old feuds again.

'In Praise of Limestone' is in many respects the happier version of 'In Transit'. It is a poem of multiple dialectics, yet eventually manages to break free from these dialectic oppositions into an area of affirmation that is neither reducible to logic nor miraculously elevated into metaphysics. The poem is also an assessment of Auden's own poetry and its past obsessions. Yet rather than once again setting up (or setting itself up against) an Oedipal trap, it treats the addictions that shape it in a loving and humorous vein. The first stanza of the poem is concerned with the paradoxical constancy of inconstancy. It starts from a position that Auden's early poems strive to achieve or signal demonstratively without much conviction: it talks about a 'we' that is characterised by a common homesickness. This homesickness is the equivalent of the striving encountered in poems such as *For the Time Being*, *New Year Letter*, *The Sea and the Mirror* and *The Age of Anxiety*. It is Auden's reduced version of certainties, their eventual shift from metaphysical promise to existential presence, even though this presence is one of absence and yearning. In the desire for that which is simultaneously in the past and in the future, homesickness manages to reconcile tradition, parents, and child with utopian hopes. It also achieves a loving rather than a critical, detached, or dismissive stance.

Consequently, in the metaphor of the limestone landscape, childhood memories, the allegorical mother figure, the young man who yearns simultaneously for Oedipal attachment and for an existence of his own, and language as the forever shifting basis of poetry meet. And this meeting does not exclude external reality either—which is represented in surface fragrances and images of butterfly and lizard, evasive and transient objects that are beyond the control of the individual will. Culture and wilderness, too, meet in the shape of 'hilltop temple', 'appearing waters' and 'Conspicuous fountains' (*CP* 414) in a poem which moves 'from a wild to a formal vineyard' without setting up hierarchies and proper oppositions. The tableau of its first stanza indeed ends in the image of a child pleasing and teasing alternately in order to receive attention. From its very start the poem relativises its own exercise and presents itself as dependent on its reader(s) and not as a detached statement, personal or metaphysical.

Its reconciliation of contradictions continues in its second stanza. There, a 'band of rivals' is seen climbing up and down the allegorical landscape 'at times / Arm in arm, but never, thank God, in step'. This is the ultimate expression of Auden's agape. It unites the libidinously charged images of his early poetry, the homosocial and often homoerotic bonding of males. Only now they are neither clearly male nor are they united by their adoration of a leader figure. They are individuals who overcome their rivalry, their individual wills, only temporarily, but do this because they have things in common, anxieties at least, and are therefore a band too. They are the products of the interaction with the sheltering yet flexible limestone landscape. Their belief is not in an overarching god, but in one 'whose temper-tantrums are moral', a god who is neither the Old Testament nor the New Testament one, while uniting both. He can be 'pacified by a clever line / Or a good lay' and is therefore also a Classical one, similar to Greek and Roman deities. All of this turns him into a postmodern concept, one that functions as a quotation from the Bible and the classics and a simultaneous reference to the cleverness and occasional smuttiness of Auden's own poetry. It remains local ('Adjusted to the local needs of valleys') and forgiving, because it is relative in the sense of remaining in tune with existence rather than standing above it.

Alternative allegories are used to describe negatively this different, because relational rather than absolute, belief. The believers in 'In Praise of Limestone' do not live in awe of a volcano 'whose blazing fury could not be fixed', nor of a jungle of 'monstrous forms and lives'. Their existence is that of valley dwellers, civilized and circumscribed, but also connected to their lives and environment 'where everything can be touched or reached by walking'. The poem yet again rejects metaphysical detachment in favour of localised existence ('Their eyes have never looked into infinite spaces'). The price that the inhabitants of this happy middle ground have to pay is that their moderate soil does not attract 'the best and worst'. Yet the poem is not convinced that these extreme Romantic positions are desirable. For those who uphold their search for essence and meanings, other soils are available: the hard granite wastes for the 'Saints-to-be'; the clay and gravel plains for 'Intendant Caesars'; and the ultimately ungiving sea for 'the really reckless'. The sea's message is for the existentialist nihilists *à la* Sartre. It asks and promises nothing, nothing but setting the individual free through nothingness. Buddhism's rejection of desire comes to mind. Yet even Auden's nihilistic sea cannot quite free itself from a sly look toward love, even though it ends up rejecting it: 'There is no love; There are only the various envies, all of them sad'.

Rather than rejecting these positions, 'In Praise of Limestone' achieves its aim by actually embracing them all: 'They were right, my dear, all of these voices were right'. It accepts plurality and different positions, but of course it also questions the validity of their exclusive stances by the very fact of its being pluralistic. Furthermore, it achieves its own act of dissidence against totalising perspectives by accepting the non-existence of love, while addressing its acceptance to 'my dear'. This 'my dear' is not the Romantic fairytale prince; it is not 'my love'. It is, rather, its conventionalised and reduced version, yet one that is attainable without sadness and envy. It is undramatic and homely. It is also backward, and perhaps even suffers from tunnel vision, but fulfils its 'worldly duty'. Its very existence, though, 'calls into question / All the Great Powers assume; it disturbs our rights', not the rights of individual, mind, but the binary concepts of right and wrong. It even challenges the poet, who—at least in his Romantic and classical modernist guise—displays a tendency to fall victim to his own puzzles, to elevate his constructions to truths and universes. The poem calls these synthetic worlds 'antimythological myth'.

'In Praise of Limestone' does not completely refrain from offering its own 'anti-mythological myth', though, even though it slyly claims to know nothing of the forgiving of sins and the rising from the dead. Yet its myth is merely an allegory, and a personal and contradictory one at that. Its limestone landscape is its vision of 'faultless love / Or the life to come'. Yet, as the poem has declared earlier, the limestone landscape is not without its tensions, nor is it concerned with a life to come—rather, its concern is with the one that is already there. Yet through its multiple contradictions 'In Praise of Limestone' has already achieved its own utopia: the poem is its own poetic paradise, and one that need not fear a Fall, because it thrives on falls.

Other, later poems take up this theme of achieved paradise within actual existence, a paradise based on contradictions and tension. 'Ode to Gaea' is such an ode to a reality, consisting of '*partibus infidelibus*' rather than certainties or idealist goals (*CP* 424). Humorous texts, such as 'The Love Feast', with its conclusion 'Make me chaste, Lord, but not yet' (*CP* 466) that echoes St Augustine, even show that, in order to be convincing, this vision of an existential paradise in the here and now must be able to step back and ridicule itself.[24] Auden's continual exercises in writing short and irreverent poems is a further indication of this happy and relaxed relativising of established certainties, including that of the status of his own poetry. 'Ode to Terminus', a poem written as late as 1968, summarises his relative and pragmatic existentialism in an address to the 'God of walls, doors and reticence' (*CP* 609).

Terminus is not a major god in the Roman pantheon. He is rather a household item, a god with a use-value rather than the indomitable forces of Venus and Mars. It is therefore telling that he should be invoked to assist 'gardeners or house-wives' against the threat of a new breed of high priests, those armed with 'telescopes and cyclotrons'. In the postwar world, it is the scientists who are the spokesmen of a new faith, yet one that is just as hostile towards existence as the old extremist religions. Scientists as the believers in the unlimited power of human intellect and reason 'keep making pronouncements about happenings / on scales too gigantic or dwarfish / to be noticed by our native senses'. In short, their teachings and interests are directed away from existence and are not in touch with it. The poem holds against these concerns of extreme rationality 'the world we / really live in', and it is a world that is irrational and non-scientific, where surfaces count and limited beliefs may be ridiculous, but provide spiritual as well as physical sustenance.

'Ode to Terminus' argues in favour of accepting limits and using them to learn to cope with existence. It does not promise answers, but through the acceptance of locality, particularity, and limitation it sees the possibility of community, at least on a small scale, and of an understanding that is a translation and a relationship. The praise of the limit is also seen as a counterbalance to the exploitation of the planet, a plundering and poisoning that results from a belief in unlimited progress. What the limit has to offer may be a translation; it may even be a lie. Yet its relativising power helps to see that the rational explanations of scientists are on a plane equal with the 'tall story' of 'self-proclaimed poets'. Its limiting influence, in which rationality and poetry come together, can make existence livable, rather than continually promising a better existence elsewhere or in the future, while destroying existence physically and spiritually in the here and now.

Notes

1. Charles Osborne's perceptive essay 'Auden as a Christian Poet' brings this to the point in the observation 'What is most interesting about Auden's "conversion" is that he remained very much as he had formerly been. He had been an extremely eccentric Marxist, and he now became an equally eccentric Christian, one in whom the Audenesque outweighed the Christian elements': Bold, *The Far Interior*, pp. 23–46 (p. 28).

2. Auden mentions these events in his contribution to *Modern Canterbury Pilgrims*, ed. James A. Pike (New York: A. R. Mowbray, 1956); quoted in Osborne, 'Auden as a Christian Poet', pp. 26–8.

3. *Theology* (November 1950), p. 412; quoted in Carpenter, *Auden*, p. 300.

4. Auden's poem 'Some say that love's a little boy', written in 1938, which culminates in the refrain 'O tell me the truth about love' (*CP* 121–2) can be read as another attempt to multiply rather than essentialise the concept of love.

5. Callan, *Carnival*, p. 254.

6. The concept is outlined most comprehensively in Jürgen Habermas, *The Theory of Communicative Action*, trans. Thomas McCarthy (2 vols., Cambridge: Polity, 1986/1988).

7. Replogle, *Auden's Poetry*, pp. 57–8.

8. Edward Callan, 'Auden's New Year Letter', in Monroe K. Spears, ed., *Auden: A Collection of Critical Essays*, Twentieth Century Views (Englewood Cliffs, NJ: Prentice Hall, 1964), pp. 1529 (p. 153).

9. Callan, 'Auden's New Year Letter', p. 158. In fairness, he also calls Kierkegaard's model non-restrictive, yet seems to miss the crucial problem that the non-restrictiveness is achieved at the cost of an obvious universalism.

10. Theodor W. Adorno, *Aesthetic Theory*, ed. Gretel Adorno and Rolf Tiedemann, trans. C. Lenhardt, The International Library of Phenomenology and Moral Sciences (London: Routledge & Kegan Paul, 1984), p. 412.

11. The parable is the starting-point of Nietzsche's influential essay 'On Truth and Lying in an Extra-Moral Sense', in *Friedrich Nietzsche on Rhetoric and Language*, trans. and ed. Sandel L. Gilman, Carole Blair and David J. Parent (New York and Oxford: Oxford University Press, 1989), pp. 246–57 (p. 246).

12. Edith Sitwell, *English Eccentrics*, revised edition (Harmondsworth: Penguin, 1971). The book was first published in 1933.

13. Auden himself acknowledged the influence of Williams' *The Descent of the Dove* in his notes to *New Year Letter*; see Hecht, *Hidden Law*, p. 210. Hecht also points out that Auden's attraction to Niebuhr's theology 'lay in his [Niebuhr's] dramatic sense of how theological matters presented themselves in the context of actual, practical life', p. 300. The titles of some of Niebuhr's books, *Christian Realism and Political Problems, Moral Man and Immoral Society*, and *Christianity and Power Politics* support this impression. Auden reviewed the last book in the *Nation*; see Carpenter, *Auden*, p. 306.

14. One of the rhetorically most forceful rejections of binary oppositions in postmodern thinking is Hélène Cixous' essay 'Sorties: Out and Out: Attacks/Ways Out/Forays', in Catherine Belsey and Jane Moore, eds., *The Feminist Reader: Essays in Gender and the Politics of Literary Criticism* (Basingstoke and London: Macmillan, 1989), pp. 101–16. On p. 102 she states: 'And the movement whereby each opposition is set up to make sense is the movement through which the couple is destroyed. A universal battlefield. Each time, a war is let loose. Death is always at work.'

15. Adorno, *Aesthetic Theory*, p. 85.

16. Ibid., p. 194.

17. *Bricolage* is a term used by Claude Lévi-Strauss to characterise mythmaking as an assemblage of pre-existent elements; *Structural Anthropology*, trans. Claire Jacobson and Brooke Grundfest Schoepf (New York and London: Basic Books, 1963). *Jouissance* is the term used by Roland Barthes for the 'pleasure of the text', a pleasure that can only be gained from interpretation and therefore from constructing as well as undoing, i.e. deconstructing, concepts, images, narratives, and characters: *The Pleasure of the Text*, trans. Richard Miller (New York: Farrar, Straus & Giroux, 1975).

18. Fuller, *Reader's Guide*, p. 162.

19. The theorist who has been most influential in introducing dialogue into the debates on aesthetics, culture and ideology is Mikhail M. Bakhtin. See in particular his *The Dialogic Imagination: Four Essays*, ed. Michael Holquist, trans. Caryl Emerson and Michael Holquist, Slavic Series, 1 (Austin: University of Texas Press,

1981). Although Bakhtin primarily refers to the novel, his concept of *heteroglossia*, a plurality of voices, is of great importance for the discussion of Auden's poetry, and is developed in the essay 'Discourse in the Novel', pp. 301–31.

20. The implications of this doubling are explored by some theorists of post-colonialism, for instance in Edward W. Said, 'Opponents, Audiences, Constituencies and Community', in Hal Foster, ed., *Postmodern Culture* (London: Pluto Press, 1985), pp. 135–59. The writings of Homi Bhabha also deal with this issue in terms such as 'hybridity'; see e.g. *The Location of Culture* (London: Routledge, 1994).

21. M. L. Rosenthal, 'Speaking Greatly in an Age of Confusion', *New York Herald Tribune* (20 July 1947), section 7, p. 3; reprinted in John Haffenden, ed., *W. H. Auden: The Critical Heritage*, The Critical Heritage Series (London *et al.*: Routledge & Kegan Paul, 1983).

22. 'The sexual act is only a symbol for intimacy'; quoted from a journal that Auden kept in 1929 in Mendelson, *Early Auden*, p. 7.

23. Auden had become a citizen of the US in 1946: Carpenter, *Auden*, p. 339.

24. The allusion is to *Confessions*, book viii, section 7, where Augustine prays: '*Da mihi castitatem et continentiam, sed noli modo*'; see Fuller, *Reader's Guide*, p. 232.

LAWRENCE RAINEY

T.S. Eliot
Immense. Magnificent. Terrible.: Reading The Waste Land

To be young, to be rich, and to be in Paris—perhaps enough to turn anyone's head. Certainly it had some such effect on John Peale Bishop (1892–1944), an aspiring poet who had graduated in 1917 from Princeton University, where his best friends had included F. Scott Fitzgerald and the soon-to-be distinguished critic Edmund Wilson. After a brief stint of service in the armed forces, Bishop had become the managing editor of *Vanity Fair*, a job he gave up in early 1922 when he married Margaret Hutchins, a young woman of independent wealth. Having turned over his position at *Vanity Fair* to Wilson, Bishop set off on his honeymoon in Europe. It was while there, in Paris, that he had briefly met Ezra Pound in August 1922 to discuss the possibility of *Vanity Fair*'s publishing *The Waste Land*, a last service on behalf of his erstwhile employer. Bishop, of course, had never read the poem and knew about it only through the rumors then circulating in the New York publishing world, rumors that Pound himself had helped set in motion. But nothing came of their discussion, and Bishop soon left to resume his honeymoon.

It was late October when he returned to Paris. He was settling in for a year to undertake some serious writing. His first book, a collection of poems and prose pieces that was titled *The Undertaker's Garland*, had been published only a few weeks earlier, and he was eager to begin on new work. On

3 November, Bishop wrote to Wilson, known to good friends as "Bunny," describing his circumstances:

> Dear Bunny:
>
> Well here we are installed in an apartment neatly placed between the Opera and the wild wild joints of Montmartre; the location has, so to say, a symbolic significance. The place belongs to two decayed members of the French gentility who, being much fallen in estate and finance have been obliged to let half their formerly enormous quarters. . . . We have then, one large salon furnished quite chastely with a touch of the grand manner; a smaller salon which we are using as a dining room and likewise as the chief living room, it being the warmest room. M[argaret] has her own bedroom and mine is large, light and sufficiently remote to make it a very excellent place to work. Imagine me then pecking zestfully at my newly repaired typewriter beside a wood fire in silence and solitude.

But in the midst of "pecking zestfully," Bishop found that something was haunting all his attempts at writing. It was *The Waste Land.* In Paris, Bishop had picked up a copy of the first issue of the *Criterion*, published only two weeks earlier and containing Eliot's poem (though without the notes, included only later when the poem was issued as an independent book).

> I am trying to work out an elaborate form which will be partly lyrical, partly descriptive, partly dramatic. . . . I need not say that the chief difficulty is to eradicate T. S. Eliot from all future work. . . . I have read *The Waste Land* about five times a day since the copy of the *Criterion* came into my hands. It is IMMENSE. MAGNIFICENT. TERRIBLE. I have not yet been able to figure it all out; especially the fortune telling episode, the king my brother and the king my father, and the strange words that look like a Hindu puzzle to me. I have not of course had the advantage of the notes which you say the book version will contain. Perhaps you can enlighten me on the following points: Mr. Eugenides (his significance), Magnus Martyr, Phlebas the Phoenician. The red rock is I take it the modern world both intellectual and mechanical. But the cock crowing, presaging the dawn and rain? And what is the experience referred to in the last section with all the DAs in it? Do you recognize *Le Prince d'Aquitaine de la tour abolie* or *shantih*?

> I don't think he has ever used his stolen lines to such terrifying effect as in this poem. And the HURRY UP PLEASE IT'S TIME makes my flesh creep.

Bishop had no time to write further but pledged to communicate again as soon as he learned anything more about *The Waste Land*.

To his surprise, he would soon learn far more than he ever expected—and from a source with remarkable authority. He hastened to notify Wilson:

> Dear Bunny,
>
> Ezra and Mrs. Pound came to dinner last night and I wished many times that you might have been here to see the great Amurricn Poet work out. There's a lot of his past that came out after he had begun to get into his cups, which was fairly soon, as well as a few points about Tears Eliot (as some Paris wit has recently christened him); the latter I feel I should at once communicate to you.
>
> TSE came abroad with the idea of working up his PhD, presumably in philosophy though of this I'm not sure, and turned up one day on Pound's doorstep. Ezra had heard of him from Harvard and at once, upon hearing that he had some poems, suggested getting out the *Catholic Anthology*, which P[ound] afterward did, just to publish Eliot whose work at that time EP had not seen. Then he advised him against vers libre.
>
> Eliot is tubercular and disposed toward epilepsy; on one occasion he decided to kill himself in Pound's house but funked at the final moment. "The Psychological Hour" in *Lustra* gives EP's reactions to TSE's wedding, which was substituted on the spur of the moment for a tea engagement at Pound's. It seems that Thomas and Vivien arrived in the hallway and then turned back, went to the registrar's and were wed, to everybody's subsequent pain and misery. She is an English lady, daughter of a member of the Royal Academy and sister of an officer in the Guards. She likewise is an invalid and according to Muriel Draper very weary and washed out. Eliot's version of her is contained in "the Chair she sat in like a burnished throne" etc. passage. By the way do you know that the HURRY UP PLEASE IT'S TIME is what the bartenders say when the English pubs are about to close? The conversation is evidently gleaned from one of the ten o'clock, just-before-closing bickers in a pub, and according to EP reflects the atmosphere immediately outside their first flat in London. Eliot, it seems, is

> hopelessly caught in his own prudent temperament. As EP says, "I am too low for any steamroller to flatten me out; I can always creep out of the way. But Eliot is incapable of taking the least chance." As one would have surmised.
>
> Mr. Eugenides actually turned up at Lloyds with his pocket full of currants and asked Eliot to spend a weekend with him for no nice reasons. His place in the poem is, I believe, as a projection of Eliot, however. That is, all the men are in some way deprived of their life-giving, generative forces. Phlebas is simply dead, like the Knight in the Gawain version of the Grail (also like Attis and the Attis dummy, see Miss Weston); the Fisher King is castrated; the one-eyed merchant a homosexual. I do not of course mean to imply that Thomas is that any more than that he is physically nutted.

Bishop went on to summarize his new understanding of Eliot's poem:

> Please disregard any queries I made before about *The Waste Land*; I think I've cleared up the meaning of the poem as far as it is possible. From Pound's account, it was originally twice as long and included Bleistein and all the old familiar faces. It's my present opinion that the poem is not so logically constructed as I had at first supposed and that it is a mistake to seek for more than a suggestion of personal emotion in a number of passages. The nightingale passage is, I believe, important. Eliot being Tereus, and Mrs. E. Philomel; that is to say that through unbalanced passion everybody is in a hell of a fix, Tereus being changed to a hoopoo and TSE a bank clerk. Thomas's sexual troubles are undoubtedly extreme.

But, as if to hint that Bishop's complacent reading of *The Waste Land* barely concealed a lingering dissatisfaction and preoccupation, he added a concluding note on the progress of his own poems: "I have written quantities or half written them to destroy them later. I don't seem to be able to get the direction right. And am much discouraged and would give a great deal for your counsel."[1] Bishop, in fact, would never quite get over *The Waste Land* or Eliot's accumulating oeuvre. The four volumes of poetry that he wrote over the course of his lifetime bear witness to a poet struggling desperately to escape the shackles of a compulsive fascination with Eliotic motifs and devices.

Bishop's two letters, neither of them published until now, are important. For apart from a brief paragraph written by James Sibley Watson, Jr., a co-editor of the *Dial* who first read *The Waste Land* in August 1922 . . . they are the only record we have of how Eliot's work was first experienced by that hypothetical beast that has haunted so many literary discussions, the well-educated general reader. And plainly that experience, as registered in Bishop's first letter, was something close to terrifying ("such terrifying effect"), terror accompanied by a sense of the poem's compulsive and uncanny power ("I have read [it] five times a day since the copy of the *Criterion* came into my hands") and its overwhelming horror (" . . . makes my flesh creep"). These experiences accumulate in a palpable sense of confusion, patent in Bishop's bewildered attempt to orient himself, to identify the nature or status of entities that are named in the poem: "Mr. Eugenides (his significance), Magnus Martyr, Phlebas the Phoenician."

Part of his confusion, of course, is cultural. An innocent abroad, Bishop doesn't yet know that "HURRY UP PLEASE IT'S TIME" is simply the closing-time call of a barman in British pubs. Likewise, he evidently assumes that "Magnus Martyr," a real church, designed by Christopher Wren in the late seventeenth century and located near the northern end of London Bridge, is on the same plane as "Phlebas the Phoenician," a wholly fictional character invented by Eliot. And he is clearly entertaining two different, perhaps incompatible readings of the poem: he is convinced that it represents a certain reckoning with the modern world (a view implicit in his comment about "the red rock"), but is also predisposed to view it in very traditional terms that regard lyrical poetry as a form of autobiography, a rehearsal of personal experience (evident in his query: "And what is the experience referred to in the last section with all the DAs in it?").

But part of Bishop's confusion has deeper roots, some of them discernible in his throw-away comment: "And the HURRY UP PLEASE IT'S TIME makes my flesh creep." When he writes his first letter, this line reverberates so much for Bishop precisely because it is uttered by a voice that lacks any clear or obvious origin; it violates our acquired habit of assigning sound to an identifiable source, or voice to an identifiable speaker. Repeated five times toward the close of part II, the last two in direct succession, it acquires an accelerating, frightening urgency, made all the more unbearable because it also has no discernible effect on the speech of that other voice which it cuts into, that of the nameless neighbor of Lil whose Cockney monologue rattles on unheeding, dementedly. For Bishop, plainly, these words become a literary counterpart to the experience of overloaded sound, a phonic order of the sort that we associate with the auditory hallucinations that afflict the psychotic and the ecstatic, or those seemingly possessed by spirits, or that we typically ascribe to divine annunciation and oracular utterance. A voice without any source or origin, such as the one that utters (to Bishop, at least) "HURRY UP PLEASE IT'S TIME," is often one that exhorts ("HURRY UP") or warns ("IT'S TIME") and acquires a note of menace that threatens subjection to an overwhelming power.[2] And it is precisely that sense of overwhelming menace, of terror, that Bishop experiences in this line ("makes my flesh creep").

Bishop, however inadvertently, has also stumbled across one of the major sources of the poem's uncanny power, our extreme uncertainty over just who is speaking at any particular moment in *The Waste Land.* That note of mysterious and oracular utterance which attends the poem's famous opening passage owes much to our bewilderment, our baffled inability to assign its voice to a speaker. And our disorientation about voice and identity only deepens when the first pronoun to appear in the poem ("Winter kept us warm . . .") ends up having a perceptibly different referent when it reappears just three lines later ("Summer surprised us, coming over the Starnbergersee"). Throughout the poem there is a deep, perennial ambiguity about the identity of that intermittent "I" who begins with commands ("Come in under the shadow of this red rock") or promises of enigmatic instruction ("I will show you fear in a handful of dust"), yet concludes with increasingly helpless questions ("Who is the third who walks . . . But who is that on the other side . . . What is that sound . . . Who are those hooded hordes . . . What is the city over the mountains," or even "Shall I at least set my lands in order?"). And is that final, perplexed, and plaintive "I" really the same individual who, when Madame Sosostris hands out Tarot cards to an unidentified recipient

> Here, said she,
> Is your card, the drowned Phoenician sailor

offers the cruel and knowing interjection:

> (Those are pearls that were his eyes. Look!)

(And if so, what has happened to transform him by the poem's end, to change him from a fierce and canny commentator into a bewildered, self-ignorant questioner?) Bishop, no doubt mistakenly and yet also insightfully, ascribes the voice who speaks HURRY UP PLEASE IT'S TIME to a recurrent order of oracular interjection (after all, it repeatedly issues commands: "Come in under the shadow . . ." "Look!" "HURRY UP"), an order fraught with uncertainty that is deeply disturbing.

Bishop's observation can be extended. For identity in *The Waste Land* is always enigmatic, shrouded in mystery. Characters rarely have names: the middle-class woman who speaks at the beginning of part II remains as nameless as the working-class neighbor of Lil and Albert. The hyacinth girl, the house-agent's clerk, the typist, the Thames-daughters—all lack names. They also lack any of the features that typically signal individual identity: eyes or hair of a certain color, bodies of a certain height or build. (Only the young man carbuncular is . . . well, carbuncular, and has "one bold stare"; the ghoulish woman in part IV has "long black hair," but it makes "whisper music"; more weirdly, only the "bats with baby faces" have human features.) They may be agents, but they seldom act. Instead, action is either delegated to dissevered body parts via synecdoche or inanimate things via personification, or else it mysteriously transpires through the passive voice: footsteps shuffle, hair spreads and glows in fiery points, the eyes and back turn upward, exploring hands encounter no defense, faces sneer and snarl; there are months that breed and mix and stir, seasons that cover, feed, and surprise, snow that is forgetful, shadows that stride behind you or rise to meet you, the evening hour that strives homeward, the human engine that waits like a taxi throbbing waiting, the currents that pick bones in whispers, dry grass that sings, towers that toll, a door that swings, limp leaves that wait for rain, a jungle that crouches; vanity requires no response, while death undoes so many; sighs are exhaled, while stockings, slippers, camisoles, and stays are piled. This is oneiric syntax, wild and Gothic, eerie and menacing because it severs that basic connection between agent and action, eerier still when punctuated by oracular mumbles uttered by uncertain voices:

> Twit twit twit
> Jug jug jug jug jug jug

or sinister sounds that issue from hollow places:

> And voices singing out of empty cisterns and exhausted wells.

Bishop, in short, was right when he detected apocalyptic menace in "HURRY UP PLEASE IT'S TIME." Alas, not for very long. For when Bishop writes his second letter to Edmund Wilson, perhaps ten days later, he has learned to attach identity to that previously mysterious voice: "By the way do you know that HURRY UP PLEASE IT'S TIME is what the bartenders say when the English pubs are about to close?" The experience of that voice is no longer an unbearable enigma; it has a source that can be situated in space and time: "The conversation is evidently gleaned from one of the ten o'clock, just-before-closing bickers in a pub, and according to EP reflects the atmosphere immediately outside their first flat in London." It even has a precise address, directly opposite 18, Crawford Mansions. The change is now complete. HURRY UP PLEASE IT'S TIME has been transformed from apocalyptic warning to everyday routine, and terrifying uncertainty has been replaced with contented calm: "Please disregard any queries I made before about *The Waste Land*; I think I've cleared up the meaning of the poem as far as it is possible. . . . It's my present opinion that the poem is not so logically constructed as I had at first supposed and that it is a mistake to seek for more than a suggestion of personal emotion in a number of passages."

Two last points should be noted about Bishop's first letter, written just after reading the poem in a version that did not contain the notes. Tellingly, it never occurs to Bishop to assess the poem in light of the Grail legends, and phrases such as "vegetation gods" or "fertility rituals" never appear in his account. Fertility may well be an intermittent concern in the poem; but the Grail materials are so peripheral to the poem's texture that a discerning, well-educated reader such as Bishop could overlook them entirely. Not so a reader who would read the poem accompanied by the notes. The other point is that even without the notes Bishop is convinced from the first that the poem is "highly constructed." All those repetitions hinting at symbolic density and development, all those insinuations of spatio-temporal connectedness of the sort found in narrative—surely they urged that the poem was "highly constructed," didn't they? That was precisely the question that would preoccupy the poem's earliest reviewers.

Consider the case of Burton Rascoe (1892–1957), then a thirty-year-old journalist whose weekly feature "A Bookman's Day Book," a diary of his week in the world of books, appeared in Sunday editions of the *New York Tribune*. Under an entry for "Thursday, October 26," Rascoe registered his receipt of "the November issue of *The Dial*," the one containing "The Waste Land." Rascoe immediately hailed it as "perhaps the finest poem of this generation," then went on:

> At all events it is the most significant in that it gives voice to the universal despair or resignation arising from the spiritual and economic consequences of the war, the cross purposes of modern civilization, the cul-de-sac into which both science and philosophy seem to have got themselves and the breakdown of all great directive purposes which give joy and zest to the business of living. It is an erudite despair. . . . His method is highly elliptical, based on the curious formula of Tristan Corbière, wherein reverential and blasphemous ideas are juxtaposed in amazing antitheses, and there are mingled all the shining verbal toys, impressions and catch lines of a poet who has read voraciously and who possesses an insatiable curiosity about life. . . . The final intellectual impression I have of the poem is that it is extremely clever (by which I do not mean to disparage it; on the contrary): it is a rictus which masks a hurt romantic with sentiments plagued by crass reality; and it is faulty

> structurally for the reason that, even with the copious (mock and serious) notes he supplies in elucidation, it is so idiosyncratic a statement of ideas that I, for one, cannot follow the narrative with complete comprehension. The poem, however, contains enough sheer verbal loveliness, enough ecstasy, enough psychological verisimilitude, and enough even of a readily understandable etching of modern life, to justify Mr. Eliot in his idiosyncracies.[3]

Rascoe's reference to "the copious . . . notes" shows that he has been reading Liveright's edition (not the November issue of the *Dial* which he is ostensibly reviewing). But more important is the way he juxtaposes "the copious . . . notes" to his charge that the poem was "faulty structurally" and his confession that he "cannot follow the narrative with complete comprehension." Contained within that juxtaposition were points of critical debate that would recur again and again in discussion of the poem. To Rascoe, as to many later readers and critics, the notes hinted at levels of narrative and/or structural coherence which jarred with his experience of the poem. To read the poem was to plummet through a series of broken sketches, antic turns, and fitful moments of oracular solemnity and lyrical intensity—a dreamworld experience that startled and disturbed. To read the notes was to find reference to "the plan," an arcane but ultimately identifiable logic that was dictating the poem's entangled movements, or perhaps even a narrative structure detectable behind its unruly opacity.

Moreover, that tension led into two other questions. One concerned *The Waste Land*'s nature, or genre. Was it "a statement of ideas," a meditative poem advancing an argument with claims on public attention, or was it some sort of "narrative"? (Rascoe used both terms within a single sentence.) Or was it perhaps something more private, an expression of some personal feelings? That question led on to another about the nature of poetry, a point that more than any other divides us from Eliot's contemporaries. For us today, a poem is an artifact of language; for them it was axiomatic that a poem communicated "emotion," perhaps not the "emotion recollected in tranquility" of Wordsworth, but "emotion" nevertheless. Consider Edmund Wilson (1890–1972), whose review of the poem appeared in the same December issue of the *Dial* which announced Eliot's receipt of the Dial Award. Yes, Wilson conceded, the poem showed that its author had a "constricted emotional experience," but his acute self-awareness of this limitation was ultimately redemptive, for it generated "intense emotion" or "strange poignancy."

> But it is the very acuteness of his suffering from this starvation which gives such poignancy to his art. And, as I say, Mr. Eliot is a poet—that is, he feels intensely and with distinction and speaks

> naturally in beautiful verse. . . . His verse is sometimes much too scrappy—he does not dwell long enough upon one idea to give it its proportionate value before passing on to the next—but these drops, though they be wrung from flint, are none the less authentic crystals. . . . The poem is—in spite of its lack of structural unity—simply one triumph after another. . . . That is also why, for all its complicated correspondences and its recondite references and quotations, *The Waste Land* is intelligible at first reading. It is not necessary to know anything about the Grail Legend or any but the most obvious of Mr. Eliot's allusions to feel the force of the intense emotion which the poem is intended to convey. . . . In Eliot the very images and the sound of the words—even when we do not know precisely why he has chosen them—are charged with a strange poignancy which seems to bring us into the heart of the singer.

Wilson seems to have intuited, however, the danger that shadowed this emphasis on "intense emotion." For why should anyone's "intense emotion" be thought to have a claim on public attention, let alone receive a significant prize? He hastily added: "And sometimes we feel that he is speaking not only for a personal distress, but for the starvation of a whole civilization—for people grinding at barren office-routine in the cells of gigantic cities, drying up their souls in eternal toil whose products never bring them profit, where their pleasures are so vulgar and so feeble that they are almost sadder than their pains. It is our whole world of strained nerves and shattered institutions."[4]

While Rascoe detected a tension between the intellectual clarity that was seemingly proclaimed by the notes and the poem's genuine opacity, and Edmund Wilson had dismissed the Grail legend as peripheral to experiencing the poem itself, Gilbert Seldes (1893–1970) sketched the outlines of a wholly different view. Seldes began his review of *The Waste Land* with an overview of Eliot's critical writings—and he was uniquely placed to do so. As managing editor of the *Dial* during 1921, he had published four of the ten essays that Eliot wrote while composing *The Waste Land* ("London Letters," which commented on the literary scene in London).[5] He himself had read Eliot's meditations on music hall and caricature; had noted Eliot's celebration of music-hall "wit" that was "mordant, ferocious, and personal," or his praise for the performer Ethel Levey, with her "fascinating inhuman *grotesquerie*" and "element of *bizarrerie*"; had observed Eliot's predilection for the extremism of the great caricaturists Rowlandson and Cruikshank, artists who possessed "some of the old English ferocity"; had witnessed Eliot's "sense of relief" at "hearing the indecencies of Elizabethan and Restoration drama"; had savored Eliot's vindication of Stravinsky's *Sacre du printemps*, a work that had transformed "the rhythms of the steppes into the scream of the motor horn, the rattle of machinery, the grind of wheels, the beating of iron and steel, the roar of the underground railway, and the other barbaric cries of modern life."[6] Moreover, the discontinuous yet coherent outline of an aesthetics of the histrionic which Eliot drew in these essays could hardly have reached a more receptive observer: Seldes had already written trenchant essays examining jazz and popular film, and one month after writing his review of Eliot he began his own landmark work, *The 7 Lively Arts*, a survey of vaudeville, popular song, the cartoon strip, slapstick film, and other forms of vernacular culture. But when he took up Eliot's critical writings, he disregarded all the Eliot essays that he himself had shepherded through the editorial process. Instead he turned directly to *The Sacred Wood* and promptly fastened on "Tradition and the Individual Talent."

Read in the light of that essay, *The Waste Land* might well seem a bit odd, a little unruly—only for a moment, though.

> It seems at first sight remarkably disconnected, confused, the emotion seems to disengage itself in spite of the objects and events chosen by the poet as their vehicle. . . . A closer view of the poem does more than illuminate the difficulties; it reveals the hidden form of the work, indicates how each thing falls into place, and to the reader's surprise shows that the emotion which at first seemed to come in spite of the framework and the detail could not otherwise have been communicated.[7]

By "framework," of course, Seldes meant the Grail legends as interpreted by Jessie Weston's *From Ritual to Romance*, the work which had informed "the plan" of Eliot's poem—or so its notes said. If only one scrutinized the poem long and diligently enough, "the hidden form" that bound together the dichotomy of text and notes would be disclosed. (Curiously, Seldes himself did not further describe this "hidden form," which remained "hidden" to his readers.)

More directly than any other critic of the time, Conrad Aiken (1890–1971) addressed the dilemmas posed by the notes. Aiken, of course, had known Eliot since his student days at Harvard, knowledge which placed him in a unique position vis-à-vis other critics. For he also knew that passages of *The Waste Land* had existed as poems or independent drafts years before the poem's publication, and years before the publication of Jessie Weston's book. But he felt that it would be unfair somehow to reveal that knowledge, as he later recalled: "How could I mention that I had long been familiar with such passages as 'A woman drew her long black hair out tight,' which I had seen as poems, or part-poems, in themselves? And now saw inserted into *The Waste Land* as into a mosaic. This would be to make use of private knowledge, a betrayal."[8] Having ruled out a more historical reckoning with the poem, Aiken proceeded to a more formal one that stressed the disparity between the poem's wild variety and the claims to extreme coherence implied by the reference to "the plan" made in the notes.

> If we leave aside for the moment all other considerations and read the poem solely with the intention of understanding, with the aid of the notes, the symbolism; of making out what it is that is symbolized, and how these symbolized feelings are brought into relation with each other and with other matters in the poem; I think we must, with reservations, and with no invidiousness, conclude that the poem is not, in any formal sense, coherent.

With great prescience, Aiken foresaw the trajectory of critical discussion of the poem: "It is perhaps important to note that Mr. Eliot, with his comment on the 'plan,' and several critics, with their admiration of the poem's woven complexity, minister to the idea that *The Waste Land* is, precisely, a kind of epic in a walnut shell: elaborate, ordered, unfolded with a logic at every joint discernible; but it is also important to note that this idea is false." Aiken, instead, placed emphasis elsewhere: "Thus the poem has an emotional value far clearer and richer than its arbitrary and rather unworkable logical value. One might assume that it originally consisted of a number of separate poems which have been telescoped—given a kind of forced unity." His sense of the poem's factitiousness even included a rudimentary account of what he called "arbitrary repetitions": "We are aware of a superficial 'binding'—we observe the anticipation and repetition of themes, motifs; 'Fear death by water' anticipates the episode of Phlebas, the cry of the nightingale is repeated, but these are pretty flimsy links, and do not genuinely bind because they do not reappear naturally, but arbitrarily." True, critics of today would not accept the easy distinction drawn between "naturally" and "arbitrarily," and Aiken's account of repetition is one that vastly oversimplifies. But Aiken astutely perceived the strains and stresses in the poem, and he fretted over what kind of unity of tone or genre might encompass them: "Could one not wholly rely for one's unity,—as Mr. Eliot has largely relied—simply on the dim unity of 'personality' which would underlie the retailed contents of a single consciousness?"

Yet he had no doubt about the poem's success or significance: "the poem succeeds—as it brilliantly does—by virtue of its incoherence, not of its plan; by virtue of its ambiguities, not of its explanations." It was, he concluded, "one of the most moving and original poems of our time. It captures us."[9]

Taken together, Rascoe, Wilson, Seldes, and Aiken had outlined the spectrum of possible responses to a perceived disparity between their experience of the poem and the kind of experience that seemed to be suggested by its notes. At one extreme of the spectrum was Gilbert Seldes, who conceded that parts of the poem at first seemed "remarkably disconnected" and "confused," but who was convinced that these difficulties would evaporate with "a closer view" that disclosed a "hidden form" in which "each thing falls into place." At the other extreme was Conrad Aiken. For him, opacity wasn't an obstacle, but the condition that informed the poem's achievement ("the poem succeeds . . . by virtue of its incoherence"). In the middle of the spectrum were Rascoe and Wilson. For them the poem, whether judged against the expectations raised by the notes or those of competent readers, was "faulty structurally" (Rascoe) or exhibited "a lack of structural unity" (Wilson). And for both there was a tension between the poem's raw beauty, its "sheer verbal loveliness" (Rascoe) or "the very images and the sound of the words" (Wilson), and its obdurate opacity, its many "idiosyncracies" (Rascoe) or unmotivated tangles: "We do not know why he has chosen them" (Wilson). For both these, too, the poem possessed a recognizable claim on public attention: it was "a readily understandable etching of modern life" (Rascoe), or it was "speaking not only for a personal distress, but for the starvation of a whole civilization" (Wilson).

Rascoe, Wilson, Seldes, and Aiken were not, of course, the only critics to review *The Waste Land* shortly after its publication; but their views and arguments laid out the fault lines that would reappear in subsequent debate. Tellingly, too, all four were American. Elevated by the Dial Award, Eliot's poem tacitly acquired a claim that it was a matter of public significance, a literary work of compelling importance. The debate that followed was a logical consequence of the institutional structures that had shaped its publication. And the contrast with the situation in England could not have been starker. Because the poem was first published there (without the notes) in the *Criterion*, a new journal struggling to find an audience, and then eleven months later was issued in the Hogarth Press edition that was limited to 460 copies, it received very little media attention: three reviews in the wake of the *Criterion* publication, a further six after the Hogarth edition—and all but one of the nine were hostile. In the United States, in contrast, there were more than fifty reviews and notices of the poem, more or less equally divided between negative and positive evaluations.[10]

When subsequent debate was taken up, it took place in the shadow of another event, at first glance one wholly unrelated to *The Waste Land*: T. S. Eliot's religious conversion. In 1928, only six years after he had published *The Waste Land*, Eliot issued *For Lancelot Andrewes*, a collection of eight recent essays preceded by a preface in which Eliot announced that he was now a "classicist in literature, a royalist in politics, and anglo-catholic in religion."[11] It was a deliberately provocative statement, and since then it has often been quoted as if it sufficed to characterize the whole of Eliot's work and life. It was an impression that Eliot himself did much to foster in subsequent years. In 1932 he published his *Selected Essays, 1917–1932*, a compilation of book reviews and essays that he had been writing. The first piece in the book was "Tradition and the Individual Talent," an essay from 1919 in which Eliot had urged that the personality of the individual artist be submerged or expunged in his work, submitting to the imperatives of a vague tradition. Perhaps innocently, Eliot even misdated the essay, assigning it to 1917 and so making it stand as the gateway to all his subsequent work, including *The Waste Land*.[12] Of the ten essays that Eliot wrote while composing *The Waste Land*, only three were included in the *Selected Essays*—all pieces which reinforced the impression that Eliot had always been a "classicist in literature." Suppressed were the other seven essays from the same period, which only recently have been reprinted for the first time (after eighty-three years).[13] The suppressed essays, which reveled in the vernacular pleasures of British music hall and caricature, had sketched an aesthetics that could be called "classicist" only by a remarkable extension of the term. But that was all in the past. Similarly, the *Selected Essays* gave special prominence to a piece which Eliot had recently written on Baudelaire, one in which he damned the French poet for "having an imperfect, vague romantic conception of Good."[14] This theological estimate of the French poet jarred against the unstinting admiration which Eliot had shown for him in 1921. Eliot's conversion to Christianity, his growing allegiance to conservative political and social views, his concern with the aesthetic and ethical force of classicism—these constituted a profound change in his thought. But it was a change that was masked by the *Selected Essays*, which instead suggested that Eliot had always been a classicist, had always had moral concerns that had only deepened with his conversion, had always viewed modernity (and so secularism) with a skeptical eye.

In the new climate of taste, one that Eliot himself did much to usher in, there was no longer a tension between the text of *The Waste Land* and the claims to coherence implied by the notes' reference to "the plan." The problem that had preoccupied the poem's early reviewers vanished from sight. The most influential critic in erasing that tension was Cleanth Brooks (1907–1994), an American critic and a devout Christian from the conservative

South. In 1937 he published "*The Waste Land*: A Critique of the Myth," an essay that profoundly shaped the course of criticism on the poem for the next forty years.[15] Brooks set out to show that the poem was "a unified whole" (136), that every detail in it contributed to a work of extraordinary structural, thematic, and poetic integrity. Characteristically, his starting point was the first of the poem's notes, the one which urged: "Not only the title, but the plan and a good deal of the incidental symbolism of the poem were suggested by Miss Jessie L. Weston's book . . ." No less characteristically, Brooks urged that the theme of the poem could best be reconstructed from Eliot's 1930 essay on Baudelaire, the one in which he had repudiated Baudelaire's "imperfect, vague romantic conception of Good." (That a term such as "Good" appears nowhere in Eliot's writings from the period when he was composing *The Waste Land* deterred Brooks not a moment.) As for critics who had earlier described a poem more entangled and disquieting than the one delineated by Brooks, they were merely victims of "the myth" that had quickly gathered around the poem.

Brooks had grown up in the American South at a time when it could still be viewed, through a haze of ahistorical nostalgia, as the last outpost of a preindustrial order, one rooted in the land and agriculture. His disdain for industry, science, popular culture, and every other index of modernity was summarized in a single word: secularization. And by a form of logic which is all too human, it turned out that secularization was damned by passage after passage in *The Waste Land*. When the poem cites a passage from Dante's description of Limbo, in canto III of the *Inferno*, Brooks notes that these "characters exemplify almost perfectly the secular attitude which dominates the modern world" (143–144). He saw no anachronism in this claim. Those depicted in Dante's canto IV are the unbaptized: "They form the second of the two classes of people who inhabit the modern waste land: those who are secularized and those who have no knowledge of the faith" (144). When the poem seemingly touches on the violation of a woman, Brooks comments drily: "The violation of a woman makes a very good symbol of the process of secularization" (147). If one had to summarize the poem one might say: "Our contemporary waste land is in large part the result of our scientific attitude—of our complete secularization" (148). And in passing he observed that "secularization has destroyed, or is likely to destroy, modern civilization" (163–164). The fishmen relaxing in a pub near St. Magnus Martyr are significant because "they have a meaningful life which has been largely lost to the secularized upper and middle classes" (170). *The Waste Land*, in short, was being beaten into shape, forced to accord with a simplistic and schematic view of history that saw the world before the industrial revolution as a coherent unity organized around religious faith, the world after it as one long, unremitting, ever-worsening horror. And Eliot himself, it must be conceded, was wont to indulge in such thinking during the 1930s—for example, "What I do wish to affirm is that the whole of modern literature is corrupted by what I call Secularism."[16] But damning secularization, for Brooks, was not quite enough. By the end of his essay he claimed: "The Christian material is at the center [of the poem]," conceding only that "the poet never deals with it directly" (171).

No less important, Brooks profoundly transformed the poem's nature. Consider his comment on the verse paragraph that makes up the poem's famous opening, with its ferocious excess of lexical, syntactic, and thematic gestures toward pattern, its uneasy progress through evanescent zones of tonal cohesion, its mercurial swing from oracular solemnity to conversational banality, from insistent pattern to empty patter. Brooks, after announcing that the poem's theme was "death-in-life," turned to its famous beginning: "The first part of 'The Burial of the Dead' introduces this theme through a sort of reverie on the part of the protagonist—a reverie in which speculation on life glides off into memory of an actual conversation in the Hofgarten and back into speculation again. The function of the conversation is to establish the class and character of the protagonist" (139). That was one way to deal with troublesome details of tone and texture: to liquidate them in the name of theme, to quash them under the impress of a new entity who appears onstage here for the first time—"the protagonist." It was also the first step in transforming the poem into a narrative.

For Brooks "the protagonist" was a very busy figure, but one whose mental states were instantly accessible to the discerning critic. When a snatch of song abruptly appears in part I, it is "perhaps another item in the reverie of the protagonist" (141). But the song has an immediate effect: "It brings to the mind of the protagonist an experience of love" (141). Elsewhere we learn:

> But the protagonist, after this reflection . . . remembers a death that was transformed into something rich and strange, the death described in the song from *The Tempest*—"Those are pearls that were his eyes." . . . The description of a death which is a portal into a realm of the rich and strange . . . assumes in the mind of the protagonist an association with that of the drowned god whose effigy was thrown into the water as a symbol of the death of the fruitful powers of nature but which was taken out of the water as a symbol of the revivified god. (See *From Ritual to Romance*.) (149–150)

True, the source and identity of any particular voice in the poem might sometimes seem mysterious. "But to the reader who knows the Weston references, the reference is to that of the Fisher King of the Grail legends.

The protagonist is the maimed and impotent king of the legends" (151). (And if the protagonist's "class and identity" were established in the poem's opening verse-paragraph, were they not undergoing a remarkable change at this point—a change so pronounced as to put the notion of "identity" in question, or even in crisis?)

But to be a narrative, it was necessary for the poem to mark progression. Yet no less an authority than the English critic F. R. Leavis, then at the height of his reputation, had already noted the poem's static character: "It exhibits no progression: 'I sat upon the shore / Fishing, with the arid plain behind me'—the thunder brings no rain to revive the Waste Land, and the poem ends where it began."[17] Brooks was determined to set that right:

> I cannot accept Mr. Leavis' interpretation of the passage, "I sat upon the shore / Fishing, with the arid plain behind me," as meaning that the poem "exhibits no progression." The comment upon what the thunder says would indicate, if other passages did not, that the poem does "not end where it began." It is true that the protagonist does not witness a revival of the waste land; but there are two important relationships involved in his case: a personal one as well as a general one. If secularization has destroyed, or is likely to destroy modern civilization, the protagonist still has a personal obligation to fulfill. Even if the civilization is breaking up—London Bridge is falling down falling down falling down—there remains the personal obligation: "Shall I at least set my lands in order?" (163–164)

It was a curious non sequitur, for demonstrating that "the protagonist" possessed a "personal obligation" was hardly tantamount to demonstrating narrative progression. Brooks returned to the charge, however, now bent on showing that "the protagonist" exhibited change and development, those features so indispensable to narrative, and he located these in an unlikely place, that final, antic swirl of quotations at the poem's end:

> London Bridge is falling down falling down falling down
> *Poi s'ascose nel foco che gli affina*
> *Quando fiam ceu chelidon*—O swallow swallow
> *Le Prince d'Aquitaine à la tour abolie*
> These fragments I have shored against my ruins
> Why then Ile fit you. Hieronymo's mad againe.
> Datta. Dayadhvam. Damyata.
> Shantih shantih shantih

Brooks seized on the fourth of these eight lines (*Le Prince d'Aquitaine à la tour abolie*), which is a quotation from a famous sonnet, "El Desdichado" (Spanish for "The Unhappy Man"), by the French poet Gerard de Nerval (1808–1855). In the French original, the immediately preceding line reads, "Je suis le ténébreux,—la veuf,—l'inconsolé," and together the two lines can be translated:

> I am the man of gloom,—the widower,—the unconsoled,
> The Prince of Aquitania, his tower in ruins.

Brooks commented: "The quotation from 'El Desdichado,' as Edmund Wilson has pointed out, indicates that the protagonist of the poem has been disinherited, robbed of his tradition. The ruined tower is perhaps also the Perilous Chapel, 'only the wind's home,' and it is also the whole tradition in decay. The protagonist resolves to claim his tradition and rehabilitate it." Brooks, by a species of logic which I have never been able to follow, could now specify not only the poem's "protagonist" but also his progress as discerned through a resolution that he reaches just before the poem's end. Yes, some aspects of the poem might seem enigmatic or disturbing; but beneath the surface there were traces of a narrative largely compatible with our everyday notions of realism. The poem gave "the effect of chaotic experience ordered into a new whole, though the realistic surface of experience is faithfully retained" (167).

Perhaps we can better understand this remark about "the realistic surface of experience" by situating it within a context much broader than that of *The Waste Land* or the critical tradition that first attended it, a context that stretches all the way back to Aristotle's *Poetics*, that seminal essay of literary theory which has exerted such a profound sway over Western cultural thought. Aristotle, we recall, was bent on refuting Plato's charge that poetry and fiction (one and the same in ancient Greece) were mendacious, and hence to be banned from a well ordered republic. Instead, he wished to assert that fiction or drama sparked a process of inference and deduction which was fundamentally the same as that of philosophy, and therefore that it issued in a form of knowledge that was different, but of equal status. The key term in prompting this process, whether in philosophy or imaginative writing, was "wonder." For wonder, he wrote in the *Metaphysics*, lay at the heart of all philosophy:

> It is through wonder that men now begin and originally began to philosophize; wondering in the first place at obvious perplexities, and then by gradual progression raising questions about the greater

> matters too, e.g., about the changes of the moon and of the sun, about the stars and about the origin of the universe. Now he who wonders and is perplexed feels that he is ignorant (thus the myth-lover [for "myth" here, read "fiction"] is in a sense a philosopher, since myths are composed of wonders).[18]

A similar process, he urges in the *Poetics* (chapter 9), is set in motion by the complex plot of a tragedy:

> Since tragic mimesis portrays not just a whole action, but events which are fearful and pitiful, this can best be achieved when things occur contrary to expectation yet still on account of one another. A sense of wonder will be more likely to be aroused in this way than as a result of the arbitrary or fortuitous, since even chance events make the greatest impact of wonder when they appear to have a purpose.[19]

A tragic plot should include actions or events that surprise us ("things [that] occur contrary to expectation"), for that sense of surprise will prompt us to wonder how the events have come about; at the same time, however, those events must exhibit spatio-temporal and logical-causal interconnectedness, for if they do not, then the process of reasoning that attempts to discern such connectedness will be in vain. The opacity of the wonderful is indispensable to tragedy, but it must always be only momentary opacity that is ultimately redeemed by reason's discernment of sequential intelligibility. Oedipus cannot be blinded just because the gods are spiteful or capricious; it must be an outcome of his earlier actions.

Later in the *Poetics* (chapter 24), however, when comparing the different characteristics of tragedy and epic, Aristotle situates the wonderful (or "the marvelous": both words translate the same term in Aristotle's Greek) in a more ambiguous context:

> While the marvellous is called for in tragedy, it is epic which gives greater scope for the irrational (which is the chief cause of the marvellous), because we do not actually see the agents [onstage]. The circumstances of the pursuit of Hector would be patently absurd if put on the stage, with the men standing and refraining from pursuit, and Achilles forbidding them; but in epic the effect is not noticed. The marvellous gives pleasure: this can be seen from the way in which everyone exaggerates in order to gratify when recounting events.

Yet only one paragraph later, when Aristotle once more takes up the topic of plot structure, he indirectly returns to the question of the marvelous via a comment on the irrational, a comment with startling implications: "Events which are impossible but plausible should be preferred to those which are possible but implausible. Plots should not consist of parts which are irrational. So far as possible, there should be no irrational component."[20] This last comment plainly contradicts the preceding one. For if every irrational (or unmotivated) component is to be excluded from a plot, and if at the same time the irrational is "the chief cause of the marvellous," then it follows that Aristotle has also excluded the marvelous from all plot construction—despite his having earlier deemed it indispensable to tragedy. Stephen Halliwell, the distinguished contemporary commentator on the *Poetics*, urges that for Aristotle wonder "lies on the boundary of the explicable and the inexplicable, and so can slip into the latter (and hence become the irrational), or, properly used, may stimulate and challenge understanding."[21] Still, it is hard to avoid the impression that the wonderful entails more vexing conundrums: we want opacity, but we also fear it; we relish transgression, but we also crave order. The wonderful marks the uneasy borderline between these contradictory desires. Tellingly, the passage from the *Iliad* that Aristotle dislikes is one of the most famous of antiquity. It occurs in book 22, when Hector and Achilles at last come together for what promises to be the climactic encounter which the work has been building toward for all the previous books. What happens, bizarrely, is nothing. Achilles chases Hector round and round before the walls of Troy, while everyone else watches, frozen in place. The forward movement of narrative is utterly suspended. It elicits a famous simile from Homer, the only simile in ancient epic which invokes a dream:

> As in a dream a man is not able to follow one who runs
> from him, nor can the runner escape, nor the other pursue him,
> So he [Achilles] could not turn him down in his speed, nor
> the other get clear.[22]

One can only guess what Aristotle would have made of *The Waste Land*'s oneiric syntax and its grim refusal of narrative connectedness.

If Brooks profoundly misread the kind of work that *The Waste Land* was, he did so partly because an Aristotelian poetics of narrative has become so pervasive in our culture that we scarcely notice its presence. But that pervasiveness may also testify to some deeper human need. Tracts of time or sound, even textual time or sound, unpunctuated by the prospect of their being integrated into meaningful networks, are unbearable. Confronted with inexplicable patterns and mazes of contradiction, we seek a hidden shapeliness that will enable us to accommodate them. Fortuity is insufferable. As Steven Connor has recently observed in a comment that has obvious relevance to a reading of "What the Thunder Said":

> The power of a voice without a visible source is the power of a less-than-presence which is also a more-than-presence. The voice that is heard in the thunder, the eruption, or the whirlwind, is a kind of compromise formation. In that it is ascribed to a god, or simply to God, the voice transcends human powers of understanding and control; but the very fact that it is so ascribed also makes it possible to begin exercising control, in the very considerable form of conferring a name. To hear the thunder as a voice is to experience awe and terror; but to hear the voice in the thunder is also to have begun to limit the powers of that voice.[23]

To hear the voice in the thunder, we might add, is to undertake a rudimentary form of spatio-temporal and logical-causal coordination of the sort that makes everyday experience comprehensible, if not bearable, and of the same sort that informs narrative. We are programmed to do this, it seems. Steven Connor ascribes our programming to various aspects of neonatal experience, Frank Kermode to our experience of learning to speak a language.[24] Whatever its source, it seems to be an indelible feature of the human mind. Brooks, though plainly a man who had a clear agenda, was also simply human.

Eliot himself, in his later years, evidently felt a need to revisit the two issues that had so decisively shaped discussion about *The Waste Land*—the status of the notes and the question of the poem's structure. In a lecture that he delivered in 1956 to an audience of 14,000 assembled in a basketball arena at the University of Minnesota, he pondered the various ways in which literary critics might be misled:

> Here I must admit that I am, on one conspicuous occasion, not guiltless of having led critics into temptation. The notes to *The Waste Land* I had at first intended to put down all the references for my quotations, with a view to spiking the guns of critics of my earlier poems who had accused me of plagiarism. Then, when it came to print *The Waste Land* as a little book—for the poem on its first appearance in *The Dial* and *The Criterion* had no notes whatever—it was discovered that the poem was inconveniently short, so I set to work to expand the notes, in order to provide a

> few more pages of printed matter, with the result that they became the remarkable exposition of bogus scholarship that is still on view to-day. I have sometimes thought of getting rid of these notes; but now they can never be unstuck. They have had almost greater popularity than the poem itself—anyone who bought my book of poems, and found that the notes to *The Waste Land* were not in it, would demand his money back. . . . No, it is not because of my bad example to other poets that I am penitent; it is because my notes stimulated the wrong kind of interest among the seekers of sources. It was just, no doubt, that I should pay my tribute to the work of Miss Jessie Weston; but I regret having sent so many enquirers off on a wild goose chase after Tarot cards and the Holy Grail.[25]

Eliot's occasional regret at having included the notes was balanced by his wan recognition that the deed was irreversible: the notes, as Stephen Dedalus might have put it, "were lodged in the room of the infinite possibilities they have ousted."

Three years later, in 1959, Eliot looked back at the much-debated question of the poem's structure. When one interviewer asked him whether Pound's excisions had changed "the intellectual structure of the poem," Eliot answered: "No. I think it was just as structureless, only in a more futile way, in the longer version." The implicit acknowledgment that the "shorter version," the published text of *The Waste Land* as we have it, was "structureless," was a long way from the claim that it was governed by a "plan." And tangled in the sidelong syntax of Eliot's response was another, more striking implication: a work might be structureless, but it could be so in ways that were "more futile" or "less futile." If we put pressure on "less futile," it might almost be thought to imply "useful" in some way, productive for literary thought and practice, provided only that a culture could find some use for it.

"In *The Waste Land*," Eliot went on in the same interview, "I wasn't even bothering whether I understood what I was saying." But that hardly mattered, he now thought. "These things, however, become easier to people with time. You get used to having *The Waste Land*, or *Ulysses*, about."[26] For a man who could be scathing about whiggish narratives of cultural progress, it was a surprisingly whiggish account of the human capacity to assimilate fortuity and disorder. The cognitive threshold for accommodating opacity, in this view, is as mutable and changeable as (let us say) our threshold for velocity (we chuckle condescendingly at the accounts of travelers who experienced vertigo when speeding along at ten miles per hour on early railroads). *The Waste Land* and *Ulysses* had indeed put unprecedented pressure on our expectations about the kinds and degrees of order that characterize a literary work; but it is a legitimate question whether we have really got "used to" the stringent indeterminacy that these works embodied. The human desire to detect pattern and reduce fortuity may be far more tenacious than Eliot imagined. Literary realism, after all, has survived the course of the twentieth century and even enjoyed a conspicuous revival in recent years. And as anybody knows who has ever taught either work to undergraduates, the struggle against easy expectations of narrative cohesion is not a battle that has been permanently won but one that is annually renewed.

For the most part, Eliot's remarks of 1956 and 1959 were politely ignored by his admirers, still laboring in the long shadow cast by Cleanth Brooks's major essay. But when Valerie Eliot published her edition of *The Waste Land* manuscripts in 1971, critical consensus began to dissolve. If nothing else, the manuscripts showed beyond doubt that *The Waste Land* had been potentially a very different poem right up to the last minute in early January 1922, when Ezra Pound had deleted some 240 lines. While there was still uncertainty about precisely when or in what sequence the various parts had been composed, it was clear that none had been produced in straightforward accordance with a "plan." The notes were beginning to recede in importance, but their recession would also prove extraordinarily slow and protracted.

At the same time, the dominance of the New Criticism, epitomized by Cleanth Brooks, was drawing to a close and already one could detect beginnings of the turn to structuralism that was to be signaled by the publication of Jonathan Culler's book *Structuralist Poetics* (1975).[27] The later 1970s and 1980s would see structuralism rapidly displaced by poststructuralism and deconstruction, then by several varieties of feminism and the rise of New Historicism, critical paradigms that stressed not the wholeness and unity of the text but its dividedness, the contradictory impulses at work beneath the surface of all language. But for the most part, criticism of *The Waste Land* has taken an increasingly biographical turn. In that respect, at least, criticism has retraced the trajectory first outlined by John Peale Bishop's two letters from November 1922, which moved from intoxicating and anxious uncertainty to a complacent preoccupation with glimpses of Eliot's private life. At the same time, the New Critical reading of the poem has never entirely vanished and continues to hold sway over the imagination of many critics. One sees its tenacious hold at work in the writing of one recent scholar who repeatedly notes "the poem's marmoreal reserve" and "monumental impregnability."[28] The notion of a neoclassical monument, so alien to the experience of the poem which its earliest readers described, still exerts a compelling power.

We cannot, of course, return to an imaginary state of pristine innocence in which the critical history of the last eighty years has been miraculously effaced. Generations of students encountered *The Waste Land* for the first time under aegis of the New Criticism, and many scholars who had that experience are to be found in English departments throughout the world, still active and still performing that invaluable task of transmitting the poem to new generations. But if the free play of attention that we ideally bring to the reading of any work is genuinely to retain its freedom, it will do so not by denying but by probing the intangible pressures exerted by a highly distinctive critical tradition, one repeatedly molded by historical contingencies as varied and intricate as those that also informed the poem's composition. Doing so, we can remain open to the pleasure of amazement and the sense of wonder that a reading of *The Waste Land* inevitably brings, attentive to the poem's vertiginous twists and turns of language, responsive to its richly varied ironic and climactic moments, receptive to its lacerating wildness and stubborn refusal to accommodate our expectations.

"IMMENSE. MAGNIFICENT. TERRIBLE." Yes, that will do as a starting point.

Notes

1. John Peale Bishop to Edmund Wilson, 3 November [1922] and [c. 10 November 1922], Yale, Beinecke Library, Edmund Wilson Papers.

2. In this discussion I am indebted to Steven Connor, *Dumbstruck: A Cultural History of Ventriloquism* (Oxford: Oxford University Press, 2000), especially chapters 1 and 2, 3–74.

3. Burton Rascoe, "A Bookman's Day Book," *New York Tribune*, 5 November 1922, section V, 8.

4. Edmund Wilson, "The Poetry of Drouth," *Dial* 73, no. 6 (December 1922): 611–616. Rpt. in Michael Grant, ed., *T. S. Eliot: The Critical Heritage* (London: Routledge, 1982), 138–144.

5. All ten essays are found in Lawrence Rainey, ed., *The Annotated "Waste Land" with Eliot's Contemporary Prose* (New Haven: Yale University Press, 2005), 138–201.

6. Ibid., 168, 169, 167, 189.

7. Gilbert Seldes, "T. S. Eliot," *Nation* 115 (6 December 1922): 614–616. Rpt. in Grant, Eliot, 144–150.

8. Conrad Aiken, "Prefatory Note (1958)," in Charles Brian Cox and Arnold P. Hinchliffe, eds., *T. S. Eliot: "The Waste Land," a Casebook* (London: Macmillan, 1978), 91.

9. Conrad Aiken, "An Anatomy of Melancholy," *New Republic* 33 (7 February 1923): 294–295. Rpt. in Grant, *Eliot*, 156–161.

10. The nine reviews, in chronological order, are an anonymous one in the *TLS* and eight others by Desmond McCarthy, Harold Monro, Edgell Rickword, Clive Bell, J. C. Squire, Charles Powell, F. L. Lucas, and Humbert Wolfe. In addition to these, published in 1922 and 1923, there were three further reviews in 1924 and 1925 devoted not specifically to *The Waste Land* but to Eliot's oeuvre to date, and written by Irish and Scottish reviewers. All twelve are listed in Rainey, *Annotated "Waste Land,"* 256–259, along with forty-seven American notices and reviews. The

reviews frequently cite one another: they make reference to four more, as yet unidentified, reviews by Edward Anthony, Keith Preston, and two anonymous reviewers in the *Christian Science Monitor* and a journal called *Measure*.

11. T. S. Eliot, *For Lancelot Andrewes* (London: Faber and Gwyer, 1928), ix.

12. On the misdating of "Tradition and the Individual Talent" in the first edition of *Eliot's Selected Essays*, see Donald Gallup, *T. S. Eliot: A Bibliography*, rev. ed. (New York: Harcourt, 1969), 47, A21.a.

13. See Rainey, *Annotated "Waste Land,"* 138–201.

14. The Baudelaire essay stands conspicuously as the first in a section treating modern authors, a position it still occupies today. The sentence by Eliot quoted here is found in his *Selected Essays* (New York: Harcourt, 1950), 380.

15. Cleanth Brooks, "*The Waste Land*: A Critique of the Myth," *Southern Review* 3 (1937–1938): 106–136. Rpt. in Cleanth Brooks, *Modern Poetry and the Tradition* (Chapel Hill: University of North Carolina Press, 1939), 136–172. Although there are some minor changes made in the reprinted version, I cite it because it is the most widely available version of the essay. All page references hereafter are given in parentheses within the text.

16. T. S. Eliot, "Religion and Literature" (1935), in *Selected Prose of T. S. Eliot*, ed. Frank Kermode (New York: Harcourt, 1975), 104–105.

17. F. R. Leavis, *New Bearings in English Poetry* (London: Chatto and Windus, 1932), 103.

18. Aristotle, *Metaphysics*, trans. Hugh Tredennich (London: Putnam's Sons, 1933), 1:13.

19. *The Poetics of Aristotle*, trans. Stephen Halliwell (Chapel Hill: University of North Carolina Press, 1987), 42.

20. *Poetics*, 60.

21. Stephen Halliwell, *Aristotle's "Poetics"* (London: Duckworth, 1986), 75 n. 41.

22. *The Iliad*, trans. Richmond Lattimore (Chicago: University of Chicago Press, 1951), XXII, 199–201.

23. Connor, *Dumbstruck*, 25.

24. Ibid., 27; Frank Kermode, *The Genesis of Secrecy* (Cambridge: Harvard University Press, 1979), 64.

25. T. S. Eliot, "The Frontiers of Criticism," in *On Poetry and Poets* (London: Faber, 1957), 109–110.

26. T. S. Eliot, "The Art of Poetry, I: T. S. Eliot," *Paris Review* 21 (Spring/Summer, 1959), 47–50, rpt. in *Writers at Work: The Paris Review Interviews*, second series, ed. George Plimpton (Harmondsworth: Penguin, 1977), 91–110, here 96, 105.

27. Ithaca: Cornell University Press.

28. Christine Froula, "Corpse, Monument, Hypocrite Lecteur. Text and Transference in the Reception of *The Waste Land*," *Text: An Interdisciplinary Annual of Textual Studies* 9 (1996): 304–314.

JANE DOWSON AND ALICE ENTWISTLE

Dialogic Politics in Carol Ann Duffy and Others

Women's dramatic monologues and dialogues participate in a perceived mainstream of contemporary British poetry which is characterised by post-modern dialogic. According to Valentin Voloshinov, all utterance is dialogic, in that it assumes an addressee, and thus the entire poetic tradition can be understood as conversational.[1] More applicable is Mikhail Bakhtin's definition of texts with a dynamic of more than one voice.[2] As earlier exemplified by Charlotte Mew and Anna Wickham, dialogic indeterminacy operates as a critique of mythical or idealised female representations and, following on from Stevie Smith, draws attention to the limits of familiar verbalisation. Multivocality particularly suits women poets because it emphasises the social origins and contexts of language. While appearing to avoid female poetic authority, a specifically female aesthetic or the privileging of female identity, they scrutinise the language of power play through dramatised personal and social interactions. These are often between men and women but also between women (notably mothers and daughters) or individuals and institutions. Textually, voices may seem to have equal status but the author can stage-manage their dramatic effects; she may challenge readers' preconceptions, direct their sympathies or collude with an implicitly female audience. Whereas the senior generation, poets such as Anne Stevenson and Fleur Adcock, sometimes synthesise male and female identities, newer

From *A History of Twentieth-Century British Women's Poetry*, pp. 212–26, 291–93.

contemporary poets retain the concept of sexual difference, albeit unfixed, by placing voices in parallel or opposition. Through 'heteroglossia' poets expose and rearrange stratified social differences. They are integral to the widespread dominance of the vernacular which problematises the lines between literary and popular cultures. Straddling the threshold of page and stage, the poems which mine Scottish and Caribbean oral traditions are often the most vibrant. Carol Ann Duffy is the obvious paradigm of protean dialogic politics; her poems are full of animated voices telling their stories with a colloquialism which cuts across the demands of the verse form.

Although dialogic criticism has become one cover-all methodology, it is particularly relevant to end-of-century poetry practice which is characterised by colloquial vividness and diversity. The impetus arises from a sensitivity towards cultural plurality and the influence of polyphonic postmodern narratives on poetry. In *Contemporary Poetry and Postmodernism: Dialogue and Estrangement* (1996), as the title suggests, Ian Gregson argues that there are two kinds of contemporary poets, 'mainstream' and 'retro-modernist'. The former group appropriate Bakhtin's dialogics for a stylistic 'mélange' while the retro-modernists are characterised by the 'estrangement' techniques described by Viktor Shlovsky. In distinguishing the movements, however, Gregson recognises that 'estrangement and the dialogic are not mutually exclusive'.[3] Much poetry can be located in the cross-currents of these developments. It can be self-consciously fictive and point to the instability of language, experience and representation without forgoing socio-literary politics. Duffy's frequently anthologised 'Standing Female Nude' destabilises the dramatic monologue's inherent assumptions by undermining art's mimetic function. In finally pointing to an unrepresented or unrepresentable self—'It does not look like me'—the subject arguably discards the male artist's distortion of her.

Similarly, Maggie Hannan draws on her experiences as a life model to contrast the masculine mediations of Schiel, Matisse and Freud with the photography of Cindy Sherman: '*she's crawling, you're crawling, the floor is dirt / where you're digging. You're naked. I am wearing that dream*'.[4] The italics, common in contemporary dialogic texts, position the reader sympathetically in relation to the subject's desperation. The alternating pronouns foreground the interactive process between 'I', 'she' and 'you' in a tenuous subjectivity. Just as 'Life Model' scrutinises the construction of femininity, Hannan 'explores the idea that we are all, in some fundamental way, created by language' throughout her collection *Liar, Jones* (1995). In her words, Hannan aims 'to capture the restlessness and unreliability of the different narratives. I try to give the subject-matter space to inhabit the different perspectives while compressing the language to the point where the unexpected is allowed to happen . . . a surprise association, a misleading echo, a reassessment of meaning. I want the poems to sound unsettling; I want them to hang like mobiles on the page.'[5] Cumulatively, women's poems negotiate between the subject as she is constituted within existing dialogic matrices and the projection beyond that to an altered state. In other words, while laying bare the fictiveness and therefore the provisionality of ready-made identity, they can construct a range of women hitherto either erased, or misunderstood, or subordinated to other voices.

Bakhtin's dialogic principles may have been depoliticised and appropriated for a utopian notion of polyphonic democracy, but they are crucial to examining the linguistic and cultural struggles inherent in the processes of self-realisation. Different voices, and their implied chronotopes, that is, 'time-spaces', may have equal status textually, but, as he points out, the modifications of representation are always evaluative:

> Someone else's words introduced into our own speech inevitably assume a new (our own) interpretation and become subject to our evaluation of them; that is, they become double-voiced. All that can vary is the interrelationship between these two voices . . . Our practical everyday speech is full of other people's words; with some of them we completely merge our own voice, forgetting whose they are; others, which we take as authoritative, we use to reinforce our own words; still others, finally, we populate with our own aspirations, alien or hostile to them.[6]

We find poets wielding the monologue and 'hidden dialogic', double-voiced or multivocal lyrics and narrative to scrutinise social assumptions about class, race or gender discrimination as filtered through mythologies, idioms and dialects. The form's demands for freely colloquial speech evade the strictures of traditional literary language and can reverse or equalise social hierarchies through the democratic medium of the page.

Duffy frequently employs heteroglossia, that is, the war of social differences maintained by language, to legitimise the speech of the underclasses or any individual who is positioned as the underdog. In her dramatic monologue 'Dummy', a ventriloquist's stooge speaks back to its manipulator, personifying the socially marginalised who are silenced to keep them in their place—'Just teach me / the right words.' At the same time, the dummy draws attention to the imprisonment of the poet's language:

> Why do you
> keep me in that black box? I can ask questions too,
> you know. I can see that worries you. Tough.[7]

The implicit inclusion of the reader in the interrogative is unsettling. In 'Yes, Officer', Duffy dramatises the police conviction of a man unable to defend himself. 'Without my own language, I am a blind man / in the wrong house.'[8] As for 'Translating the English, 1989', the collage of voices cleverly indicate the anachronisms and contradictions in so-called British culture. The polyphonic 'Comprehensive' interrogates the ideal of racial harmonisation in the face of monolithic nationalism. The parallel narratives of Jewish, African, Moslem, Indian and working-class white children present the reader with insoluble yet shared states of alienation. Glancing at her treatment of gender, Gregson is alert to the disguised polemic in Duffy's arrangement of voices:

> Because she has urgent political motives [Carol Ann Duffy] has felt it necessary to place a limit on postmodern free play; in this her motives are analogous to those of James Fenton. The power of her work arises from the persuasiveness both of her depiction of the distortive ways in which women are represented (the subtle, apparently 'natural' means of representation, the complex ramifications of the ends of representation) and of her condemnation of these distortions. Moreover, she manages to do both, to depict and to condemn, through the deployment of the dialogic tactics which are available to novelised poets.[9]

Many poets are Duffyesque in traversing the line between postmodern defamiliarisation and poetry's expressive function to give voice to Britain's socially deprived, foreigners and women. *On the Game*, the third section of Linda France's richly textured third collection *Storyville* (1997), is a sequence of dramatic lyrics about the social and emotional politics of prostitution. The first is a dramatic monologue which rejects the predatory logic sold to a vulnerable girl: 'Don't think I'm the only one snagged in the loop / of those big black lies: *easy money / just a job; don't worry, you're in control.*'[10] U. A. Fanthorpe presents characters in socially marginal situations compassionately. She avoids detached voyeurism with universal access points, like railway buffets, illnesses, mothers-in-law and job applications. Italics and parentheses often denote the depths of unspoken feeling. In *Strange Territory* (1983), Elizabeth Bartlett draws upon her working-class environment for urban backcloths of pubs, factories, alleyways and off-licences but seldom introduces class diction into her pertinently conversational poems, often based on her experiences within the health and social services. *Look, No Face* (1991) largely consists of monologues by people who are on the edge—battling with love, marriage breakdown, mental illness or rejection. 'Appointment' is the internalised dialogue between a suicidal woman and a Freudian doctor to whom she recounts her dreams:

> Why do you think this is? he said, and she
> cleverly side-stepped the trap of mythology,
> explaining about not being able to cope with
> children, husband, love, and that other myth
> of women who could sew and garden, bake
> and remember the sequence of pills to take.[11]

As Carol Rumens usefully observes, 'A dialogue with tradition is going on in much of Bartlett's work. The poems often enact interesting negotiations between the formal "big stanza" with its regular metre and rhyme, and vernacular looseness. Her line-formation never breaks faith with the rhythms of modern English speech. Yet the metrical "ghost" is a vital presence and reference. It not only satisfies the reader's often neglected need for melody, but allows the work to subvert, play with and ironically comment on English traditions and at the same time draw strength from them. Generations of love poems and elegies underwrite some of her grittiest settings.'[12]

The poetry of Sylvia Kantaris is often formally conventional but packed with voices. The *Lad's Love* sequence, set in the Britain of the 1980s and 1990s, is rooted in a statistic cited in the explanation prefacing the poem that 'Men now outnumber women in the 16–35 age group by 212,000. The toy boy phenomenon could make sense (*Observer*).' The dramatisation of a partnership between a middle-aged woman and her younger lover is initially light-hearted but the narrative darkens as the relationship deteriorates. In 'Domestic', a conversation with the police produces compassion for both parties:

> 'We see dozens of domestics every week,'
> one of the cops said, reassuringly.
> Seems I was lucky that I hadn't snuffed it
> totally—just throttled and my head and face bashed up.
> Oh, we were growing more domestic by the minute
> since grants and housing benefit were cut
> and my lover had nowhere else but here to live
> so he said I had to die 'because of poll tax'.
>
> 'Is this man your son?' they'd asked.
> Final irony. Pity I couldn't laugh.
> He used to joke: 'If anybody ever asks you that,

> say I'm your dad.' I saw him out in handcuffs.
> If it's true that each man kills the thing he loves
> it was himself he really meant to finish off.[13]

The sonnet's connotations of lyrical sentiment are raided by the politically charged interchange. The link between family violence and poverty takes the personal on to a more national scale. Although principally a monologue, we see here the widespread 'hidden dialogicality', where 'the second speaker is present invisibly, his [*sic*] words are not there, but deep traces left by these words have a determining influence on all the present and visible words of the first speaker'.[14] In this way Jackie Kay's 'Condemned Property' is a harrowing monologue of violence to a mother by her adolescent son. The mother's secret misery reaches out to the reader:

> There is something the matter with my eyes.
> They are weeping like drains and changing colour.
> *What could you have done, what could you?*
> I talk to myself in this baby-voice
> I used to use for my son, *tell Mum*.[15]

Exploiting the grimness of drains, Kay works the metaphor to set the scene, confide emotion and point to the lack of available words for it.

In the fantasy realism of the dramatic monologue, the woman poet can wield authority over personal relations, social taboos and the reader's sympathies. Many of these poems satirise or undermine the constricting voices of education and the family on the developing female. Duffy's enjoyable 'Head of English' was an early jibe at the conflict between 'a real live poet' and a traditionalist English school curriculum: 'We don't / want winds of change about the place.'[16] 'Litany' dramatises the young girl's negotiation between the sanitised vocabulary preserved by her mother's coterie of cellophane-wrapped women and the uncensored slang of a boy in the playground. Significantly, she thrills with power at reciting his forbidden swear words in their face: 'Language embarrassed them'. Such female-centred monologues most palpably emphasise the power dynamics of language in social interchanges. Duffy's popular collection *The World's Wife* (1999) supremely resurrects the silenced or marginalised while investigating available representation. As indicated in the title, her thirty 'heroines', from Mrs Midas and Frau Freud to Queen Kong, are everywoman types. Conflating the worlds of history, literature, myth and the contemporary reader has become something of a classic device for women, but Duffy's potent irony and parody are distinguished by 'in-your-face' vernacular and sexuality. Enhanced by live reading, the monologues appeal to a female community although at their crudest the power-balance is simply reversed. They may seem ingenuous because of their entertainment value but Duffy confronts the formulaic influences of myth in the variety of personalities and their stories. For some, troublesome partnerships are unresolved; others come out victorious. Here is Eurydice, deflating the entire literary tradition and its hegemonic institutions:

> And given my time all over again,
> rest assured that I'd rather speak for myself
> than be Dearest, Beloved, Dark Lady, White Goddess, etc., etc.
>
> In fact, girls, I'd rather be dead.
>
> But the Gods are like publishers,
> usually male,
> and what you doubtless know of my tale
> is the deal.
>
> Orpheus strutted his stuff.[17]

In colluding with the speaker and the direct address to the 'girls', she excludes and alienates the male reader. Likewise, Vicki Feaver combines the fanciful with realism in her Forward Prize-winning 'Judith' and 'The Handless Maiden'. In the latter, as Feaver's footnote explains, according to the Grimms' fairytale, the maiden's hands are restored for good conduct after seven years while in a Russian version they return when she saves her drowning baby: 'And I cried for my hands that sprouted / in the red-orange mud—the hands / that write this, grasping / her curled fists.'[18] Since to write with sprouting hands is too far-fetched, the moral closure of fairytale is undermined.

In their male-centred dramatic monologues, women particularly exploit the relationship between the poet as dramatist and the reader. In its kinship with the soliloquy of tragic drama, the medium assumes sympathy for the protagonist, but Lavinia Greenlaw's haunting 'Hurting Small Animals' only *appears* to allow the reader's complicity with the swanker who has assaulted a girl on a party 'pick up'. His cocky intonation is antagonising: 'We went outside and fucked her in the car park / but it was no good, she got a bit loud.'[19] This 'internal polemic', that is 'a sideways glance at someone else's hostile word', propels us towards the absent eighteen-year-old victim.[20] The information that her brother taught her to destroy helpless creatures questions whether it is a biological or social imperative for men to vanquish women and whether or not gendered attributes are transferable. In Duffy's 'Psychopath', the form invites sympathy for, but we are repelled by, the blatant boasts of a man who has abducted a girl from a fairground, sexually violated her and thrown her into the canal:

> You can woo them
> with goldfish and coconuts, whispers in the Tunnel of Love.
> When I zip up the leather, I'm in a new skin, I touch it
> and love myself, sighing Some little lady's going to get lucky
> tonight. My breath wipes me from the looking glass.[21]

In also allowing the criminal to disclose his own social and emotional deprivation, Duffy may challenge the social forces behind archetypal masculinity but she does not diminish the 'hero's' moral void. This is the 'hidden polemic', where, as Bakhtin puts it, 'Every struggle between two voices within a single discourse for possession or dominance in that discourse is decided in advance, it only appears to be a struggle.'[22] In Duffy's disturbing evocation of child abuse, 'Lizzie, Six', the adult voice dominates with three-quarters of the lines but the reader recoils from it. The disconcerting effect is produced by this structural tension and the absence of overt moral judgement:

> What are you thinking?
> *I'm thinking of love.*
> I'll give you love
> when I've climbed this stair[23]

Again, the poet's concealed polemic is asserted via the intonation. Sympathy is directed towards the italicised childlike innocence in conflict with the menacing adult. Similarly, Selima Hill's 'A Voice in the Garden' depicts the imprints of an elderly neighbour's secret pursuit of a young girl on the adult woman's memory.[24]

In addition to dramatised voices which imply an audience, many poems consist of reported dialogue between two speakers or the 'hidden dialogue' of two voices constructed in the consciousness of a single speaker. These voices in conflicting, consensual or competitive dialogue particularly expose the power dynamics of self-in-relation. The voices in Carol Rumens's sestina 'Rules for Beginners' belong to distinct characters who are both external to and internalised by the *Educating Rita* type of mature women who grasped at newly available education but met with opposition at home: 'Her husband grumbled—"Where's the dinner, mother?" / "I'm going down the night-school for an O level."'[25] Although temporarily escaping from stifling domestic demands, this woman still fulfils her traditional womanly duties. In Duffy's 'A Clear Note', the voices of three generations construct and contest the continuum of women's suppression within the family unit. The youngest urges the implicitly female reader to fracture the cycle:

> Listen. The hopes of your thousand mothers
> sing with a clear note inside you.
> *Away, while you can, and travel the world.*
>
> I can almost hear her saying it now.
> *Who will remember me?* Bleak decades of silence
> and lovelessness placing her years away
> from the things that seem natural to us.[26]

Here, there is a consensual sympathy between the grandmother, mother and daughter. In 'Big Girls', by the up-and-coming Tracey Herd, they are in conflict:

> *Granny's here.* Her mother's voice was bright
> with pleasure. She turned away in spite.
> *Hello,* she mumbled and dropped her eyes back
> to the book she was reading. It was a book
> for Big Girls. The knowledge stuffed her
> with pride. Granny could go to Hell.[27]

We are asked to side with each generation, strapped in their particular version of womanhood. Although the youngest rebels, she is implicitly prey to the marketing and commodification of contemporary femininity. U. A. Fanthorpe's 'Washing Up' interjects a mother's phrases into her daughter's wistful attempts to connect with her memory, whereas Feaver's dramatic 'Woman's Blood' links menstruation, the initiation into womanhood, with inherently murderous mother/daughter relations.[28] Hill's twenty-page sequence on a lifelong tricky affiliation between sisters also investigates the implications of gender determinacy. The highly dialogic narrative surrounds the death of their mother but through reminiscence the schisms connect with the girls' formative childhood: 'she thinks *she thinks she loves me but she doesn't, / she doesn't understand a word I say*'.[29]

The largest group of poems features the dialogue of genders where, as before, the significant other's voice is reworked into the identity created through internal monologue. Contemporary women poets are not, however, simply reflecting a self/other dependency; by simulating dialogues they fictionalise relationships and manufacture female identities which blur the boundaries of 'lived experience' and the imaginary. By dissolving the binary opposition between private and public, they release women to politicise their personal experiences. As Gregson comments, 'It is not a question of the bland tolerance of difference but of a profound sense that the self has no meaning except in interrelation with others, and that the lived experience of the self can only be expressed through determined efforts to evoke the otherness with which the self continuously interacts.'[30] Since the 'other' is absent, the female speaker manipulates the reported dialogue to create her own identikit. In poems about the end of a relationship, such as Ann Sansom's 'Voice' or 'And Please Do Not Presume' by Deryn Rees-Jones, female power is often reasserted directly—'don't use the *broken heart again* voice'.[31] Control can be reclaimed by humour and by stretching the limits of the plausible. Where pain and loss are central, the speaker can find restitution by possessing the discourse, as in Rees-Jones's 'It Will Not Do': 'It will not do that I don't shout or cry or rant or plead / show you the door marked exit that I ought.'[32] Mimi Khalvati's 'Stone of Patience' has a mythical realism in its narrative framework: '"In the old days," she explained to a grandchild bred in England, / "in the old days in Persia"'. The speech marks are dropped and the first person voice fuses with the poet's to relate the pain of sexual domination and the shame of illegitimate children:

> a voice that says
> *oh come on darling, it'll be all right, oh do let's.*
> How many children were born from words such as these?
> I know my own were; now learning to repeat them, to outgrow
> a mother's awe of consequences her body bears.[33]

Internalised dialogue constitutes the fractured consciousness of individual female subjectivity. As Sarah Maguire comments on her collection *Spilt Milk* (1991): 'Above all, what I've tried to do in these poems is to push out of the lyric tradition, with its connotations of hermetic intimacy, into the broader contexts of the historical and the social, without employing the exhortations of the polemic, without losing sensuality or richness of language. A small attempt at transgressing yet another boundary.'[34]

The 'time-space' is frequently an amalgam of the recognisable and the remote which exposes and also transcends cultural politics. Moniza Alvi's *Carrying My Wife* (2000) consists of a husband's addresses to an imaginary wife: 'My wife was a rare occurrence / and a common occurrence.' The self-contained metaphor, 'She created a hiding place / in the empty supermarkets of the moon', is the central mediator between the familiar and the strange.[35] Alvi states that 'In a sense the poems are autobiographical, and writing from a male or "husband" viewpoint has been a way of distancing myself from the sensations and difficulties portrayed, and then zooming in closely. I found surreal aspects of relationships emerged ... I suppose I am attracted by fantasy and the strange-seeming and find there some essence of experience.'[36] In Rees-Jones's 'Service Wash', the line between external and imaginary perceptions, and between masculinity and femininity, becomes hard to define. A lonely impoverished laundry-man creates a woman's identity from the clothes he handles. Sympathy is invited for the tragic figure of this attendant, along with his wife and the bellboy, who are all social inferiors to the rich owner of the dress which he tries on: 'I could have cried. / My breasts hung empty.' In a turnaround of Freudian prescriptions, does he latently desire to *be* a woman? Towards the end, however, the narrative seems to go beyond the land of unspoken desires with the incantatory repetition of 'sometimes':

> Sometimes I think an afternoon will last for ever.
> Sometimes I think the world is flat. Go on. Convince me.
> Sometimes I think I'll fall in love again.[37]

The speaker's sexuality, the woman's identity, and even her existence, remain uncertain since they are contiguous with the dreamstate of the male narrator. The direct address to the reader—'Go on. Convince me'—sends the chronotope to the fictive page and the first person pronoun could be the poet's. The strangeness but liberation of altered consciousness is not new but characterises much end-of-century poetry. In 'Superman Sounds Depressed', Jo Shapcott seizes the masculinity emblematised by the cartoon hero, to feed and examine women's fantasies of being desired:

> And I want us to eat scallops,
> and I want to lick the juice from her chin
>
> as though I could save the world that way,
> and I won't even ask what passion is for.[38]

The chronotope is more vividly a 'borderzone' between levels of consciousness.

Kay often suffuses quotidian familiarity with the surreal to deny definitive signification: 'I think I will always be interested in identity, how fluid it is, how people can invent themselves, how it can never be fixed or frozen

... I like mixing fact with fiction and trying to illuminate the border country that exists between them.'[39] As in her collection *Other Lovers* (1993), same-sex relations and passions can especially be coded through unspecified dialogic interchange. The central sequence charts the making and breaking of a love relationship which is vividly intimate yet universal. In 'Mouth', displaced images evoke the unpresentable pain of love turning to hate: 'Words like dead gulls thrown out the sea; / your mouth froths like a drowning man' (p. 58). Fact and fiction share the same territory in memory and Feaver's 'The Singing Teacher' is a retrospective tragedy of a disabled woman's passion for a young girl: 'Oh, Miss Cree, forgive me / for what twisted through you / like a corkscrew.'[40] Feaver typically moves between particularised and imaginary chronotopes in her love poems, such as 'Lacrimae Hominis', a meditation on the male partner's inability to cry, or 'French Lesson', where the speaker tries on a new identity via a foreign language.[41]

Although dialogism does not substitute the universalising authority of masculine discourse with an identifiable female poetic voice, it avoids the linguistic difficulties for women encased between the expressive or the antirepresentational, the personal or the public. Kay's bestselling *The Adoption Papers* (1991), originally a radio drama, exemplifies how multivocality articulates and maintains difference but bypasses the binary opposites of conventional versions of gender and race. The parallel narratives construct the actual and psychological interplay between a birth mother, the adopting mother and the adopted child. Also in *The Adoption Papers*, topical poems introduce debates about environmental and economic abuses and nonheterosexual arrangements. 'Photo in the Locket' explores the alliance between a black and a white girl through intermingling the girls' and their parents' voices. The hidden dialogic in 'Dance of the Cherry Blossom' invites sympathy for two men dying of AIDS: 'Both of us are getting worse / Neither knows who had it first' (p. 50). Similarly, the dramatis personae in 'Mummy and Donor and Deirdre' compel emotional understanding: 'Tunde said Do you know who your daddy is? / I said yes he's a friend of a friend of mummy's' (pp. 54–55). 'Sign', from *Other Lovers*, sums up how these occluded individual testimonies can seem like pebbles thrown at an overwhelming giant of dominant rhetoric:

> All this
>
> *distance*
>
> between one language and another, one
> culture and another; one religion
> and another. The *little languages*

squashed, stamped upon, cleared out
to make way
for the big one, better tongue. (p. 21)

Dialogic representation of Anglo-Asian duality is aimed as much against Western homogenising of Indian culture as it is against inscribing it:

The multicultural poem does not expect
The reader to 'understand' anything,
After all, it is used to being misunderstood.

It speaks of a refraction
It wants more dialogue
between the retina of the light
It says, 'get rid of your squint'

It lives the chapter in history
They can't teach you in school.[42]

Sujata Bhatt's multilingual creativity is a weapon against the invisibility of hybridity since it maintains differences and holds them alongside each other. In contrast, Irish poets have tended to operate within their dominant lyric tradition but to some extent the younger women define themselves antithetically to stereotyped Irish sentiment by starkly vernacular English. Rita Ann Higgins's 'The Deserter' is the unsentimental dramatic monologue of a woman whose man has died: 'But in his favour / I will say this for him, / he made a lovely corpse.'[43] In 'Federal Case', Julie O'Callaghan mimics both the addiction for a 'Big Mac' and the disapproval of it: 'Maybe it's a mortal sin cuz / I've got a yen for some junk food.'[44] Knowingly, she pitches slang at literary correctness. Such universalising colloquialisms appear anarchic, not least because they discard the nationalist ideal of unification.

Scottish poets plunder the rich resources of their English heritage, Scottish dialects and Gaelic languages. Liz Lochhead was among the first to exploit the range of native dialects and exhibit a knotty relationship with her repressive heritage. Similarly, Kathleen Jamie recognises that nationalistic pulls to a unified Scottish identity are not advantageous to women:

Scotland, you have invoked her name
just once too often
in your Presbyterian living rooms.

She's heard, yea
even unto heathenish Arabia
your vixen's bark of poverty, come down
the family like a lang neb, a thrawn streak,
a wally dug you never liked
but can't get shot of.[45]

As Helen Kidd explains, 'Scots English is recognisable by certain tropes, whereas women do not have a language that is specifically female, nor a specific set of dialects which are identifiable by women from other cultural contexts. What we do have, however, is a sense of the subversive qualities of language: ironies, digressions, musicalities, as well as a sense of the dangers of certain male discourses which place the female subject in a subordinate position.'[46] At the same time, the national mother tongue disadvantages the English reader. Scots dialects and phonetics both expose and refresh its traditions. Jamie's 'Forget It' asks whose history is preserved and questions whether the poem's function is to reclaim it:

Who wants to know? Stories
spoken through the mouths
of closes: who cares
who trudged those worn stairs,
or played in now rubbled back greens?
What happened about my granddad? Why
did Agnes go? How come
you don't know

that stories are balm,
ease their own pain, contain
a beginning, a middle—
and ours is a long driech
now-demolished street. *Forget it*![47]

Just as the pronunciation of 'Forget It' is up for grabs, so is the resolve to maintain or discard memory. As for other colonised peoples, there is a fine line between holding on to past racial suppression and being stuck there. In other poems in this newest collection, *Jizzen* (1999), Jamie shifts further between realism and the yet-to-be.

With African rhythms, Dub poems and Creole dialects, Caribbean poets investigate and keep alive their histories. Colloquial multivocality retains women's role as custodians of the oral tradition. In 'Language Barrier',

Valerie Bloom imbues traditional English quatrains with the nonstandardness of nation language:

> But sayin' dis an dot yuh know
> Sometime wi cyan understan one anodda
> Even doah wi all lib yah
> An chat de same patwa[48]

The necessity of pronouncing the words phonetically comments upon the flatness of page text while the sense dispels any ideal of a homogenous Caribbean experience. Bloom is committed to the social inclusiveness of orality and her performances are often participatory. Grace Nichols tends more to disempower the colonising assumptions of English by cross-fertilising oral and literary traditions. In *i is a long-memoried woman*, she switches from the first person singular Creole voice—'from dih pout / of mih mouth' to the choric standard English: 'Yet we the women / whose praises go unsung / whose voices go unheard' (p. 12). Jean 'Binta' Breeze creates character types who speak for, and potentially to, a community who are united by their marginality and sense of African as well as Caribbean pasts. Whether in 'The First Dance' or 'Dis Lang Time Girl', their politics centralise her experiences as a Jamaican emigrant in England.[49] For Breeze, Dub poetry '"is a public voice, a political voice of social commentary that works to a rhythm . . . there's a strong sense of rhythm which is the rhythm of reggae. It's poetry which combines a love of language with a sense of rhythm and music while at the same time recording our stories and oral observations."' Through evoking powerful emotions with the physicality of her theatre and her vocal range, she raises awareness about history, war or the stereotyping of Third World poverty, penetrating 'into the lives of ordinary people'. For her, colonialism '"is an academic term. Let's call it what it is—international theft of resources and robbery of people's land. Colonialism doesn't say that."'[50] Breeze's dialogicality, from the dramatic monologue to the multivocal performance piece, stretch and thus question the perimeters of 'poetry'. Frequently woman-centred, they produce complex female identities which are always in motion: 'I have a really strong sense of my own voice, as a woman, because I write a lot of voices.'[51] As C. Innes puts it, in differing ways these poets 'challenge, often with subversive wit and humour, essentialist concepts of women and race, or monolithic views of culture and insist upon the interplay of multiple heritages and voices in a Britain where they "have arrived".'[52] Patience Agbabi's 'UFO WOMAN (PRONOUNCED OOFOE)' is the monologue of an African-Caribbean finding herself perceived as an alien in England:

my two-tone hand with its translucent palm,
life line, heart line, head line, children, journeys,
prompting the '*Why's it white on the inside*
of your hand?' '*Do you wash? Does it wash off?*'
Or my core names, Trochaic, Dactylic,
Galactic beats from ancient poetry,
names they make me repeat, make them call me
those sticks-and-stones-may-break-my-bones-but names.

In times of need I ask the oracle.
Withdrawing to my work station I press
HELP. I have just two options. HISTORY:
The screen flashes subliminal visuals
from the old days which I quickly translate:
Slave ship: space ship, racism: spacism.

Resignedly I select HERSTORY:[53]

Significantly, Agbabi has discarded Creole to play with the possibilities of manipulating more eclectic cultural discourses. The scene ends with a positive future vision of 'not aloneness but oneness', thus picking up the gauntlet from her 'Transformatrix', a rhythmic celebration of female linguistic freedom:

Give me a stage and I'll cut form on it
give me a page and I'll perform on it.

Give me a word.
any word.[54]

Notes

1. See extract from 'Discourse in life and Discourse in Art', Voloshinov/ Bakhtin, *The Bakhtin Reader: Selected Writings of Bakhtin, Medvedev, Voloshinov*, ed. Pam Morris (London: Edward Arnold, 1994), pp. 160–73.
2. See Chapter 5, notes 13 and 14.
3. Ian Gregson, *Contemporary Poetry and Postmodernism: Dialogue and Estrangement* (Basingstoke: Macmillan, 1996), p. 9.
4. Maggie Hannan, 'Life Model', (*Liar, Jones*, 1995), *New Blood*, ed. Neil Astley (Newcastle upon Tyne: Bloodaxe Books, 1999), pp. 141–42.
5. Hannan, *New Blood*, p. 140.
6. M. M. Bakhtin 'Problems of Dostoevsky's Poetics' (1963), *The Bakhtin Reader: Selected Writings of Bakhtin, Medvedev, Voloshinov*, ed. Pam Morris (London: Edward Arnold, 1994), pp. 105–7.

7. Carol Ann Duffy, 'The Dummy', *Selling Manhattan* (London: Anvil Press, 1987), p. 20.

8. Duffy, 'Yes, Officer', ibid., p. 31.

9. Gregson, *Contemporary Poetry*, p. 106.

10. Linda France, 'Selling Yourself Short', *Storyville* (Newcastle upon Tyne: Bloodaxe Books, 1997), p. 62.

11. Elizabeth Bartlett, 'Appointment', *Two Women Dancing New and Selected Poems* (Newcastle upon Tyne: Bloodaxe Books, 1995), p. 202.

12. Rumens, Introduction to Bartlett, *Two Women Dancing*, p. 15.

13. Sylvia Kantaris, *Lad's Love* (Newcastle upon Tyne: Bloodaxe Books, 1993), p. 58.

14. Bakhtin, 'Problems of Dostoevsky's Poetics', p. 108.

15. Jackie Kay, 'Condemned Property', *Other Lovers* (Newcastle upon Tyne: Bloodaxe Books, 1993), p. 54.

16. Carol Ann Duffy, 'Head of English', *Standing Female Nude* (London: Anvil Press, 1985), p. 12.

17. Carol Ann Duffy, 'Eurydice', *The World's Wife* (London: Picador, 1999), pp. 58–61.

18. Vicki Feaver, 'The Handless Maiden', *The Handless Maiden* (London: Jonathan Cape, 1994), p. 12.

19. Lavinia Greenlaw, 'Hurting Small Animals', *New Women Poets* (1987), ed. Carol Rumens (Newcastle upon Tyne: Bloodaxe Books, 1990), p. 165.

20. Bakhtin, 'Problems of Dostoevsky's Poetics', p. 108.

21. Duffy, 'Psychopath', *Selling Manhattan*, pp. 28–29.

22. Bakhtin, 'Problems of Dostoevsky's Poetics', pp. 107, 112.

23. Duffy, 'Lizzie, Six', *Standing Female Nude*, p. 13.

24. Selima Hill, 'A Voice in the Garden', *Saying Hello at the Station* (London: Chatto & Windus, 1984), p. 29.

25. Carol Rumens, 'Rules for Beginners' (*Unplayed Music*, 1981), *Thinking of Skins: New and Selected Poems* (Newcastle upon Tyne: Bloodaxe Books, 1993), p. 60.

26. Duffy, 'A Clear Note', *Standing Female Nude*, pp. 27–31.

27. Tracey Herd, 'Big Girls', *No Hiding Place* (Newcastle upon Tyne: Bloodaxe Books, 1996), p. 40.

28. U. A. Fanthorpe, 'Washing up', *A Watching Brief* (Calstock: Peterloo Poets, 1987) pp. 30–31; Feaver, 'Women's Blood', *Handless Maiden*, p. 19.

29. Hill, 'My Sister's Sister', *Violet* (Newcastle upon Tyne: Bloodaxe Books: 1997), pp. 11–32.

30. Gregson, *Contemporary Poetry*, p. 7.

31. Ann Sansom, 'Voice', *Romance* (Newcastle upon Tyne: Bloodaxe Books, 1994), Deryn Rees-Jones, 'And Please Do Not Presume', *The Memory Tray* (Bridgend: Seren, 1994); Maura Dooley, ed., *Making for Planet Alice: new women poets* (Newcastle upon Tyne: Bloodaxe Books, 1997), pp. 163, 151.

32. Rees Jones, 'It Will Not Do', *Making for Planet Alice*, p. 152.

33. Mimi Khalvati, 'Stone of Patience', *In White Ink* (Manchester: Carcanet, 1991); *Making for Planet Alice*, pp. 112–13.

34. Sarah Maguire, 'On *Spilt Milk*', *PBS Bulletin* (1991), repr. in *Don't Ask Me What I Mean: Poets in their own words*, eds. Clare Brown and Don Paterson (London: Picador, 2003), p. 171.

35. Moniza Alvi, 'Missing', *Carrying My Wife* (Newcastle upon Tyne: Bloodaxe Books, 2000), p. 3; Astley, *New Blood*, p. 108.

36. Alvi, *New Blood*, p. 107.

37. Rees-Jones, 'Service Wash', *The Memory Tray; Making for Planet Alice*, p. 149.

38. Jo Shapcott, 'Superman Sounds Depressed', *Her Book: Poems 1988–1998* (London: Faber, 2000), pp. 46–47.

39. Kay, *New Blood*, p. 73.

40. Feaver, 'The Singing Teacher', *Handless Maiden*, p. 18.

41. Feaver, 'Lacrimae Hominis', 'French Lesson', ibid., pp. 43, 32.

42. Sujata Bhatt, 'The Multicultural Poem', *Augatora* (Manchester: Carcanet, 2000), pp. 100–3.

43. Rita Ann Higgins, 'The Deserter' (*Philomena's Revenge*, 1992), *Sunnyside Plucked: New and Selected Poems* (Newcastle upon Tyne: Bloodaxe Books, 1996), p. 63.

44. Julie O'Callaghan, 'Federal Case' in 'Opening Lines: *Dramaticules*', *What's What?* (Newcastle upon Tyne: Bloodaxe Books, 1991), p. 34.

45. Kathleen Jamie, 'The Queen of Sheba', *Mr and Mrs Scotland are Dead: Poems 1980–1994* (Tarset: Bloodaxe Books, 2002), p. 114.

46. Helen Kidd, 'Writing Near the Fault Line: Scottish Women Poets and the Topography of Tongues', *Kicking Daffodils: Twentieth-Century Women Poets*, ed. Vicki Bertram (Edinburgh University Press, 1997), p. 100.

47. Kathleen Jamie, 'Forget It', *Jizzen* (London, Picador, 1999), pp. 5–7.

48. Valerie Bloom, 'Language Barrier', *Touch Mi Tell Mi* (London: Bogle-L'Ouverture, 1983), pp. 41–42.

49. Both poems are in 'Poetry in Performance' Vol. 1 (London: 57 Productions, 2002). For an incisive discussion, see Denise de Caires Narain, 'Speaking and performing the Creole Word: the work of Valerie Bloom, Jean "Binta" Breeze, Merle Collins and Amryl Johnson', *Contemporary Caribbean Women's Poetry: Making Style* (London: Routledge, 2001), pp. 89–147.

50. Jean 'Binta' Breeze, interview with Henry Palmer, *new internationalist* 31 (March 1999).

51. 'A Round-Table Discussion on Poetry in Performance', *Feminist Review* 62 (Summer 1999), p. 33.

52. C. Innes, 'Accent and Identity: Women Poets of Many Parts', *Contemporary British Poetry: Essays in Theory and Criticism*, eds. James Acheson and Romana Huk (New York: State University of New York Press, 1996), p. 339.

53. Patience Agbabi, 'UFO WOMAN (PRONOUNCED OOFOE)', *Transformatrix* (Edinburgh: Payback Press, 2000), pp. 15–16.

54. Agbabi, 'Transformatrix', ibid., p. 11.

TIM KENDALL

Fighting Back over the Same Ground: Ted Hughes and War

'When I first started writing,' Ted Hughes acknowledged, 'I wrote again and again and again about the First World War.'[1] He ascribed that compulsion to three factors: the stories told by his father, who had survived his regiment's massacre at Gallipoli; a love of Wilfred Owen's poetry; and the West Yorkshire landscape where he grew up believing that 'the whole region is in mourning for the first world war'.[2] Despite his best efforts, Hughes never managed to free himself from his subject. In *Wodwo* (1967) he was already writing poetry designed to 'get rid of the entire body of preoccupation': 'I finally decided that really [the First World War] had nothing to do with me.'[3] The exorcism failed: a series of poems in *Wolfwatching* (1989) returned Hughes to his first inspiration in the wartime experiences of his father and uncle. Those poems are among the most visible signs of a pressure which shapes his writing career.

War is the abiding concern of Hughes's poetry. As a teenager beginning to write in the early 1940s, he viewed contemporary conflict through the lens of the past, and the fear that his elder brother's war would prove as terrible as their father's became his 'permanent preoccupation'.[4] His post-war poetic maturity continued to perceive experience through that lens: Hughes characterizes his poems as 'battleground[s]' where his imagination, excited by 'the war between vitality and death', celebrates 'the exploits of the warriors of either side'.[5] Writing about the natural world, he therefore appears less a war poet *manqué* than a war poet by other means. This position requires some defending because, notwithstanding his own prompts and observations, the bulk of critical writing on Hughes remains silent about war.[6] Primitivism, shamanism, Trickster myth, pastoral, post-pastoral, ecology, parapsychology—it sometimes seems that there is no context so esoteric that it has not been used to explain Hughes's work. War is considered only in passing, if at all, and is typically assumed to be representative of something larger: 'war itself is the occasion rather than the subject of the best "war poems" in *The Hawk in the Rain*. Their subject is death and grief.'[7] The inverted commas in this example from Terry Gifford and Neil Roberts insinuate that Hughes's 'war poems' are not really war poems at all. Wilfred Owen, to whom Hughes professes a fundamental indebtedness, rates barely a mention in most critical studies.

Whatever insights the various approaches to Hughes have afforded, their blindness to his belief that experience cannot be disentangled from the influence of war guarantees that they miss the forming impulse of his poetry. That impulse, Hughes recognized, originates in a war fought on the home front as well as internationally: 'Owen, when I came to know his poems, grew to represent my father's experience, and later on [Keith] Douglas my brother's (who was in North Africa through the same period). So that pattern of antithetical succession was prefigured, for me, and quite highly charged.'[8] Casting Owen as poetic father and Douglas as older brother, Hughes positions himself squarely within a tradition of war poetry, transforming it into a family drama where he as latecomer must negotiate between two rival males who struggle for supremacy. Owen or Douglas? It is the question which, Hughes implies in an introduction to Douglas's work, challenges and categorizes the most important of their English poetic successors. Hughes maintains that Owen's style was 'duly taken over, with only a few modifications, by, for instance, Philip Larkin'.[9] In the final sentence of his essay, he pays a similar compliment to Douglas:

> And like Owen, after producing a few examples of what could be done with [his style], he died and left it to others.
>
> TED HUGHES [1987][10]

This is as much a signing up as a signing off. Having already situated Larkin in the Owen tradition, Hughes adds his own name as first in the list of Douglas's successors. The antithesis which critics routinely detect in the rival achievements of Larkin and Hughes is predetermined and 'prefigured' by the 'polar opposition of Owen and Douglas'.[11] Hughes credits those two poets with begetting the dominant traditions of post-war English poetry.

Hughes's account of modern literary history (perhaps itself a product of the First World War's '*versus* habit'[12]), and his own self-portrayal as a belated war poet, endorse Francis Hope's judgement that 'In a not altogether rhetorical sense, all poetry written since 1918 is war poetry.'[13] Finding that inheritance riven by a power struggle, Hughes displays a loyalty to Douglas in his prose that does not accurately represent the imaginative sympathies of his early poetry. His preoccupation with the First World War pre-dates his discovery in the late 1950s of Douglas's work, and, accordingly, Owen rather than Douglas is the presiding spirit of *The Hawk in the Rain* (1957). The first poem of a first collection provides significant clues as to how the poet views himself, and how he wishes to be viewed by others. The title poem which opens *The Hawk in the Rain* projects Hughes as a nature poet, but one who experiences nature in terms of First World War combat:

> I drown in the drumming ploughland, I drag up
> Heel after heel from the swallowing of the earth's mouth,
> From clay that clutches my each step to the ankle
> With the habit of the dogged grave . . . [14]

'[T]he ground was not mud, not sloppy mud, but an octopus of sucking clay . . . relieved only by craters full of water,' Wilfred Owen told his mother. 'Men have been known to drown in them.'[15] The ploughland, the sucking mud, the reference to drowning, the constant proximity of death, the struggle against the carnivorous earth—Hughes might be describing a battlefield landscape from the First World War. However, the only enemy is the environment: 'banging wind kills these stubborn hedges, || Thumbs my eyes, throws my breath, tackles my heart, | And rain hacks my head to the bone'. This illustrates a problem which besets much of Hughes's work: shearing wartime atrocity from its specific historical contexts, his poetry risks sounding absurdly overwritten. As a result, the collection's group of poems explicitly about the First World War loses its force. 'Bayonet Charge' describes a soldier 'Stumbling across a field of clods towards a green hedge | That dazzled with rifle fire',[16] but despite a similar landscape, the poem's language fails to match the intensity of 'The Hawk in the Rain'. Hughes's portrayals of violence rarely concern themselves with the necessary calibrations, so that getting caught in a bad storm sounds at least as dangerous as a bayonet charge into gunfire. Hughes's language fights the First World War, going over the top even when his subjects do not.

When Hughes speaks, almost a decade later, of 'the terrible, suffocating, maternal octopus of English poetic tradition',[17] his ungainly borrowing of Owen's octopus metaphor proves that one unspoken battle in 'The Hawk in the Rain' is between the ephebe and an inescapable precursor. Thinking of his poetic predecessors, Hughes cannot see past Owen, who has become both father and mother. In 'Bayonet Charge', Hughes's unnamed protagonist 'plunged past with his bayonet toward the green hedge', as the luxuries of 'King, honour, human dignity, etcetera' were discarded: the sentiment is Owen, *passim*, and the plunging might have been taken from either 'Dulce et Decorum Est' ('He plunges at me, guttering, choking, drowning')[18] or Owen's only poetic description of a bayonet charge, 'Spring Offensive' ('plunged and fell away past this world's verge').[19] 'Bayonet Charge' is something less than Hughes's best work, but it allows the son to relive his biological father's experience in the same vicarious way that he rewrites the poetry of his poetic father. Similarly, in 'My Uncle's Wound' Hughes takes his uncle back to the battlefield where a bullet had 'picked him up by the hip-bone / And laid him in a shell-hole';[20] the poet's ambition to appropriate the experience for himself—'I wanted the exact spot'—springs from a desire to understand (and, perhaps, to be wounded in war) which is also a profound jealousy that he can never achieve the authority of the combatant poet. In Hughes's early poetry the need to re-create wartime experiences proves stronger than the need for originality, whatever the aesthetic cost: his stage-managed performances rely on familiar props, as telegrams open more terribly than bombs ('Griefs for Dead Soldiers'), photographed young men never age ('Six Young Men'), and death's spectators stand helpless as ghosts ('The Casualty').

Over a decade after writing the war poems of *The Hawk in the Rain*, Hughes may have provided one reason for his failure:

> Perhaps the more sure of itself a truth is, the more doubtful it is of the adequacy of words. This struck me forcibly once when I was collecting material for what I hoped would be a long poem about the campaign on Gallipoli during the First World War. I read memoirs and histories, eloquent and detailed. But however eloquent and detailed such writings are, one always half dismisses them, because they are inevitably false. The actuality must always have been different—in every way that really matters. . . . The same principle works in all sorts of situations. At every point, a man's deeper sufferings and experiences are almost impossible for him to express by deliberate means.[21]

Hughes moves characteristically from the First World War to other 'situations': the lens of war again colours experience 'at every point'. His positing of an antagonistic relationship between truth and language befits a First World War mentality in which language has become corrupted by propaganda. Yet this distrust fails to distinguish what Owen calls the truthfulness of true poets from the lies, distortions, and euphemisms engendered by war. Hughes's preoccupation with the First World War provokes a near-fatal conviction that for the true poet (and, for that matter, the true historian) to be truthful, he must renounce language. Unsurprisingly, his long poem about Gallipoli was never written.

Hughes's account does not give a date to this crisis, but his second collection, *Lupercal* (1960), betrays what may be consequent ruptures: whereas *The Hawk in the Rain* contains six poems directly about war, *Lupercal* has none. The omission ought to make redundant Hughes's attempt in *Wodwo* to persuade himself that the First World War has nothing to do with him. Whereof the poet cannot speak, thereof he must remain silent: unable to write the truth about war, Hughes stops writing about war altogether. Only once, at the end of 'Mayday on Holderness', does the old preoccupation resurface, albeit in circumstances suggesting that the poet is operating under duress:

> The North Sea lies soundless. Beneath it
> Smoulder the wars: to heart-beats, bomb, bayonet.
> 'Mother, Mother!' cries the pierced helmet.
> Cordite oozings of Gallipoli,
>
> Curded to beastings, broached my palate,
> The expressionless gaze of the leopard,
> The coils of the sleeping anaconda,
> The nightlong frenzy of shrews.[22]

Hughes's long poem about Gallipoli has shrunk to these convulsing fragments. No longer does he try to write representational war poetry; instead, the images constitute the horrific return of what has been repressed, broaching (both meanings: initiating and piercing) the poet's palate. Hughes depicts Gallipoli as his 'beastings'—the colostrum which provided his earliest nutrition. That formative influence, no doubt aided by a pun on 'beast', invades the animal kingdom as well. Hughes's sustained fascination with predators is flavoured by the 'Cordite oozings' of war.

'Mayday on Holderness' admits that war is the prior condition which nourishes Hughes's work. But after the mixed results of *The Hawk in the Rain*, *Lupercal* understands that poetic re-enactments of battle cannot seem other than mannered exercises. Hughes's breakthrough comes in realizing—to reverse the opinion of Gifford and Roberts—that war, the subject of his poetry, need not also be its occasion. So, while the title of 'Wilfred Owen's Photographs' may seem to promise a war poem in the old style, it delivers an account of a parliamentary debate in which Parnell called for the abolition of the British Navy's cat-o'-nine-tails. Hughes reports elsewhere the source for his otherwise mystifying title:

> Owen carried about, in his pocket, photographs of trench horrors which he would evidently have liked to see magnified and put on public display in London, his idea being to shock his non-participant fellow citizens into an awareness of the new day dawning in the trenches.[23]

Hughes bypasses the debate about whether those photographs existed, and his 'evidently' shows the strains of disguising guesswork as fact. Naturally enthusiastic about the validity of photographs which are not dependent on corrupted language, he applauds Owen's role as the purveyor of truth to a society which seeks to deny its own nature. It is a role for which Hughes is the willing successor as he pushes beyond the gentility principle to betray the animal passions in the parlour or the death-skull hidden behind the complacent smirks of acquaintances. Hughes finds in Owen's motives the template for all such revelations, and by seeming to cite the photographs as anterior to Parnell's parliamentary performance, he ensures that the First World War remains the point of origin to which the meaning of all other experiences should be referred. There is, nevertheless, a complication. Not content with embellishing the story of Owen's photographs, Hughes distorts Owen's temperament in the process. Far from pushing the truth of war into the shocked faces of his 'non-participant fellow citizens', Owen spoke only once about his photographs, and never showed them—a withholding which Jon Stallworthy attributes to his 'characteristic delicacy'.[24] In Hughes's misreading comes a sign that some new external force has disrupted his dependence on the First World War which fashioned his imagination. Hughes remakes Owen in another's image: the poet who photographed war's horrors, and who made plans to have his photographs published, was Keith Douglas.

Like Owen, Douglas goes underreported in discussions of the influences on Hughes's work; as Edna Longley notes, 'studies of Hughes—far more abundant than of Douglas—make little room for an obvious ancestor and inspiration'.[25] Again, Hughes's prose writings make the case explicitly, and again they have been taken at less than their word. 'Speaking of Keith Douglas in 1964,' Seamus Heaney observes, 'Hughes could have been speaking of himself';[26] 'Hughes's comments on Keith Douglas's language shed light on his own practice,' Paul Bentley maintains;[27] Gifford and Roberts use terminology from Hughes's account of Douglas to demonstrate 'his own most characteristic style';[28] Ekbert Faas finds in *Wodwo* a strategy reminiscent of something Hughes had defined 'in the later poetry of Keith Douglas'.[29] These are throw-away remarks which give the impression of a happy coincidence: not one of the critics stops to wonder why Hughes should sound like he is discussing his own poetry when he discusses Douglas's. Hughes himself, in his introduction to Douglas's poetry, is explicit about his obligation, praising 'an achievement for which we who come after can be grateful': 'His poetry in general seems to be of some special value. It is still very much alive, and even providing life.'[30] As Sylvia Plath reported to her mother in June 1962, she and Hughes felt Douglas's loss with keen immediacy: 'Both of us mourn this poet immensely and feel he would have been like a lovely big brother to us. His death is really a terrible blow and we are trying to resurrect his image and poems'.[31] Evidence for that admiration comes not least from *Lupercal*, where Douglas's influence is among the most significant factors to distinguish the collection from its predecessor, *The Hawk in the Rain*, especially in its attitudes to violence.

Drowning in the mud of his battlefield landscape, the poet of 'The Hawk in the Rain' had noticed the hawk hanging effortlessly above him, 'Steady as a hallucination in the streaming air'.[32] This is a hubris punished by the hawk's imagined death at the poem's end, as the 'ponderous shires crash on him'. By contrast, Hughes's persona remains earthbound and embattled, a passive sufferer without hope of reprieve. In *Lupercal*'s 'Hawk Roosting', poetry has taken wing and become predatory, giving voice to the hawk which proudly asserts its right to kill where it pleases. Hughes himself provides the best assessment of this psychology, discovering

> one of those characters of supreme, heartless professionalism but supreme 'essence', such as Gourdjieff describes, gazing a whole day over the sights of a rifle, waiting for the traveller. What is distinctive about it is just that 'essence', that individualized temper superior to all circumstances, the diamond quality that has already survived the ultimate ordeals, a salamander quality that can act, and can remain intact and effective—and even feel at home—in the fires of the end.[33]

Hughes happens to be talking about Douglas's 'How to Kill', yet his commentary perfectly captures the essence of his own killer, a hawk undistracted by 'falsifying dream[s]': 'My manners are tearing off heads'.[34] The hawk's 'supreme, heartless professionalism' flies 'Through the bones of the living', and it asserts ownership of Creation without concerning itself with finicking debates about its entitlement to behave in this way: 'No arguments assert my right'. The hawk's is a temper 'superior to all circumstances'; 'The sun is behind me', it boasts, turning the life-giving force of the universe into a supporter and a hunting aid.

Hughes's selective interpretation of Douglas's poem applies more satisfactorily to the narrower tonal range of his own. 'Hawk Roosting' is 'How to Kill' rewritten for the natural world, although Hughes neglects both Douglas's metaphysical dimension and his nimble transactions between the brutal and the delicate. Roy Fuller's misguided criticism of Douglas as an 'incipient fascist'[35] isolates and recoils from the single aspect of Douglas's work which most influences Hughes: the belief that killing and being killed, as Hughes argues in relation to Douglas's poetry, are the touchstone epiphanies of 'the cruelty—or indifference—of a purely material Creation.'[36] This is the same upper-case 'Creation' to which the hawk refers: 'It took the whole of Creation | To produce my foot, my each feather: | Now I hold Creation in my foot || Or fly up, and revolve it all slowly'. Might is right, and there is no higher court of appeal. However, the open invitation of 'Hawk Roosting' to extrapolate back to the human realm incurs serious difficulties. Hughes has stated that he wrote the poem with the idea that 'in this hawk Nature is thinking';[37] but a nature which thinks is no longer nature. The literary and historical sources have not been fully subsumed: in the same interview Hughes goes on to admit that the hawk sounds like 'Hitler's familiar spirit'. Turning nature into a Nazi, he makes Nazism seem natural.

The evident dangers of this interchange between human society and the natural world lead Hughes to agitate on behalf of his portrayals of violence. His riposte to those critics who condemn such portrayals as glorifying militarism follows a line of defence—or, more accurately, counterattack—inspired by the war poets' insistence that a society which requires its young men to kill strangers and die on its behalf is obliged not to turn away from truthful reports of wartime experience, no matter how horrific and morally discomfiting they may be. Hughes's modern-day equivalent of this hypocritical desire to evade is the 'vigorous human carnivore' who leaves the room sickened by 'the behaviour of predators killing and eating' on television:

> For all who are horrified by this predation on the screen, our own internal involvement in the killing and eating of animals can only exist as an equally horrifying crime. And beneath it, but inseparable from it, moves our extraordinary readiness to exploit, oppress, torture and kill our own kind, refining on the way all the varieties of the lie and all the pleasures of watching others suffer.[38]

The Nazism of 'Hawk Roosting'—if it can be called Nazism—becomes justified by Hughes's belief that most of us are, in effect, Nazis: given the opportunity, he continues, 'most people will dutifully, zealously, zestfully inflict ultimate pain on others'. Like his story of Owen's photographs, Hughes aims to depict a violence which shocks society with this truth about itself and its actions. However, the ambition differs from that of Owen and other First World War poets in one critical respect: whereas Owen mourns soldiers who 'die as cattle',[39] Hughes dwells on active violation rather than passive suffering. Talking of the spectacle of 'lions killing and eating a zebra' on our television screens, he allows no doubt that we as humans should identify with the predators and not their prey.[40] As the relationship between 'How to Kill' and 'Hawk Roosting' already suggests, it is Douglas who informs this predator's vision and the moral questions which accrue. The central drama of Douglas's poetry, in which the survivor or killer surveys the dead, provides Hughes with a tableau for considering what he calls 'this strange tacit criminality of ours'.[41]

Lupercal interrogates this criminality through its abundance of corpses. Everywhere the poet stumbles across death and what remains after death, whether it be the last wolf killed in Britain, the woman sinking into the hospital pillow, the stoat nailed to a door, the pig spread across a barrow, the shore's flotsam of indigestible bones (one of which becomes a 'cenotaph'—again shadowed by memory of war[42]), the two pike high and dry in the willow-herb, or the ragged dog-fox hanging from a beam. One source for this morbid fascination is Edward Thomas's 'The Gallows', described by David Bromwich as the 'ur-Hughes poem',[43] in which the keeper shoots and hangs up weasels, crows, and magpies. Its influence is most conspicuous in Hughes's 'November' which ends, like Thomas's poem, by confronting a row of carcasses on an oak:

And many other beasts
And birds, skin, bone and feather,
Have been taken from their feasts
And hung up there together,
To swing and have endless leisure
In the sun and in the snow,
Without pain, without pleasure,
On the dead oak tree bough.
(Thomas, 'The Gallows')[44]

The keeper's gibbet had owls and hawks
By the neck, weasels, a gang of cats, crows:
Some, stiff, weightless, twirled like dry bark bits

In the drilling rain. Some still had their shape,
Had their pride with it; hung, chins on chests,

Patient to outwait these worst days that beat
Their crowns bare and dripped from their feet.
(Hughes, 'November')[45]

The poems arrive at similar destinations by significantly different routes. Thomas, writing during the First World War, never flinches from the victims' fate. Each stanza tells the same story and ends with the inevitable deathly refrain. Having been seen alive in the sun with their families, thieving and murdering, talking and acting, the animals are 'taken from their feasts': the poem presents an idyllic before and a dismal after, paralleling the outbreak of the First World War, to engage the reader's sympathy. However, Hughes's 'November' claims no prior knowledge of the animals' existence, and generates no pathos for their deaths. The poem starts with another corpse—'The month of the drowned dog'—and takes a detour to gaze at a tramp surprisingly alive: 'I took him for dead, || But his stillness separated from the death | Of the rotting grass and the ground.' The blurred distinction between living and dead is learnt from Douglas, but so is the poem's technique of steering between external facts and internal psychology. Whereas Thomas effaces himself in 'The Gallows', Hughes not only looks, but looks at himself looking: 'I stayed on under the welding cold || Watching the tramp's face glisten'. It is a way of implicating the self in the scene, so that the act of looking enters the moral realm, and judgement can be passed on the living as well as the dead. That judgement is damning, because the vision of the keeper's gibbet uncovers a transferred hostility. 'November' embodies a powerful refinement of, in Hughes's terms, 'the pleasures of watching others suffer'. The tramp has no more 'shape' or 'pride' than the recently slain animals which, like him and with equal futility, outwait the weather. Having mistakenly assumed the tramp dead, the poem makes every effort to restore that first impression.

Hughes considers the highest human inspiration to be predatory, and compares Mozart's brain with the thrush's 'bullet and automatic | Purpose' as it eats worms or the shark hungrily attacking its own blood-wound ('Thrushes').[46] The corpses in *Lupercal* therefore constitute victims of artistic violence; as Bromwich has argued, Hughes's 'tender intimacy with dead things, or with things void of all impulse, is the repose of a spent aggression'.[47] The equanimity with which the gamekeeper's gibbet is seen in 'November' suggests a passion satisfied after the subliminally angry encounter with the tramp. It is less Thomas's 'The Gallows' than Douglas's '*Vergissmeinnicht*', complimented by Hughes for being 'as final and universal an image of one of the ultimate battle experiences as exists on any page',[48] which provides the model for such poetry. Inspecting the dead enemy three weeks after the fury of battle, Douglas admits to feeling almost contented. Hughes's version of this confrontation between living and dead, transferred into the animal realm, is 'View of a Pig', the title of which explains why Hughes should write about the carcass at all: the ethics and psychology of viewing, as much as the object on view, excite the poem. 'View of a Pig' is not a sustained gaze, as Hughes and others have claimed.[49] Rather, it consists of a disappointment constantly reiterated: the pig is 'less than lifeless', 'too dead', 'Too deadly factual'.[50] The poet wants his emotions provoked, but thumps the carcass 'without feeling remorse', and finds it 'Too dead now to pity'. Owen's characteristic response, of pity, is not possible. Nor is Douglas's: Douglas had felt 'amused' (in another important poem for Hughes, 'How to Kill') at the sight of a dead German, but Hughes glumly observes that his pig 'was not a figure of fun'. Hughes considers bringing the dead to life by remembering the 'earthly pleasure' the pig once enjoyed, but quickly dismisses it as 'off the point'. Nevertheless, he temporarily circumvents his own objection and breaks out of the scene's inertia:

> Once I ran at a fair in the noise
> To catch a greased piglet
> That was faster and nimbler than a cat,
> Its squeal was the rending of metal.
>
> Pigs must have hot blood, they feel like ovens.
> Their bite is worse than a horse's—
> They chop a half-moon clean out.
> They eat cinders, dead cats.

Douglas recalls in '*Vergissmeinnicht*' how the German had once tried to kill him. Hughes's attempt to turn the object of his gaze into a dangerous antagonist is inevitably less successful (as illustrated by the comic descent into the eating of cinders and dead cats), despite assigning to the pig a predator's bite and a vicious squeal. The poem fails to generate and spend its aggression, and ends with the resigned acknowledgement that the dead pig had 'long finished with' the porcine distinctions of its living brethren. 'I stared at it a long time,' the poet insists, but the pig resolutely refuses to meet his challenge. The poem is an exercise in frustration: no matter how long he stares and how hard he thumps, the war poem that Hughes wants to write cannot be written about a pig.

'View of a Pig' communicates a telling discontent with its own accomplishment: like *Lupercal* as a whole, it fails for reasons which Hughes, later determining to 'get rid of the entire body of preoccupation', fully appreciates.

Whether re-creating trench warfare or transposing the dramas of war on to the natural world, his first two books lack the immediacy and ethical danger evidenced by the poetry of his older family members, Owen and Douglas. Hughes is never able to disown their influence: for example, *Crow*'s 'black beast' is Douglas's 'bête noire';[51] the serpent's 'dark intestine' to which 'Theology' assigns humankind is the 'volatile huge intestine' which swallows everything in Douglas's 'Time Eating';[52] and the trench horrors of *Wolfwatching* (in the Owen-titled 'Anthem for Doomed Youth', for example) resurrect an early ambition to enact the father's experience and the father-poet's style. Yet, from *Wodwo* onwards, Hughes endeavours to break out of the gloomy, ghost-ridden repose of what he describes in 'Anthem for Doomed Youth' as 'war's drizzling afterdawn'.[53] *Wodwo* is the work of a poet no longer satisfied with his own belatedness. Its opening poem, 'Thistles', signposts a new attitude to the war poets' legacy. Each of the thistles is

> a revengeful burst
> Of resurrection, a grasped fistful
> Of splintered weapons and Icelandic frost thrust up
>
> From the underground stain of a decayed Viking.
> They are like pale hair and the gutturals of dialects.
> Every one manages a plume of blood.
>
> Then they grow grey, like men.
> Mown down, it is a feud. Their sons appear,
> Stiff with weapons, fighting back over the same ground.[54]

The poem refers to the First World War legend that poppies draw their colour from the blood of the dead men buried amongst their roots. In doing so, it owes a debt to Blunden's 'I must go over the ground again' via Douglas's 'Returning over the nightmare ground'.[55] 'Thistles' therefore 'fight[s] back over the same ground', except that Hughes for the first time finds a prior myth which denies the war its privileged place as prime mover. Challenging his indebtedness even as he confesses it, Hughes portrays history as cyclical: violence becomes resurrected into each new generation, reducing the First World War to merely a local instance of some archetypal and organic pattern. Hughes clears imaginative space for himself not by disavowing the inevitability of fighting the wars of the fathers, but by stressing that the fathers were themselves bound to this repetitive inheritance. There can be no escape from the battleground in which Hughes's poetry finds itself obliged to operate.

Hughes's new approach to war has been initiated by his need to establish a less subordinate relationship with his war-poet predecessors. The thistles are his befitting emblems of adversity, the products of a panoramic vision which refuses to be confined within the narrower prospects apparent in *The Hawk in the Rain* and *Lupercal*. A new, historically unspecific figure crosses the poetic terrain of *Wodwo*, spotted first when a fern dances 'like the plume | Of a warrior returning' ('Fern').[56] His kin reappear in 'The Warriors of the North', which indulges in some dubious genealogy to discover the blood of marauding Vikings in 'the iron arteries of Calvin'.[57] The 'blood-crossed Knight' or 'Holy Warrior' finally reveals his true identity in 'Gog' as he rides across the womb of stone and 'Out under the blood-dark archway'.[58] This is no Sir Gawain slaying wolves and wodwos while honourably pursuing his pilgrimage. The warrior is identified as man—*vir* perhaps more than *homo*—whose weapons of lance or gun may be historically determined, but whose bellicose nature confirms that war is an unavoidable part of the human (or at least, human male's) condition. Similarly, in 'Karma', Hughes insists that violence ordains evolutionary design: 'a hundred and fifty million years of hunger | Killing gratefully as breathing | Moulded the heart and the mouth || That cry for milk'. To distinguish between the many wars and atrocities of history misses the point of their karmic repetitiveness:

> When the world-quaking tears were dropped
> At Dresden at Buchenwald
> Earth spewed up the bones of the Irish.
>
> Queen Victoria refused the blame
> For the Emperors of Chou herding their rubbish
> Into battle roped together.
>
> The seven lamented millions of Zion
> Rose musically through the frozen mouths
> Of Russia's snowed-under millions.[59]

And so on, potentially ad infinitum: 'Karma', like 'Hawk Roosting', is sustained by Hughes's belief that we are most of us willing to inflict ultimate pain on others. Queen Victoria may have refused the blame, but we, presented with what is in effect another of Wilfred Owen's photographs, are encouraged to admit our criminal humanity.

Hughes is recorded as saying in 1962 that 'you can't deal directly with Vietnam horror, it's much more effective to set it in the time-scale of history.'[60] (That generalized 'you' does not seem to accommodate the war's combatants.)

Acknowledging the civilian's inability to forge a poetry of witness, Hughes insists on a perspective wide enough to begin transforming history into myth. Recent wars become more manageably proportioned when they can be interpreted as the consequences of an unalterable law, in which soldiers are haunted by dead predecessors and doomed successors, all 'concentrating | Toward a repeat performance'.[61] Yet, despite his determination to distance himself from the wars of Owen and Douglas, Hughes cannot give them up. 'Bowled Over' and 'Scapegoats and Rabies' (the latter published only in the American edition of *Wodwo*) revisit the battlefield of modern warfare, while 'The Wound' is an unperformable and virtually unreadable psychodrama of a shell-shocked survivor. And 'Out', the poem which Hughes wrote to coax himself away from the First World War, resists its author's palpable designs with a success which accentuates the impossibility of his task.

The tripartite structure of 'Out' attempts to map the poet's progress towards freedom. The title refers to being armed on the battlefield, but also gestures to Hughes's desire to rid himself of the damned spot of war. The poem's first section, ironically titled 'The Dream Time', observes the 4-year-old child as his father's 'luckless double' trapped by war's remnants and unable to 'move from shelter'. However, the following section finds release even for the war-dead: rewriting Christian resurrection ('the dead man in the cave'), Hughes shows the 'reassembled infantryman' reborn as 'just another baby'; and for once he resists the temptation to pursue the cycle to the next instalment of destruction.[62] The prospect of new beginnings leaves the third section to denounce the poppy and all that it represents as responsible for weighing down the poet's 'juvenile neck'. As if finally shaking off that yoke, Hughes ends by rejecting the rites of remembrance, including the 'cenotaphs' which nourished him for so long:

> So goodbye to that bloody-minded flower.
>
> You dead bury your dead.
>
> Goodbye to the cenotaphs on my mother's breasts.
>
> Goodbye to all the remaindered charms of my father's survival.
>
> Let England close. Let the green sea-anemone close.[63]

Goodbye to all that: but it is an equivocal kind of renunciation which must still express itself in the language of the thing it renounces. Nor does a poet capable of describing his mother's nipples as cenotaphs seem a likely candidate for successful rehabilitation. Hughes's recidivistic mind, moulded by war and the literature of war, cannot deny its own identity, whether by outright abdications or by attempting to escape into the natural world. A poem he writes two decades later, about narcissi swaying in the wind, suddenly and unexpectedly evokes

> a rustling, silent film
> Of speeded-up dancing
> And laughing children
> From the 1918 Armistice.[64]

But for Hughes's poetry, the Armistice is never signed.

Notes

1. From a transcript of Ted Hughes reading at the Adelaide Festival, Mar. 1987, accessed at http://www.zeta.org.au/-annskea/Adetaide.htm on 15 May 2003.
2. Ted Hughes, 'The Rock', in Geoffrey Summerfield (ed.), *World: Seven Modern Poets* (Harmondsworth: Penguin, 1974), 126.
3. Ted Hughes at the Adelaide Festival, Mar. 1987.
4. Ted Hughes, 'Postscript 1: Douglas and Owen', in *Winter Pollen: Occasional Prose*, ed. William Scammell (London: Faber, 1994), 215.
5. Hughes, 'The Rock', 126.
6. The closest to an exception is Dennis Walder, whose *Ted Hughes* (Milton Keynes: Open University Press, 1987) spends 14 pages considering Hughes and war.
7. Terry Gifford and Neil Roberts, *Ted Hughes: A Critical Study* (London: Faber, 1981), 84.
8. Hughes, 'Postscript 1: Douglas and Owen', 215.
9. Hughes, 'Introduction', in Keith Douglas, *The Complete Poems*, ed. Desmond Graham (Oxford: Oxford University Press, 1987), p. xxvi.
10. Ibid, p. xxvii.
11. Ibid, p. xxi.
12. Paul Fussell, *The Great War and Modern Memory* (Oxford: Oxford University Press, 1975), 79–82.
13. Francis Hope, quoted in Jon Silkin, *Out of Battle: The Poetry of the Great War* (Oxford: Oxford University Press, 1972), 347–8.
14. Hughes, *Collected Poems*, ed. Paul Keegan (London: Faber, 2003), 19.
15. Wilfred Owen to Susan Owen, 16 Jan. 1917, in *Collected Letters*, ed. Harold Owen and John Bell (Oxford: Oxford University Press, 1967), 427.
16. Hughes, *Collected Poems*, 43.
17. Hughes, 'Keith Douglas', in *Winter Pollen*, 213.
18. Wilfred Owen, *The Complete Poems and Fragments*, i: *The Poems*, ed. Jon Stallworthy (London: Chatto & Windus, Hogarth Press, and Oxford University Press, 1983), 140.
19. Ibid. 193.
20. Hughes, *Collected Poems*, 101.
21. Hughes, 'Orghast: Talking without Words', in *Winter Pollen*, 122–3.

22. Hughes, *Collected Poems*, 60–1.

23. Hughes, 'Introduction', in Douglas, *The Complete Poems*, p. xxxi.

24. Jon Stallworthy, *Wilfred Owen* (Oxford and London: Oxford University Press and Chatto, 1974), 222.

25. Edna Longley, '"Shit or Bust": The Importance of Keith Douglas', in *Poetry in the Wars* (Newcastle: Bloodaxe, 1986), 94.

26. Seamus Heaney, 'Englands of the Mind', in *Preoccupations: Selected Prose 1968–1978* (London: Faber, 1980), 157.

27. Paul Bentley, *The Poetry of Ted Hughes: Language, Illusion & Beyond* (Harlow: Longman, 1998), 27.

28. Gifford and Roberts, *Ted Hughes*, 27.

29. Ekbert Faas, *Ted Hughes: The Unaccommodated Universe* (Santa Barbara, Calif: Black Sparrow Press, 1980), 18.

30. Hughes, 'Keith Douglas', 215, 212.

31. Sylvia Plath, quoted in Cornelia Pearsall, 'Complicate Me When I'm Dead: The War Remains of Douglas and Hughes', a paper given at the MLA, San Diego, 27 Dec. 2003.

32. Hughes, *Collected Poems*, 19.

33. Hughes, 'Introduction', p. xxv.

34. Hughes, *Collected Poems*, 69.

35. Roy Fuller, quoted in William Scammell, *Keith Douglas: A Study* (London: Faber, 1988), 210.

36. Hughes, 'Introduction', p. xxiii.

37. 'Ted Hughes and *Crow*', interviewed by Ekbert Faas, *London Magazine*, 10/10 (Jan. 1971), 10.

38. Hughes, 'Poetry and Violence', in *Winter Pollen*, 256.

39. Owen, 'Anthem for Doomed Youth', in *Complete Poems and Fragments*, i. 99.

40. Hughes, 'Poetry and Violence', 257.

41. Ibid.

42. Hughes, 'Relic', in *Collected Poems*, 78.

43. David Bromwich, 'Ted Hughes's *River*', in *Skeptical Music: Essays on Modern Poetry* (Chicago: University of Chicago Press, 2001), 164.

44. Edward Thomas, 'The Gallows', in *Collected Poems*, ed. R. George Thomas (Oxford: Oxford University Press, 1981), 115–16.

45. Hughes, 'November', in *Collected Poems*, 81–2.

46. Hughes, 'November', in *Collected Poems*, 82.

47. Bromwich, 'Ted Hughes's *River*', 166.

48. Hughes, 'Introduction', p. xxv.

49. See Ted Hughes, *Poetry in the Making* (London: Faber, 1969), 58–61.

50. Hughes, *Collected Poems*, 76.

51. Hughes, *Collected Poems*, 223; Douglas, *Complete Poems*, 118.

52. Hughes, *Collected Poems*, 161; Douglas, *Complete Poems*, 71.

53. Hughes, *Collected Poems*, 762.

54. Ibid. 147.

55. See Scammell, *Keith Douglas*, 105. I am indebted to Dawn Bellamy for extending the connection between Blunden and Douglas to include Hughes.

56. Hughes, *Collected Poems*, 153.

57 Ibid. 167.

58. Ibid. 163–4.
59. Ibid. 167–8.
60. Hughes, quoted by Rand Brandes, 'Hughes, History and the World in Which We Live', in Keith Sagar (ed.), *The Challenge of Ted Hughes* (Basingstoke: Macmillan, 1994), 142.
61. Hughes, 'Scapegoats and Rabies', *Collected Poems*, 187.
62. Hughes, *Collected Poems*, 165–6.
63. Hughes, *Collected Poems*, 166.
64. Hughes, 'Narcissi', ibid. 709.

KEITH SAGAR

D.H. Lawrence *'New, Strange Flowers':* Pansies, Nettles *and* Last Poems

Between the beginning of 1923 and the end of 1928 Lawrence wrote only a handful of poems. When he resumed, it was to write a very different kind of poetry from *Birds, Beasts and Flowers.* Whatever reservations we may have about *The Plumed Serpent,* the American fiction certainly engaged the whole of Lawrence's imaginative effort in a way the fiction of the immediate post-war years had not. The return to Europe in 1925 coincided with a restoration of Lawrence's concern with and for the human world, and that concern expressed itself in fiction (and in the imaginative prose of *Etruscan Places*) up to the completion of *The Escaped Cock* in July 1928.

Lawrence had never fully recovered from the haemorrhages of July 1927. Neither inhalation treatment at Baden nor six weeks at Les Diablerets at four thousand feet had done any good. In July 1928 he wrote his last works of fiction. From this time forth he had the strength to produce only short newspaper articles, essays, poems, paintings, and the unfinished *Apocalypse.*

In October the Lawrences went to the island of Port-Cros to stay with the Aldingtons, who had a fortress there. La Vigie. Frieda had brought a raging cold from Italy and gave it to Lawrence, who struggled up to the Vigie but was too ill to go out again. The following week he had haemorrhages again, and stayed in bed reading the deeply hurtful reviews of *Lady Chatterley's Lover,* 'the most evil outpouring that has ever besmirched the literature of our country', according to John Bull [CH 278]. Aldington recalled:

> It seems to me one up to Lawrence that he went tranquilly on with his writing although he was so ill, and was angry and bitter about the attacks on him in England. Every morning he sat up in bed, wearing an old hat as protection against an imaginary draught, and produced a short story or one of the little essays of *Assorted Articles*. He must also have been working secretly on *Pansies*, for two of them were inspired by books he read on the island. One was Aldous Huxley's *Point Counter Point* and the other a book on Attila. [CB iii. 254]

In fact, Lawrence wrote no short stories there, though he did finish his translation of Il Lasca's *The Story of Dr Manente*, corrected the proofs of 'The Blue Moccasins', and lengthened 'Rawdon's Roof' by five pages. The essays were 'Is England Still a Man's Country?', 'Sex Versus Loveliness' and 'Do Women Change?'

Lawrence actually blamed Aldington and Huxley for his illness on Port Cros. On 28 October he wrote to Huxley:

> If you can only palpitate to murder, suicide, and rape, in their various degrees—and you state plainly that it is so—*caro*, however are we going to live through the days? Preparing still another murder, suicide, and rape? But it becomes of a phantasmal boredom and produces ultimately inertia, inertia, inertia and final atrophy of the feelings. Till, I suppose, comes a final super-war, and murder, suicide, rape sweeps away the vast bulk of mankind. It is as you say—intellectual appreciation does not amount to so much, it's what you thrill to. And if murder, suicide, rape is what you thrill to, and nothing else, then it's your destiny—you can't change it mentally. [. . .] It's amazing how men are like that. Richard Aldington is exactly the same inside, murder, suicide, rape—with a desire to be raped very strong—same thing really—just like you—only he doesn't face it, and gilds his perverseness. It makes me feel ill, I've had more hemorrhage here and been in bed this week. [L vi. 601]

The first draft of *Pansies* must have been started at this time. The second poem, 'What Matters', is very close to this letter:

> As one of our brightest young intellectuals said to me:
> What matters is what we thrill to.
> We are ultimately determined by what we thrill to
> And, of course, thrilling is like loving, you have no choice about
> it. . . .

No, when it comes to thrills, there are really very few.
Judging from the fiction it is possible to read, I should say rape was rather
thrilling
or being raped, either way, so long as it was consciously done, and slightly subtle. [CP 531–2]

The poem goes on to discuss murder and suicide. The first poem, 'The Noble Englishman', is also a savage attack on Aldington, as are several others. It is not surprising that Lawrence kept his poems to himself on Port Cros.

'What Matters' is not a bad poem, but any reader must be aware at once of the superiority of the letter. It is the depth of Lawrence's personal commitment and caring which gives the informal prose of the letter its irresistible sweep and urgency. The poem attempts to take the matter out of the area of the personal, but there is not a sharp enough edge to the satire to make up for the loss of weight, of total seriousness.

The first poem to achieve that simplicity of pure perception which is to be characteristic of the best pansies is the fifth poem in the manuscript, 'Roses', which Lawrence chose to discard:

Nature responds so beautifully.
Roses are only once-wild roses, that were given an extra chance,
So they bloomed out and filled themselves with coloured fulness
Out of sheer desire to be splendid, and more splendid. [831]

There soon followed several more beautiful tiny poems, of four or five lines. 'The Gazelle Calf' and 'Little Fish' are well known. 'New Moon' is equally fine:

The new moon, of no importance
lingers behind as the yellow sun glares and is gone beyond the sea's
edge;
earth smokes blue;
the new moon, in cool height above the blushes,
brings a fresh fragrance of heaven to our senses. [467]

Here, perhaps, is the first faint hint of the theme of death. In *Last Poems* the yellow sun of life will again sink into the sea, and a full moon will preside over the passage through blue darkness to renewed life.

The nineteenth and twentieth poems, 'The Mess of Love' and 'Fidelity', seem to be by-products of the essay 'Do Women Change?' (written between

5 and 8 November). The essay ends with the statement that love is a flow; it flowers and fades: 'If flowers didn't fade they wouldn't be flowers, they'd be artificial things. But there are roots to faded flowers and in the root the flow continues and continues' [P II 542]. 'The Mess of Love' goes no further than the essay. 'Fidelity' reaches the conclusion of the essay by its mid-point:

> Embalmed flowers are not flowers, immortelles are not flowers;
> flowers are just a motion, a swift motion, a coloured gesture;
> that is their loveliness. And that is love. [476]

(The poems themselves are to be just such transient coloured gestures.) But the poem goes deeper. All life is a flow, not only that which seems, by the human time-scale, ephemeral. At the opposite pole is the slow flowing of a sapphire

> the sapphire of fidelity.
> The gem of mutual peace emerging from the wild chaos of love.
> [477]

Richard Hoggart has characterized Lawrence's distinctive voice in *Pansies* as 'the voice of a down-to-earth, tight, bright, witty Midlander . . . slangy, quick, flat and direct, lively, laconic, sceptical, nonconforming, nicely bloody-minded'. Indeed, that voice is often heard; but so are many others. Often, and we have heard it already, there is the tender voice of true feeling, the naked voice of the man without a mask. At the other extreme, there are the voices not his own, in poems where he exercises his great gift of mimicry, as, for example, in 'What Ails Thee?', a dialogue, as it might be, between a gamekeeper and his uncompliant mistress, impervious to the 'Robbie Burns touch' [540].

The first title Lawrence intended to use for his new poems was *Pensées*. Some of Pascal's *Pensées* are like sharp little poems: 'Le nez de Cléopatre: s'il eût été plus court, toute la face de la terre aurait changé'. But, rather than any sense of debt to or affinity with Pascal, it was probably more his need to write what could be produced without taxing imaginative effort, his desire to communicate with a larger audience than that which 'art' poetry commands, and his need, time being short now, to encapsulate his ideas, which led him to jot down loosely versified thoughts, the poetic equivalent of the newspaper articles he was writing at the same time. And the possibility of the pun on pansies must have occurred to him at an early stage. The pansy was a perfect flower for his purpose. He needed something unpretentious and unselfconscious and ephemeral. He wanted his poems to have the quality which had so attracted him in Etruscan art:

> Myself, I like to think of the little wooden temples of the early Greeks and of the Etruscans: small, dainty, fragile, and evanescent as flowers. [. . .] all vivid and fresh and unimposing. The whole thing small and dainty in proportion, and fresh, somehow charming instead of impressive. [SEP 32]

Poems such as the man who had died, smiling to himself, might have casually jotted down. Most of all he wanted to avoid the kind of art which seems 'too much cooked in the artistic consciousness' [206].

The word pansy in fact derives from the French pensée. But by analogy with daisy, which means day's eye, Lawrence may have also thought of the false derivation of pansy from Pan's eye. Each pansy is intended to be 'a true thought, which comes as much from the heart and the genitals as from the head. A thought, with its own blood of emotion and instinct running in it like the fire in a fire-opal' [CP 417]. They are therefore the thoughts of the demon, at their best as subversive of ordinary thinking as Blake's 'Proverbs of Hell'. The 'Retort to Jesus', for example, is the demon's retort:

> And whoever forces himself to love anybody
> begets a murderer in his own body. [653]

At the end of *More Pansies* the demon announces himself in 'Demon Justice' and 'Be a Demon!'

Lawrence's demonic or 'true thought' is very different from Pascal's. He defined it in the later poem 'Thought':

> Thought is the welling up of unknown life into consciousness,
> Thought is the testing of statements on the touchstone of the conscience,
> Thought is gazing on to the face of life, and reading what can be read,
> Thought is pondering over experience, and coming to a conclusion.
> Thought is not a trick, or an exercise, or a set of dodges,
> Thought is a man in his wholeness wholly attending. [673]

Four times in three consecutive poems comes the imperative 'think!', as if Lawrence were giving us a crash course in this kind of thinking. The first of these is called 'Think—!':

> Imagine what it must have been to have existence
> in the wild days when life was sliding whirlwinds, blue-hot weights,

> in the days called chaos, which left us rocks, and gems!
> Think that the sapphire is only alumina, like kitchen pans
> crushed utterly, and breathed through and through
> with fiery weight and wild life, and coming out
> clear and flowery bluc! [529–30]

To think is to imagine. These poems are exercises for the atrophied imagination, little acts of pure attention producing fragments of life-knowledge.

Lawrence's own life-knowledge, acquired by this means, he confidently opposes to orthodox scientific knowledge in, for example, 'Self-Protection'. This is the first of many poems, most of them in *Last Poems*, where a scientific or philosophical theory is wittily undermined, and then replaced by a theory which Lawrence makes to seem like the merest common sense, though in fact a product of his own uncommon sensibility. Here it is the theory of 'protective coloration' in animals, which makes 'self-protection the first law of existence'. The vulgar error to be demolished is deliberately expressed in lifeless and abstract formulary prose. As it turns to look at living creatures, the language comes alive:

> A tiger is striped and golden for his own glory.
> He would certainly be much more invisible if he were grey-green.

Sheer vivacity of language almost guarantees the validity of Lawrence's alternative theory:

> As a matter of fact, the only creatures that seem to survive
> Are those that give themselves away in flash and sparkle
> and gay flicker of joyful life;
> those that go glittering abroad
> with a bit of splendour. [523]

* * *

The Lawrences left Port Cros ('that poky island') on 17 November for Bandol. Lawrence's room at the Hotel Beau Rivage looked south over the sea. Four days later he wrote to Maria Huxley:

> It is incredibly lovely weather, and the place very lovely, swimming with milky gold light at sunset, and white boats half melted on the white twilight sea. [L vii. 21)

The world seemed simplified down to its elements, sun, moon and sea:

> We don't know how lovely the elements are.
> Why trouble about people?
> The sun is so lovely.
> If a man looked at me for one moment as the sun does
> I could accept men.
> If twilight came in the eyes of women
> As it comes over the milk-blue sea, hinting at gold and darkness,
> Oh lovely women! [CP 840]

As sometimes happens in *Pansies*, the freshness and simplicity of the original perception in the first draft is lost as Lawrence later 'develops' it into something more like conventional thoughts. Neither 'Elemental' nor 'I Wish I Knew a Woman' can preserve the freshness of their source-poem 'The Elements'.

Gazing every day out to sea at the setting sun of November, Lawrence felt his own affinity with it:

> A few gold rays thickening down to red
> as the sun of my soul is setting
> setting fierce and undaunted, wintry
> but setting, setting behind the sounding sea between my ribs.
> The wide sea wins, and the dark
> winter, and the great day-sun, and the sun in my soul
> sinks, sinks to setting and the winter solstice
> downward, they race in decline
> my sun, and the great gold sun. [455]

Many of the poems in *Pansies* fall into clusters of several variations on the same theme. A group which Lawrence may have begun on 23 November is typical. The theme is 'peace', especially that inward peace which comes from roots that go 'deep beyond the world of man', bringing him a 'natural abundance' and nobility which Lawrence contrasts with mere riches [499]. Within each group there are usually some poems of bald, prosaic assertion which fall flat:

> I would rather sit still in a state of peace on a stone
> than ride in the motorcar of a multimillionaire
> and feel the peacelessness of the multimillionaire poisoning me.
> [498]

Others develop from the same basic thought towards real poems in two distinct directions. Some are amusing, mocking or self-mocking, colloquial, with deft manipulation of tone and rhythm ('What Would you Fight For'). Some, beginning flatly, become real poems, new efforts of attention and discovery, as soon as they become concrete and metaphorical. 'Poverty', for example, is nothing until the tenth line, when Lawrence ceases to assert in the abstract and looks at 'this pine tree near the sea, / that grows out of rock, and plumes forth, plumes forth':

> With its roots it has a grand grip on its daily bread,
> and its plumes look like green cups held up to the sun and air
> and full of wine. [498]

The best poem in this group is, perhaps, 'Glory':

> Glory is of the sun, too, and the sun of suns,
> and down the shafts of his splendid pinions
> run tiny rivers of peace.
> Most of his time, the tiger pads and slouches in a burning peace.
> And the small hawk high up turns round on the slow pivot of
> peace.
> Peace comes from behind the sun, with the peregrine falcon, and
> the owl.
> Yet all of these drink blood. [496]

* * *

The young Welsh novelist Rhys Davies stayed with the Lawrences for the last weekend in November:

> At this time in Bandol he was writing the satirical poems to be called *Pansies* and also painting one or two pictures. He told me he would write no more novels; Lady Chatterley's Lover was to be his last long work of fiction, the last large attempt to tell men and women how to live. For all his fury and rages, he got immense fun out of writing *Pansies*. He would write them in bed in the mornings, cheerful and chirpy, the meek sea air blowing in from the enchanting little bay outside his window ... There was something perky and bird-like about him thus, and he was intensely happy and proud of the Pansies; he would read out the newest ones with delight, accentuating the wicked sharp little pecks in them. [CB iii. 273–4]

goose
far off upon the misty waters of the depths of space
silently swimming and sleeping, and pressing the flood
with webbed fecundity, plunging the seed of life in the wet wilderness
and honking with a horn-like annunciation of life from the marshes of
chaos
something thrills in me, and I know
the next day is the day of the goose, the wild swan's day. [841]

Man has, apparently, forfeited his right to woman. If he questions her about the fatherhood of the 'little beast' she bears

will there be a whistle of wings in the air, and an icy draught?
will the singing of swans, high up, high up, invisible
break the drums of his ears
and leave him forever listening for the answer? [439]

According to the painting *Singing of Swans*, it will leave him worse than that. There angry swans swoop over men who are insanely destroying each other; dies irae, the swan-song of the race.

* * *

Most of the subsequent poems in the manuscript, the December poems, are satirical. A major breakthrough comes with Lawrence's discovery of the satirical value of rhyme. 'In Nottingham' seems merely petulant and small-minded in its original near-prose. Rhythm and rhyme transform it into the twinkling but cutting comedy of 'Nottingham's New University'. 'Red Herring' brings a new gusto into the collection:

My mother was a superior soul
a superior soul was she
cut out to play a superior role
in the god-damn bourgeoisie. [490]

In 'No! Mr Lawrence' the dull thud of the final rhyme undermines the speaker's would-be sophistication. In 'The Little Wowser' Lawrence turns his wit wryly against himself:

I think of all the little brutes
as ever was invented
that little cod's the holy worst.
I've chucked him, I've repented. [493]

On 15 December Lawrence described these poems to Maria Huxley: 'I have been doing a book of *Pensées* which I call pansies, a sort of loose little poem form; Frieda says with joy: real doggerel' [L vii. 64]. The first draft was finished by 23 December: 164 poems in two months. Immediately Lawrence wrote a little foreword defending his pansies:

> If some are only in bud, and some are a bit shrivelled-looking, c'est la vie, mon cher! That's how life is! And if there is no system, think of pansies pansily marching one after the other, still as wooden soldiers forming fours around a general! It's enough system for pansies that they all turn to the sun, and droop when they feel like it. [DF 183]

And if they have a 'peppery sort of little smell' that makes the reader sneeze, that too is part of the whole living flower: 'Live beauty will always be a bit 'shocking', and pansies will always have their roots in dung and humus'. Within a few days Lawrence wrote a much longer foreword, making bolder claims. Most of this foreword is a defence against the charge of obscenity. Prophetically, Lawrence wrote: 'Obscene means today that the policeman thinks he has a right to arrest you, nothing else' [CP 418]. By 7 January Lawrence had typed out the poems, revising and adding to them. Both copies of the typescript were sent to Pollinger on that date, and were seized by the police. At the beginning of February Lawrence 'typed them all out afresh—and revised many of course' [L vii. 176]. Secker refused to print fourteen of the more outspoken poems, so Lawrence arranged for a private edition which would include them, together with the longer foreword. For the Seeker trade edition he produced in April yet a third version of the foreword, close to the original one, and 'perfectly proper'.

The reviewers were predictably worried by the general hatred of modern life expressed in the poems, but most were prepared to take the poems on Lawrence's terms. The anonymous review in the *Times Literary Supplement* ended:

> And, while there is much modern poetry which does not seem to express anything that the poet greatly wished to say, there is scarcely a line of Mr. Lawrence's verses which does not sound like

> a piece of the author's mind, in both the obvious and the idiomatic sense of the phrase. [CH 311]

* * *

In March 1929 Lawrence went to Paris to arrange for the publication of a popular edition of *Lady Chatterley's Lover.* There he succumbed to big-city 'grippe':

> I haven't been well in Paris. Sometimes one feels as if one were drifting out of life altogether—and not terribly sorry to go. These big cities take away my real will to live. [L vii. 235]

By the end of April the Lawrences were settled in Majorca, which gave Lawrence just the relaxation he needed:

> I agree this isn't a good place for work. I have tried to paint two pictures—and each time it's been a failure and made me all on edge. So I accept the decree of destiny, and shall make no further attempt to work at all while I am in Spain. [L vii. 286]

But Lawrence did write fifty or sixty more pansies before leaving Majorca on 18 June.

In the seven months from May to November 1929, Lawrence wrote over three hundred poems. Except for those he prepared for publication, the twenty-seven in *Nettles*, the six which appeared in the 1930 *Imagist Anthology*, and the two published by the *London Mercury* in 1930 ('Bells' and 'The Triumph of the Machine'), none of these received their final revision, And many would undoubtedly have been discarded.

The demon has two distinct voices, the mischievous or jeering voice he uses to needle his enemies, and the lyrical voice, sometimes sparkling, sometimes intense and quietly rhapsodic, of his own true thinking. *More Pansies* (to adopt Aldington's title) opens with a dozen poems in the first voice, attacking various kinds of self-important people. Then, in the second voice, comes 'Andraitx—Pomegranate Flowers', a glimpse of people who are not at all self-important, insistent or self-advertising, but whose flame of life is all the brighter for being cupped in silence and darkness, like the pomegranate's 'short gasps of flame in the green of night', 'small sharp red fires in the night of leaves':

> And noon is suddenly dark, is lustrous, is silent and dark
> men are unseen, beneath the shading hats;

> only, from out the foliage of the secret loins
> red flamelets here and there reveal
> a man, a woman there. [CP 606]

The demon speaks from that dark interior of man where 'flow the heart's rivers of fulness, desire and distress' [607]. The demon is a man's naked self, when he has cast off his moral clothing:

> And if stark naked I approach a fellow-man or fellow-woman
> they must be naked too,
> and none of us must expect morality of each other:
> I am that I am, take it or leave it.
> Offer me nothing but that which you are, stark and strange.
> Let there be no accommodation at this issue. [608]

A man's demon is what keeps him 'in the rooted connection with the centre of all things' [610]. One of the names of the demon is Lucifer, who lost none of his brightness in falling, and is now due to replace the orthodox angels 'tarnished with centuries of conventionality' [614].

Frieda's sister Else called Lawrence's paintings Satanisch. Lawrence replied:

> Perhaps you are right; Lucifer is brighter now than tarnished Michael or shabby Gabriel. All things fall in their turn, now Michael goes down, and whispering Gabriel, and the Son of the Morning will laugh at them all. Yes, I am for Lucifer, who is really the Morning Star. The real principle of Evil is not anti-Christ or anti-Jehovah, but anti-life. I agree with you, in a sense, that I am with the anti-christ. Only I am not anti-life. [L vii. 331–2]

Another of the demon's names is the Holy Ghost:

> The Holy Ghost is the deepest part of our consciousness
> wherein we know ourselves for what we are
> and know our dependence on the creative beyond. [CP 621]

But modern life is a sinning against the Holy Ghost, repudiating and persecuting the demon until 'we destroy the most essential self in us'. For these self-inflicted wounds 'there is no remedy'.

In his introduction to *Pansies* Lawrence stressed the healing function of these poems:

> Or, if you will have the other derivation of pansy, from *panser*, to dress or soothe a wound; these are my tender administrations to the mental and emotional wounds we suffer from. Or you can have heartsease if you like, since the modern heart could certainly do with it. [CP 417]

(Did he know that the Elizabethans first cultivated the pansy because they believed it to contain a cure for inflammation of the lungs?)

The wound that most concerns him here is the broken connection between man and the living cosmos. In 'Fatality', he suggests that the only healing of that wound might be death:

> Death alone, through the long processes of disintegration
> can melt the detached life back
> through the dark Hades at the roots of the tree
> into the circulating sap, once more, of the tree of life. [617]

In 'Healing', he is less fatalistic. Here Lawrence sees himself as the patient as well as the healer:

> I am ill because of wounds to the soul, to the deep emotional self
> and the wounds to the soul take a long, long time, only time can help
> and patience, and a certain difficult repentance
> long, difficult repentance, realisation of life's mistake, and the
> freeing
> oneself
> from the endless repetition of the mistake
> which mankind at large has chosen to sanctify. [620]

One form that mistake has taken has been to substitute for 'dependence on the creative beyond' dependence on the machine. In 'The Triumph of the Machine', 'the man in the machine', that is the perverse will endlessly, mechanically repeating the same mistake, persecutes 'the native creatures of the soul' until they rebel and drive him mad. Then 'the edifice of our life will rock in the shock of the mad machine, and the house will come down' [624]. It is a vision of holocaust, for 'over the middle of the earth will be the smoky ruin of iron'. The 'native creatures' will survive, but only 'in the ultimate, remote places'. It is difficult to know from the first version of the poem whether the swan, the lark and the lambs of the poem's ending are still symbols of the demon within the hearts of those men who never capitulated to the machine, or whether the catastrophe eliminates man, and releases them into their animal being to begin a new day without men in the far places.

The revised version of the poem drops the apocalyptic ending completely. Now Lawrence asserts that so long as one heart harbours them, the wild creatures cannot die. 'And at last [. . .] they will hear a silence fall [. . .] as the machine breaks finally down.' It is the demon who triumphs now, in the form of a sprout of hornbeam rending the asphalt roads

> And then at last
> all the creatures that were driven back into the uttermost comers of the
> soul
> they will peep forth. [958]

* * *

The Lawrences left Majorca on 18 June, Lawrence to visit the Huxleys at Forte dei Marmi, Frieda to London to see the exhibition of Lawrence's paintings at the Warren Gallery. On 5 July the police raided the gallery and confiscated thirteen pictures deemed obscene because of the depiction of pubic hair. On the same day Lawrence was struck down in Forte with stomach pains. He travelled to Florence the following day, but was so ill that Orioli put him to bed in his own flat and sent for Frieda.

As we can see from such titles as the Blakean 'Dark Satanic Mills', 'What have they done to you?' and 'Cry of the masses', several of the poems written at Forte had expressed feelings of outraged and tender fellow-feeling:

> And though the pomegranate has red flowers outside the window
> and oleander is hot with perfume under the afternoon sun
> and I am 'il Signore' and they love me here,
> yet I am a mill-hand in Leeds
> and the death of the Black Country is upon me
> and I am wrapped in the lead of a coffin-lining, the living death of my
> fellow men. [630]

But Lawrence was so deeply hurt by the raid ('The dirty swine would like to think they made you weep' [L vii. 364]) that he repudiated his fellow men with almost incoherent disgust:

> I love my neighbour
> but
> are these things my neighbours?
> these two-legged things that walk and talk
> and eat and cachinnate, and even seem to smile
> seem to smile, ye gods!
>
> Am I told that these things are my neighbours?
>
> All I can say then is Nay! nay! nay! nay! nay! [CP 644]

Later that month, in Baden, Lawrence seems to be returning to his preoccupation with leadership. He defines true democracy as 'demos serving life', which means that 'the many must obey the few that look into the eyes of the gods' [650]. But when he turns to look himself into the eyes of the gods, a group of lovely poems follows. He sees a woman, shy and alone, washing herself under a tap, 'and the glimmer of the presence of the gods was like lilies, / and like water-lilies' [651]. The tall white corn, as it yields to the scythe, is 'the fallen stillness of god', 'the pale gold flesh of Priapus dropping asleep'. Alone, their presence makes the air still and lovely to him:

> And I fall asleep with the gods, the gods
> that are not, or that are
> according to the soul's desire,
> like a pool into which we plunge, or do not plunge. [652]

This sequence of twenty-eight poems about the gods, and what happens to us if we deny them, ends with a return to the image of the pansy, now yielding its essential heartsease:

> There is nothing to save, now all is lost,
> but a tiny core of stillness in the heart
> like the eye of a violet. [658]

Lawrence's effort in these poems 'to save the streaked pansy of the heart from being trampled to mud' carried over into the splendid essay 'The Risen Lord', where the risen Christ faces his greatest test, 'to be a man on earth':

> Now comes the true life, man living his full life on earth, as flowers live their full life, without rhyme or reason except the

> magnificence of coming forth into fullness [. . .] But this time, it would no longer be the fight of self-sacrifice that would end in crucifixion. This time it would be a freed man fighting to save the rose of life from being trampled on by the pigs. [P II 575]

One of the attributes of the risen Lord is 'the accomplished acceptance of His own death'. Lawrence's own health had declined to the point where he allowed himself to be persuaded to go with his mother-in-law to the Kurhaus Plattig. The Baroness had not accepted her death:

> She is 78, and is in a mad terror for fear she might die; and she would see me or anyone else die ten times over, to give her a bit more strength to drag on a few more meaningless years. It is so ugly and so awful, I nearly faint. I have never felt so down, so depressed and ill, as I have here these ten days: awful! [L vii. 399]

Such resistance to death implies also 'a rancid resistance / to life':

> Old men, old obstinate men and women
> dare not die, because in death
> their hardened souls are washed with fire, and washed and seared
> till they are softened back to the life-stuff again, against which they
> hardened themselves. [CP 663]

For Lawrence, closeness to death enhanced his appreciation of life:

> we can but touch, and wonder, and ponder, and make our effort
> and dangle in a last fastidious fine delight
> as the fuchsia does, dangling her reckless drop
> of purple after so much putting forth
> and slow mounting marvel of a little tree. [667]

By the end of July, Lawrence had rallied enough to write 'some nice stinging nettles, and let's hope they'll sting the arses of all the Meads and Persians of slimy London' [L vii. 411]. Frederick Mead was the eighty-two-year-old magistrate before whom Lawrence's paintings were to be tried on 8 August. In 'Innocent England' Lawrence takes up the fight against the 'hard-boiled conventionalists' with a comic verve which suggests that he is writing now not with the helpless savagery of a man at bay, but from a position of inner strength, like the twinkling mockery of the gods:

A wreath of mist is the usual thing
in the north, to hide where the turtles sing.
Though they never sing, they never sing,
don't you dare to suggest such a thing
or Mr Mead will be after you.
—But what a pity I never knew
A wreath of English mist would do
as a cache-sexe! I'd have put a whole fog. [CP 580]

* * *

But the improvement in Lawrence's health was short-lived. At the end of August, Lawrence and Frieda went to Rottach, in Bavaria, to be near Lawrence's friend Max Mohr, who was a doctor as well as a writer. Lawrence spent the first week in bed. Max Mohr brought three doctors from Munich. They prescribed a diet which included arsenic, and made Lawrence worse. 11 September was his forty-fourth birthday. In his heart of hearts he knew it would be his last.

As early as 1916, Lawrence had affirmed a very positive attitude towards death:

> Do I fear the strange approach of the creative unknown to my door? I fear it only with pain and with unspeakable joy. And do I fear the invisible dark hand of death plucking me into the darkness, gathering me blossom by blossom from the stem of my life into the unknown of my afterwards? I fear it only in reverence and with strange satisfaction. For this is my final satisfaction, to be gathered blossom by blossom, all my life long, into the finality of the unknown which is my end. [RDP 18]

Now that courage was to be put to the ultimate test. Could it be maintained through the process of actual dying? At the Kurhaus he had written of turning 'to the adventure of death, in eagerness':

I have always wanted to be as the flowers are
so unhampered in their living and dying,
and in death I believe I shall be as the flowers are.
I shall blossom like a dark pansy, and be delighted
there among the dark sun-rays of death.
I can feel myself unfolding in the dark sunshine of death

> to something flowery and fulfilled, and with a strange sweet perfume.
> Men prevent one another from being men
> but in the great spaces of death
> the winds of the afterwards kiss us into blossom of manhood. CP 677]

Death, he believes, will call out from him whatever in him can answer to the perfume of the pansy, the blueness of the gentian. And that will be his essential manhood. Did Lawrence literally believe that after death he would in some sense retain his humanity, manhood and identity? He could only discover what he truly believed by giving his whole attention to whatever images of death life brought him.

Frieda recalled:

> I remember some autumn nights when the end seemed to have come. I listened for his breath through the open door, all night long, an owl hooting ominously from the walnut tree outside. In the dim dawn an enormous bunch of gentians I had put on the floor by his bed seemed the only living thing in the room. [NI 213]

Four drafts having survived, we can follow the process by which Lawrence explored deeper and deeper levels of meaning in these Bavarian gentians. The first draft was called 'The State of Grace' [PP 228].[1] The idea of the poem is similar to that of the next poem in the manuscript, 'Flowers and Men', which begins 'Flowers achieve their own floweriness and it is a miracle' [CP 683]. By recognizing that miracle, a man's soul can enter and share the 'dark-blue godhead' of the gentian. The poem is largely descriptive. In spite of the perception that the gentians make a 'dark-blue gloom / in the sunny room', there is no image of the gentians as torches. Nor, in spite of the line 'HOW deep I have gone', is there any journey. But the first revision (interlinear) seized on that opportunity, cancelling 'in your marvellous dark-blue godhead' in favour of 'since I embarked on your dark blue fringes', and changing 'What a baptism for / my soul' to 'What a journey . . . '. The Christian terminology having disappeared, the title becomes 'Glory of darkness'. The next revision (marginal) opens up a new mythic dimension with the perception of the gentian as a dark doorway to Hades, through which Persephone has just gone back to her bridegroom, and to her 'wedding in the winter dark' [PP 229]. But in developing this idea, the theme of the journey of the poet's soul into darkness is completely lost. This he takes up in a different context in 'Ship of Death', leaving the unrealized potentialities of the 'Glory of darkness' drafts to be developed later.

On 30 August Lawrence wrote describing Rottach to Orioli: 'It is quite beautiful, and very peaceful, cows and haymaking and apples on tall apple trees, dropping so suddenly' [L vii. 455]. Three days later he was visited by his sister-in-law Else and her lover Alfred Weber. According to Frieda, when Lawrence was alone with Weber, he said to him: 'Do you see those leaves falling from the apple tree? When the leaves want to fall you must let them fall' [NI 213]. Obviously she misremembered, since no leaves would have been falling so early. It was the apples themselves Lawrence had spoken of. They provided him with the opening of 'Ship of Death':

> I sing of autumn and the falling fruit
> and the long journey towards oblivion
> The apples falling like great drops of dew
> to bruise themselves an exit from themselves. [PP 221]

Years earlier, he had responded in a similar way to medlars and sorb apples:

> The fibres of the heart parting one after the other
> And yet the soul continuing, naked-footed, ever more vividly embodied
> Like a flame blown whiter and whiter
> In a deeper and deeper darkness
> Ever more exquisite, distilled in separation. [CP 281]

Now, however, there is a new. more deeply personal urgency. The image of the falling apples is abruptly dropped, with no further development, in this draft, as Lawrence moves on to what will be, the title tells us, the controlling image:

> Have you built your ship of death, oh, have you?
> Build then your ship of death, for you will need it! [PP 221]

We hear nothing more of the ship for the moment, as the poem considers the plight of the soul for which no ship has been built 'thrust out onto the grey grey beaches of shadow / the long marginal stretches of existence crowded with lost souls'.

> Pity the poor gaunt dead that cannot die [. . .]
> but must roam like outcast dogs on the margins of life. [222]

This long section of 'Ship of Death' is later to be dropped from 'The Ship of Death' and become four separate poems, 'Difficult Death', 'All Souls' Day', 'The Houseless Dead' and 'Beware the Unhappy Dead'.

Now Lawrence turns to the ship he must build for his own soul 'with oars and food / and little dishes, and all accoutrements dainty and ready for the departing soul'. The primary source of this image is the 'little bronze ship of death' [SEP 17] which symbolized, for the Etruscans, 'the mystery of the journey out of life, and into death; the death journey, and the sojourn in the after-life' [60]. This, not only to the Etruscans, but to all the 'peoples of the great natural religions', was but 'a continuing of the great wonder-journey of life' [174]. Another important source, and a conscious one, given the Whitmanesque opening 'I sing of autumn . . . ', was Whitman's 'Passage to India', from which these lines must have come strongly back to him:

> O we can wait no longer,
> We too take ship O soul,
> Joyous we too launch out on trackless seas,
> Fearless for unknown shores on waves of ecstasy to sail.
> Amid the wafting winds (thou pressing me to thee, I thee to me,
> O soul,)
> Caroling free, singing our song of God,
> Chanting our chant of pleasant exploration. [WW 378]

At last the 'shirt of the spirit's experience' melts away, the boat 'dissolves like pearl', and the soul slips into 'the womb of silence in the living night' [PP 223]. How literally we are to take the word 'womb' is indicated by the cancelled phrase 'sperm-like', and the question with which the poem ends: can it be that the 'last lapse of death, into pure oblivion' is also 'procreation' [224]? In the later version of the poem, the idea of procreation is replaced by that of resurrection; but if we think of the Buddhist concept of the soul re-entering the womb-door after death, the two concepts cease to be distinct.

In spite of, or perhaps because of, his closeness to death at Rottach, Lawrence also wrote there, just before 'Glory of darkness' and 'Ship of Death', the most life-affirming poem in *More Pansies*, 'God is Born'. It is also a triumph of mimetic art. The poem derives from Lawrence's response to the Etruscan idea of 'the vitality of the cosmos':

> The universe, which was a single aliveness with a single soul, instantly changed, the moment you thought of it, and became a dual creature with two souls, fiery and watery, for ever mingling and rushing apart, and held by the great aliveness of the universe in

> an ultimate equilibrium. But they rushed together and they rushed apart, and immediately they became myriad: volcanoes and seas, then streams and mountains, trees, creatures, men. [SEP 57]

The opening lines of the poem mime the straining of chaos to bring forth identities:

> The history of the cosmos
> is the history of the struggle of becoming.
> When the dim flux of unformed life
> struggled, convulsed back and forth upon itself,
> and broke at last into light and dark
> came into existence as light,
> came into existence as cold shadow. [CP 682]

The verse itself struggles towards the phrase 'light and dark', thrusting them to their polar extremes with that resistant phrase 'came into existence as'. The separation of light and dark in turn creates the opposites of hot and cold, which in turn generate the next pair, condensation and evaporation—the birth of the waters and the atmosphere. Gradually all the constituents of chaos are polarized, the whole process witnessed by and participated in by the delighted atoms. It is the permanent rocking balance between these pairs of mighty opposites which is life. If that were lost, all would collapse again into chaos. The words embody the ideas, ultra-tangible, as if the poem were giving them their very first incarnation. Each stanza ends with the recognition and celebration of miracle. Throughout the aeons, as the lizard swirls his tail finer than water, as the peacock turns to the sun, and could not be more splendid, as the leopard smites the small calf with a spangled paw, perfect, the universe trembles: God is born! God is here! Lizard, peacock and leopard have one line each, but are there, splendid and perfect, with only one descriptive adjective between them, 'spangled'; for it is action, a distinctive life-mode, which conveys identity, not merely appearance. Even a flower, the narcissus, is itself for what it does: it 'lifted a tuft of five-point stars / and dangled them in the atmosphere'. How, after these, can the emergence of man be rendered as anything but an anti-climax? The greatest poetry is very simple. Here Lawrence goes with striking simplicity to the heart of the matter:

> And when at last man stood on two legs and wondered,
> then there was a hush of suspense at the core of every electron:
> Behold, now very God is born!
> God Himself is born!

We know how crucial a moment that was in evolution, when man, by standing upright, freed his hands for all sorts of creative purposes, and somehow also freed his spirit to perceive and worship the wonder of the universe. The verb to wonder can carry all the weight it needs to carry because Lawrence has already so vividly demonstrated in this poem, and in so many others, what it means.

At Rottach Lawrence heard from Frederick Carter, and resumed the relationship that was to lead to the writing of his last book, *Apocalypse*. When Carter tried, years later, to sum up Lawrence's essential beliefs, he concentrated particularly on Lawrence's deep belief in man's capacity for wonder and worship before the fall:

> Man, he asserted, then mastered things not by thought of the conscious kind only, or so much, as by the thrust of the underconscious will and desire in him. Thence came the pure physical mastery that set him upright on his two legs in defiance of nature's rule for the animal creation. Man has a pure physical poise that no other creature possesses, the power of balance, a sense of positive and negative, of good and evil—the beginnings of things as they are. [BM 54]

It was because he held so high an estimate of man's capacities, and man's place in the natural order, that Lawrence was so outraged by what men had done to themselves and to each other. The desire to hurt, in *Nettles* and the more satirical *Pansies*, is only a desire to pierce the hard shell of the modern ego, which must be done before the healing process can begin. To sting was also, perhaps, an end in itself, Lawrence's only means of defending himself against those who had persecuted Lady Chatterley and the paintings. But it was not simply a matter of revenge, since, through Lawrence, these men were, he knew, doing dirt on life itself, denying the gods in themselves and other men.

When he left Rottach in mid-September, Lawrence was physically no better, but had purged himself of anger. His next collection of poems, he told the Brewsters, would be called *Dead Nettles* 'because they were to have no sting in them' [RC 309]. All his strength and attention would be needed now to build that ship of death we know as *Last Poems*.

* * *

For months Lawrence had longed for the Mediterranean. It did not disappoint him. Ten days after his arrival in Bandol, he wrote to Else on 4 October:

> I still love the Mediterranean, it still seems young as Odysseus, in the morning. [. . .] When the morning comes, and the sea runs silvery and the distant islands are delicate and clear, then I feel again, only man is vile. [L vii. 509]

In this spirit Lawrence wrote the opening poems of *Last Poems*. In the spirit, also, of the beginning of 'Passage to India':

> The Past—the dark unfathom'd retrospect!
> The teeming gulf—the sleepers and the shadows!
> The past—the infinite greatness of the past!
> For what is the present after all but a growth out of the past?
> [WW 372]

So Lawrence in these poems, as in *Apocalypse*, which he worked on in parallel with them, discovers 'a new vision in harmony with the memories of old, far-off, far, far-off experience that lie within us' [A 54]. In this sense, the pagan gods and heroes of the ancient Mediterranean (in more than one sense Middle of the World) were more alive to Lawrence than the smoking liners which 'cross like clockwork the Minoan distance' [CP 688].

Though these are bright morning poems, with all the freshness of the dawn of our civilization, they are also poignantly autumnal, equally aware of the waning of the year. The sun 'goes slowly down the hill', while the ascending moon looks down on him like a queen. But the moon is no longer, for Lawrence, 'cursed Syrea Dea', the maleficent all-consuming female. She is now the goddess who 'gives men glistening bodies', and 'only cares / that we should be lovely in the flesh, with bright, crescent feet' [687). He has now covered 'the grand pagan calm which can see the woman of the cosmos wrapped in her warm gleam like the sun, and having her feet upon the moon, the moon who gives us our white flesh' [A 121]. On 29 October Lawrence wrote to Carter:

> In my opinion the great pagan religions of the Aegean, and Egypt and Babylon must have conceived of the 'descent' [of the soul into the body] as a great triumph, and each Easter of the clothing in flesh as a supreme glory, and the Mother Moon who gives us our body as the supreme give of the great gift, hence the very ancient Magna Mater in the East. [L vii. 545]

In 'Invocation to the Moon' Lawrence, at the gate of her mansion, sees that gift. Many of these poems speak of a gate or door. They are rites of passage for the soul. Hermes stands at the gate because he is the messenger or herald who moves freely between the words of men and gods. As psychopomp he brings back to this world the souls which are to be born again.

In *Apocalypse* Lawrence tells us that the Twins, the Kabiri are the ancient gods of gateposts', 'guardians of the gate'. Their function is to 'open the gates that birth may come through between them' [116]. According to Lawrence's understanding of pagan religion, the purpose of spirit, its raison d'être, is to animate the physical world. Consequently, its separation from the body can only be temporary, a transition (experienced by the soul as oblivion) from a worn out body to a new incarnation. The moon symbolizes this transition because she herself waxes and wanes, passes through a period of total eclipse, then renews herself. Her 'garden' is of silver bells and cockle-shells, magical transformations of living flora and fauna ('Of his bones are coral made') quite contrary to the vividly coloured but ephemeral flowers and creatures in the garden of the sun. The moon's garden holds beautiful representations and relics of life which serve to preserve the soul's attachment to the physical world by memory through the period of its withdrawal from that world:

> Now lady of the Moon, now open the gate of your silvery house
> And let me come past the silver bells of your flowers, and the
> cockle-shells
> into your house, garmentless lady of the last great gift:
> who will give me back my lost limbs
> and my lost white fearless breast
> and set me again on moon-remembering feet
> a healed, whole man, O Moon! [CP 696]

This strong desire to re-enter the womb-door is the opposite of Buddhism, whose spiritual disciplines are designed to strengthen the soul in its efforts to close the womb-door and resist the pull back into the great wheel of Karma. In *Apocalypse* Lawrence claims that with the Orphics the tedious idea of 'escaping the wheel of birth' had begun to 'abstract men from life' [A 131]. On the contrary, Lawrence wishes his 'soul to remain as long as possible—wrapped in the dark-red mantle of the body's memories' [PP 223], and to emerge from brief oblivion back on the shores of life.

Several of the best of *Last Poems* have a common strategy. They begin with some widely held, seriously taken belief or proposition, which seems to Lawrence specious or absurd, and proceed, wittily and passionately, to demolish it, not by mere counter-argument or analysis, but simply by making us see the reality through his own direct perception of it. 'Demiurge' is the first of these. The vulgar error is Platonic idealism:

They say that reality exists only in the spirit
that corporal existence is a kind of death
that pure being is bodiless
that the idea of the form precedes the form substantial.
But what nonsense it is!
as if any Mind could have imagined a lobster
dozing in the under-deeps, then reaching out a savage and iron claw!
Even the mind of God can only imagine
those things that have become themselves:
bodies and presences, here and now, creatures with a foothold in creation
even if it is only a lobster on tip-toe. [CP 689]

In 'Red Geranium and Godly Mignonette' the same idea generates wicked but genial comedy:

You can't imagine the Holy Ghost sniffing at cherry-pie heliotrope.
Or the Most High, during the coal age, cudgelling his mighty brains
even if he had any brains: straining his mighty mind
to think, among the moss and mud of lizards and mastodons
to think out, in the abstract, when all was twilit green and muddy:
'Now there shall be tum-tiddly-um, and tum-tiddly-um,
hey-presto! scarlet geranium!'
We know it couldn't be done. [690]

Lawrence knew also, modulating to total seriousness, how it could be done:

But imagine, among the mud and the mastodons
God sighing and yearning with tremendous creative yearning, in that dark
green mess
oh, for some other beauty, some other beauty
that blossomed at last, red geranium, and mignonette.
He knows by analogy with the creative process within himself:
Even an artist knows that his work was never in his mind,
he could never have thought it before it happened.
A strange ache possessed him, and he entered the struggle,
and out of the struggle with his material, in the spell of the urge

> his work took place, it came to pass, it stood up and saluted his
> mind. [690]

A later example of this type of poem is 'Anaxagoras'. Anaxagoras claimed that since all things are mixed, even pure white snow must contain an element of blackness:

> That they call science, and reality.
> I call it mental conceit and mystification
> and nonsense, for pure snow is white to us
> white and white and only white
> with the lovely bloom of whiteness upon white
> in which the soul delights and the senses
> have an experience of bliss. [708]

At first glance it might seem that Lawrence is proceeding by mere contradiction. What is in fact happening in such poems is that Lawrence is demonstrating the difference between the thinking of fallen and unfallen man. Thinking which is abstract, conceptual, mechanical, which has lost its hold on phenomena and sensory experience, which is no longer informed by man's many other ways of knowing, is the thinking of fallen man which can bring only ungodly knowledge and corruption. Lawrence submits himself wholly to the experience of snow, and is faithful in his thinking to that incontrovertible reality.

In 'The Man of Tyre', the proposition to be tested and found wanting is 'that God is one and all alone and ever more shall be so' [692], a proposition already mischievously undermined by the nursery language in which it is stated, so out of keeping with the serious philosophical 'pondering' which is supposed to have generated it. To go 'down to the sea' is to confront and be cut down to size by a vast reality anterior to all human attempts to reduce it to intellectual propositions, the sea 'where God is also love, but without words' [695]. The man of Tyre is not mocked, or only very gently, for he is at least open to that reality, and to the human revelation of the divine he is granted in the form of a naked woman wading shorewards 'with her back to the evening sky'

> both breasts dim and mysterious, with the glamorous kindness of
> twilight
>   between them
> and the dim blotch of black maidenhair like an indicator,
> giving a message to the man—

> So in the cane-brake he clasped his hands in delight
> that could only be god-given, and murmured:
> Lo! God is one god! But here in the twilight
> godly and lovely comes Aphrodite out of the sea towards me!
> [CP 693]

As Michael Kirkham has pointed out,[2] the man's delight is more than sexual. She is, like the moon in her nakedness, 'more wonderful than anything we can stroke' [695]. Her divinity is also bound up with her relation to sea and sky, the ebb and flow of her movements. At first sight she is purely of the workaday world, a woman washing clothes in a pool. But as she lays her shift on the shore and wades out to 'the pale green sea of evening', away from the watcher, she suggests the body detaching itself from the world, committing itself to the deep and the dark. But the woman does not drown or disappear. Pouring sea-water over herself, like a baptism, she turns and returns shorewards, transfigured by 'the glamorous kindness of twilight', re-enacting the birth of Venus from the foam. Her intimation of renewal cannot be separated from her sexuality. The unspoken message to the man indicated by her maidenhair is that the source of new life is within her. It is through the eternal female and only through her that man has access to the 'bath of life' which the sea symbolizes.

The poem itself, in keeping with its delicacy and muted tones, makes no such overt statement. We sympathize with the puzzlement of the man, unable to reconcile revelation with doctrine. 'Lo! God is one god! But [. . .]' Is he admitting that doctrine must be hived off from experience? Is he admitting exceptions to his rule? Or is he wondering whether, if God is one god, the name of that one god might be Aphrodite?

Between 'The Man of Tyre' and 'Invocation to the Moon' come two more poems about the sea, answers to the false proposition that the sea is loveless. The dolphin is another token of the capacity of the cold sea to create new warm life, the sea as the womb of life. But such births can only follow a meeting and mingling of opposites, symbolized by the rainbow. The Etruscans, according to Lawrence, knew the sea in this way:

> The dolphin leaps in and out of it suddenly, as a creature that suddenly exists, out of nowhere. He was not: and lo! there he is! The dolphin which gives up the sea's rainbows only when he dies. Out he leaps; then, with a head-dive, back again he plunges into the sea. He is so much alive, he is like the phallus carrying the fiery spark of procreation down into the darkness of the womb. [SEP 60]

The poems, with their perfect control of rhythm, their flexibility and athleticism, their exuberance, are themselves like dolphins, leaping gaily between the elements of reality and myth:

> and up they come with the purple dark of rainbows
> and flip! they go! with the nose-dive of sheer delight;
> and the sea is making love to Dionysos
> in the bouncing of these small and happy whales. [CP 693]

It is amazing that Lawrence could write such poems on days after in all probability, he had been kept awake all night by incessant coughing. Frieda recalled such days:

> But then at dawn I believe he felt grateful that another day had been given him. 'Come when the sun rises,' he said, and when I came he was glad, so very glad, as if he would say: 'See, another day is given me'. The sun rose magnificently opposite his bed in red and gold across the bay and the fishermen standing up in their boats looked like eternal mythological figures dark and alive against the lit-up splendour of the sea and sky. His courage and unflinching spirit doing their level best to live as long as he possibly could in this world he loved so much, gave me courage too. [NI 302]

Nor did he flinch from the effort to imagine his departure to another world. He took up again the 'Glory of darkness' drafts. At first the crucial idea of the gentians as torches still did not come despite the 'smoking blueness of Pluto's gloom' [PP 229]. First they were 'sheaf-like', an image which could lead nowhere, then

> many cups sharp-lipped, erect, oh very erect
> long and erect and fathomless, dark sharp cups of pure blue darkness,
> and burning with dark-blue power.

The cups were no better than the sheaves. But the word 'burning' surely brought with it the image Lawrence needed. He went back over the preceding lines, changing them to:

> Bavarian gentians, big and dark, only dark
> darkening the day-time, torch-like with the smoking blueness of Pluto's

gloom,
ribbed and torch-like, with their blaze of darkness spread blue
down flattening into points, flattened under the sweep of white day
torch-flower of the blue-smoking darkness, Pluto's dark-blue daze

and so on to the now familiar ending, where the torches guide him

to the sightless realm where darkness is awake upon the dark
and Persephone herself is but a voice
or a darkness invisible enfolded in the deeper dark
of the arms Plutonic, and pierced with the passion of dense
gloom,
among the splendour of torches of darkness, shedding darkness
on the lost bride and her groom.

But there are implications of the Persephone story not followed through here. If she is pierced with passion on this her wedding night, does not that imply her renewal and return journey? Nor is it clear what the marriage of Persephone has to do with the poet's own soul journey, which the ending loses sight of. Also, with those jettisoned lines, Lawrence had thrown out a crucial word, 'erect'.

On the next page of the notebook, he starts again, and now, for the first time, releases all the poem's potentialities, follows through its images with the boldness of a great metaphysical poem. Outwardly the gentians are phallic—'ribbed hellish flowers erect'; inwardly they are womb-like. They are both Pluto and Persephone. Persephone, the life of the vegetation, and, here, of the body, is no longer 'the lost bride'. She goes to her marriage, to be 'ravished' by Pluto, pierced once more by his 'passion of the utter dark'. To be pierced by that darkness is to be violated and to die, yet at the same moment to be fertilized. Death is a nuptial to which the gentians summon and guide the poet. As wedding-guest he is himself to witness and perhaps participate in this process, to be enfolded in darkness, violated. Only such violation can break down the self, marry it to darkness, so that it can emerge renewed from the darkness which is also the womb of all life:

Give me a flower on a tall stem, and three dark flames,
for I will go to the wedding, and be wedding-guest
at the marriage of the living dark.

At the time he wrote this, Lawrence was studying, and attempting to reconstruct, 'the mystery of the individual adventure into Hades' which, it seemed to him, must have been the pagan source for the business of the seven seals in the Book of Revelation. The 'three dark flames' reveal that 'Bavarian Gentians' in its final form has become Lawrence's personal re-enactment of this mystery:

> The initiate [the wedding-guest] is bodily dead. There remains, however, the journey through the underworld, where the living 'I' must divest itself of soul and spirit, before it can at last emerge naked from the far gate of hell into the new day. For the soul, the spirit, and the living 'I' are the three divine natures of man [the 'three dark flames']. The four bodily natures are put off on earth. The two divine natures can be divested in Hades. And the last is a stark flame which, on the new day, is clothed anew and successively by the spiritual body, the soul-body, and then the 'garment' of flesh, with its fourfold terrestrial natures. [A 104]

'Bavarian Gentians' can only enact the early stages of this mystery. It stops short of the re-emergence and the new day. The remaining stages need further poems to work through, culminating in the final version of 'The Ship of Death'.

In 'Bavarian Gentians' the bride was enfolded in deepest darkness. In 'Silence', the poet wishes to be enveloped in Silence, 'great bride of all creation', 'embedded in a shell of Silence [. . .] the silence of the last of the seven great laughs of God' [CP 698]. These 'seven creative thunders' are described in *Apocalypse*. They are also 'seven new words' which will 'bring the new cosmos into being', but the seer is forbidden to write them down: 'We must wait for the actuality' [A 114]. The holy silence, then, is the 'silence of passing through doors', the 'great hush of going from this into that':

> Lift up your heads, O ye Gates!
> for the silence of the last great thundrous laugh
> screens us purely, and we can slip through.

At the end of October, Lawrence turned again to 'The Ship of Death'. The long first draft is broken down now into several poems. In particular, the sections of concern for the fate of those who have no ship of the soul are stripped away, leaving a much clearer narrative line—the need to build the ship of death, the preparations, and the journey—and this is then filled out with new material. It is clearly stated at the outset that the journey is a metaphor for 'the long and painful death/ that lies between the old self and the new' [PP 225]. The ship is now described as a 'little ark', suggesting both

Noah's ark ('already the flood is upon us') and the ark of the covenant ('the ark of faith'). The image of the flood allows Lawrence to extend the threat of death to 'all of us': 'and soon it will rise on the world, on the outside world'. This brings the poem into accord with *Apocalypse*, where he speaks of two simultaneous processes, 'the destruction of the old Adam and the creation of new man', and the 'general or universal message of the destruction of the old world and creation of the new' [A 114]. Whether the individual is literally dying or not, he will be unable to cope with life and change unless he has accepted death. Otherwise, instead of slipping through the gateway to new life, he will 'slip entirely through the fingers of the hands of god / into the abyss of self-knowledge / knowledge of the self-apart-from-god' [CP 701], or join the hosts of the walking dead in the 'bursten cities' [704].

Much more dramatically, with much more conviction and immediacy than before, Lawrence now describes the disappearance of the ship into utter darkness:

> And everything is gone, the body is gone
> completely under, gone, entirely gone.
> The upper darkness is heavy on the lower,
> between them the little ship
> is gone
> she is gone.
> It is the end, it is oblivion. [PP 226]

New too is the moving imagery of dawn which follows:

> A flush of rose, and the whole thing starts again.
> The flood subsides, and the body, like a worn sea-shell
> emerges strange and lovely.
> And the little ship wings home, faltering and lapsing
> on the pink flood,
> and the frail soul steps out, into her house again
> filling the heart with peace. [227]

It is very wistful and poignant. It seems cruel to probe something so tender. Yet it seems to me too wishful and imprecise, like a fairy-tale. There is no attempt to find imagery that will give any clue as to how the renewal is brought about. Is it the same soul stepping into the same body in the same world? If so, the imagery is more appropriate to healing than to rebirth. All the sexual and procreative imagery of the earlier version has been dropped, imagery which had equated the process he describes with familiar processes of nature. In the last analysis, there seems a reluctance to let go of the self, the 'living 'I'', the last 'stark flame'; a reluctance understandable enough were it not for Lawrence's insistence, in so many other poems in this collection, that abandonment of self is a prerequisite for rebirth. It can be argued that a willingness to enter oblivion is itself an abandonment of self. But if, in oblivion, the soul loses irrecoverably all memory of body, self and world, what sense does it make to speak of it as the 'living 'I'', or to suggest that it is still the same soul? How do 'the body' and 'the heart', implying the same body and heart, become habitable again after death? The image of the 'worn sea-shell' does not help.

It may be that Lawrence himself was not happy with this version of 'The Ship of Death', since there exists another, apparently later, version, reduced to less than a quarter of its length. The journey itself is given in a mere four lines:

> Rigging its mast with the silent, invisible sail
> That will spread in death to the breeze
> Of the kindness of the cosmos, that will waft
> The little ship with its soul to the wonder-goal. [CP 965]

Perhaps he regretted his attempt to spell out the mystery, for, as he says in 'Know-All':

> Man knows nothing
> till he knows how not-to-know. [726]

Even in the magnificent spiritual and poetic achievement of 'Bavarian Gentians' and 'The Ship of Death', Lawrence found himself betrayed back to the world of that which we can presume to understand. Did he now feel himself seduced by the Orphic myths and esoteric oriental doctrines which enable us to invest with attributes whatever lies beyond the life of the body? That is forbidden knowledge and a violation of the tabernacle:

> But anyone who shall ascribe attributes to God or oblivion
> let him be cast out, for blasphemy.
> For God is a deeper forgetting far than sleep
> and all description is a blasphemy. [726]

Can we imagine poems which would eschew all description? Perhaps they would be like Tamil Vacanas, or some poems by such post-war Eastern European poets as Popa and Pilinszky, or the Epilogue poems in Hughes's *Gaudete*—to an English reader still 'new, strange flowers' indeed.[3]

There follows Lawrence's last important poem on death, and best, 'Shadows', with no description of God or oblivion, no attempt to use myth or esoteric lore as a key, no imagery beyond that of 'earth's lapse and renewal'. Each section of the poem begins 'And if . . . ', laying claim to no knowledge, no certainties:

> And if, in the changing phases of man's life
> I fall in sickness and in misery
> my wrists seem broken and my heart seems dead
> and strength is gone, and my life
> is only the leavings of a life:
> and still, among it all, snatches of lovely oblivion, and snatches of
> renewal
> odd, wintry flowers upon the withered stem, yet new, strange
> flowers
> such as my life has not brought forth before, new blossoms of
> me—[727]

We have ourselves been witness to this miracle. Out of this chronic sickness and wasted body (he had less than four months to live) have come such a profusion of new, strange flowers, *Pansies* and *Last Poems*.

Perhaps it was at this point that Lawrence returned to 'The Ship of Death', stripped it of the falling apples and the Hamlet posturings, and dropped the attempt to describe the unknowable, leaving the journey only, 'so still / so beautiful, over the last of seas.'

Notes

1. I have given references for the early drafts of 'Bavarian Gentians' and 'the Ship of Death' as PP rather than CP because Mandell gives all the interlinear revisions not in CP.
2. Kirkham 110–12.
3. See Nicholas Bishop, *Re-Making Poetry: Ted Hughes and a New Critical Psychology* (Hemel Hempstead: Harvester Wheatsheaf, 1991); and Sagar, Keith, 'The Poetry Does not Matter,' in *Critical Essays on Ted Hughes*, ed. Leonard M. Scigaj (Boston: O.K. Hall, 1992).

Bibliography and Reference Key

1. Works of D. H. Lawrence

The Cambridge University Press Edition

A Kalnins, Mara, ed. *Apocalypse and the Writings on Revelation*, 1980.

AR Kalnins, Mara, ed., *Aaron's Rod*, 1988.
BB Eggert, Paul, ed. *The Boy in the Bush*, 1990.
FCL Mehl, Dieter, ed., *The Fox, the Captain's Doll, The Ladybird*, 1992.
K Steele, Bruce, ed., *Kangaroo*, 1994.
L i Boulton, James T., ed. *The Letters of D. H. Lawrence*, vol. i, 1979.
L ii Zytaruk, George J. Zytaruk and James T. Boulton, eds, 1981.
L iii Boulton, James T. and Andrew Robertson eds, 1984.
L v Boulton, James T. and Lindeth Vasey, eds, 1989.
L vii Sagar, Keith and James T. Boulton, eds, 1993.
PS Clark, L. D., ed., *The Plumed Serpent*, 1987.
RDP Herbert, Michael, ed., *Reflections on the Death of a Porcupine*, 1988.
SCAL Greenspan, Ezra, Lindeth Vasey and John Worthen, eds, *Studies in Classic American Literature*, 2003.
SEP De Filippis, Simonetta, ed., *Sketches of Etruscan Places and Other Italian Essays*, 1992.
SL Baron, Helen and Carl Baron, eds, *Sons and Lovers*, 1992.
STH Steele, Bruce, ed. *Study of Thomas Hardy*, 1985.
TI Eggert, Paul, ed. *Twilight in Italy*, 1994.
WL Farmer, David, Lindeth Vasey and John Worthen, eds, *Women in Love*, 1987.
WRA Mehl, Dieter and Christa Jansohn, eds, *The Woman Who Rode Away and Other Stories*, 1995.

Other editions

CP De Sola Pinto, Vivian, and Warren Roberts, eds, *The Complete Poems of D. H. Lawrence* (Harmondsworth: Penguin Books, 1977).
DF Farmer, David, 'An Unpublished Version of D. H. Lawrence's Introduction to *Pansies*', *Review of English Studies* 21 (May 1970).
F Lawrence, D. H., *Fantasia of the Unconscious and Psychoanalysis and the Unconscious* (Harmondsworth: Penguin Books, 1971).
MM Lawrence, D. H., *Mornings in Mexico* and *Etruscan Places* (Harmondsworth: Penguin Books, 1960).
P Mcdonald, Edward D., ed., *Phoenix: The Posthumous Papers* of *D. H. Lawrence* (Harmondsworth: Penguin Books, 1978).
P II Roberts, Warren and Harry T. Moore, eds, *Phoenix II: Uncollected, Unpublished and Other Prose Works by D. H. Lawrence* (London: Heinemann, 1968).

2. Other References

Place of publication London unless otherwise stated

AA Gilbert, Sandra, *Acts of Attention: The Poems of D. H. Lawrence* (Ithaca, New York and London: Cornell University Press, 1972).
BGE Nietzsche, Friedrich, *Beyond Good and Evil*, trans. Helen Zimmern (New York, 1964; first published 1909–11), Sect. 295.
BM Carter, Frederick, *D. H. Lawrence and the Body Mystical* (Denis Archer, 1932).
CB Nehls, Edward, ed., *D. H. Lawrence: A Composite Biography*, 3 vols. (Madison: University of Wisconsin Press, 1957–9).
CH Draper, R. P. ed., *D. H. Lawrence: The Critical Heritage* (Routledge, 1979).
D Kerenyi, C., *Dionysos* (Routledge, 1976).

DH Auden, W. H., *The Dyer's Hand* (Faber, 1963).
DHLR Cowan, James C. et al. eds, *The D. H. Lawrence Review.*
EY Worthen, John, *D. H. Lawrence: The Early Years 1885–1912* (Cambridge: Cambridge University Press, 1991).
GB Frazer, G., *The Golden Bough* (Macmillan, 1957).
GM Graves, Robert, *The Greek Myths*, vol. i (Harmondsworth: Penguin Books, 1960).
FS Potter, Stephen, *D. H. Lawrence: A First Study* (Cape, 1930).
HTF Campbell, Joseph, *The Hero with a Thousand Faces* (Princeton, NJ: Princeton UP, 1972).
JW Nietzsche, Friedrich, *The Joyful Wisdom*, trans. Thomas Common (New York: Macmillan, 1924).
MC Tedlock, E. W., ed., *Frieda Lawrence: The Memoirs and Correspondence* (Heinemann, 1961).
MG Baring, Anne, and Jules Cashford, *The Myth of the Goddess: Evolution of an Image* (Viking, 1991).
NI Lawrence, Frieda, *Not I, But the Wind* (Heinemann, 1935).
PP Mandell, Gail Porter, *The Phoenix Paradox: A Study of Renewal Through Change in the Collected Poems and Last Poems of D. H. Lawrence* (Northern Illinois U.P. 1984).
RC Brewster, Earl and Achsah, *D. H. Lawrence: Reminiscences and Correspondence* (Secker, 1934).
PR Chambers, J. D., ed., *D. H. Lawrence: A Personal Record by E. T. (Jessie Chambers)*, 2nd edition (Frank Cass, 1965).
RU Haeckel, Ernst, *The Riddle of the Universe*, tr. J. McCabe (New York: Harper, 1901).
WBY Yeats, W. B., *The Collected Poems* (Macmillan, 1950).
WG Graves, Robert, *The White Goddess* (Faber, 1961).
WP Hughes, Ted, *Winter Pollen: Occasional Prose* (Faber, 1994).
WW Holloway, Emory, ed., *Walt Whitman: Complete Poetry & Selected Prose and Letters* (Nonesuch Press, 1938).

Chronology

1840	Thomas Hardy is born on June 2 in Upper Bockhampton.
1865	William Butler Yeats is born on June 13 in Ireland. (Joseph) Rudyard Kipling is born on December 30 in Bombay.
1871	Hardy's *Desperate Remedies* is published.
1872	Hardy publishes *Under the Greenwood Tree.*
1873	Hardy publishes *A Pair of Blue Eyes.*
1874	Hardy publishes *Far from the Madding Crowd.*
1878	Hardy publishes *The Return of the Native.*
1885	David Herbert (D. H.) Lawrence is born on September 11 in Eastwood.
1886	Hardy publishes *The Mayor of Casterbridge.* Kipling publishes *Departmental Ditties and Other Verses.*
1887	Hardy publishes *The Woodlanders.*
1888	Hardy publishes *The Wessex Tales*, a collection of short stories. Thomas Stearns Eliot is born on September 26 in St. Louis, Missouri.
1889	Yeats publishes *The Wanderings of Oisin and Other Poems.*
1891	Hardy publishes *Tess of the d'Urbervilles* and *A Group of Noble Dames.*

1892	Hardy's first version of *The Well-Beloved* is serialized. Yeats publishes *The Countess Kathleen and Various Legends and Lyrics*. Kipling publishes *Ballads and Barrack-Room Ballads*.
1893	Wilfred Owen born on March 18 in Oswestry, in Shropshire, England.
1894	Hardy publishes a collection of poems, *Life's Little Ironies*. Kipling publishes *The Jungle Book*.
1895	Hardy publishes *Jude the Obscure*. Yeats publishes *Poems*.
1897	Hardy publishes *The Well-Beloved*. Kipling publishes *Captains Courageous*.
1898	Hardy publishes *The Wessex Poems*.
1899	Outbreak of the Boer War. Yeats publishes *The Wind among the Reeds*.
1901	Queen Victoria dies; Edward VII becomes king. Kipling publishes *Kim*. Hardy publishes *Poems of the Past and the Present*.
1902	The Boer War ends. Kipling publishes *Just So Stories*.
1903	Kipling publishes *The Five Nations*.
1904	Hardy publishes Part 1 of *The Dynasts;* Part 2 is published in 1906; Part 3 in 1908.
1907	Kipling wins the Nobel Prize for Literature. Wystan Hugh Auden is born on February 21 in York, England.
1908	Yeats' eight-volume *Collected Works in Verse and Prose* is published.
1909	Hardy publishes *Time's Laughingstocks*.
1910	King Edward VII dies; King George V rules. Kipling publishes *If*.
1911	Lawrence publishes *The White Peacock,* his first novel.
1913	Hardy publishes *A Changed Man*. Lawrence publishes *Sons and Lovers* and *Love Poems and Others*.
1914	Outbreak of World War I. Hardy publishes a collection of poems, *Satires of Circumstance*. Dylan Thomas is born on October 27 in Wales. Yeats publishes *Responsibilities*.
1915	Eliot's "The Love Song of J. Alfred Prufrock" is published in *Poetry*. Lawrence publishes *The Rainbow*.

1916	Lawrence publishes *Amores.*
1917	The United States enters World War I. Eliot publishes *Prufrock and Other Observations.* Hardy publishes *Moments of Vision,* a poetry collection. Lawrence publishes *Look! We Have Come Through!* Owen is hospitalized because of combat wounds; meets fellow patient Siegfried Sassoon. Yeats publishes *The Wild Swans at Coole.*
1918	World War I ends. Owen killed in action in northeast France on November 4. Lawrence publishes *New Poems.*
1919	Versailles Treaty is signed. Hardy's first *Collected Poems* is published.
1920	Eliot publishes *Poems* and *The Sacred Wood.* Lawrence publishes *Women in Love.* Owen's *Poems,* edited by Sassoon, is published.
1921	Hardy publishes *Late Lyrics and Earlier.* Yeats publishes *Michael Robartes and the Dancer.* Lawrence publishes *Tortoises.*
1922	Eliot publishes *The Waste Land* and *Sweeney Agonistes.* Philip (Arthur) Larkin is born on August 9 in Coventry, Warwickshire, England.
1923	Lawrence publishes *Birds, Beasts and Flowers.* Yeats wins Nobel Prize for Literature.
1925	Eliot publishes *Poems, 1909–25.* Hardy publishes *Human Shows,* a poetry collection.
1927	Eliot becomes a British citizen and publishes *Journey of the Magi.*
1928	Eliot publishes *For Lancelot Andrewes: Essays on Style and Order.* Hardy dies on January 11; his poetry collection *Winter Words* is published; Florence Emily Hardy publishes *The Early Life of Thomas Hardy.* Lawrence publishes *Lady Chatterley's Lover.* Yeats publishes *The Tower.* Auden's first book, *Poems,* is privately printed.
1929	U.S. stock market crash initiates the Great Depression. Lawrence publishes *Pansies.*
1930	Eliot publishes *Ash-Wednesday.* Hardy's *Collected Poems* posthumously published. Florence Emily Hardy publishes *The Later Years of Thomas Hardy.* Ted Hughes is born on August 17. Lawrence dies on March 2.
1931	Eliot publishes *Thoughts After Lambeth.*

1932	Auden publishes *The Orators*.
1933	Eliot publishes *The Use of Poetry and the Use of Criticism*. Yeats publishes *The Winding Stair*.
1934	Eliot publishes *After Strange Gods—A Primer of Modern Heresy*. Thomas publishes his first volume of poetry, *Eighteen Poems*.
1935	Eliot's *Murder in the Cathedral* produced and published.
1936	Edward VIII succeeds King George V on January 20; he abdicates on December 11. George VI becomes king. Eliot publishes *Collected Poems, 1909–35*. Thomas publishes *Twenty-five Poems*. Auden publishes *Look, Stranger!* Kipling dies on January 18 in London.
1938	The Munich Pact is signed. Yeats publishes *New Poems*.
1939	Outbreak of World War II. Seamus Heaney is born on April 13 in Northern Ireland. Eliot's *Family Reunion* produced and published. Thomas publishes *The Map of Love*. Auden emigrates to the United States and becomes an American citizen. Yeats dies in France on January 28; his wife and sister publish *Last Poems and Two Plays*.
1940	Thomas publishes *Portrait of the Artist as a Young Dog*. Auden publishes *Another Time*.
1941	Auden publishes *The Double Man*.
1943	Eliot's *Four Quartets* published.
1944	Auden publishes *For the Time Being*. Eavan Boland is born on September 24 in Dublin.
1945	World War II ends. Eliot publishes *What Is a Classic?* Auden publishes *The Collected Poetry*. Larkin publishes *The North Ship*.
1946	Thomas publishes *Deaths and Entrances*. Larkin publishes *Jill* (novel).
1947	Auden publishes *The Age of Anxiety: A Baroque Eclogue*, for which he wins the Pulitzer Prize for Poetry. Larkin publishes *A Girl in Winter* (novel).
1948	Eliot wins the Nobel Prize for Literature.
1949	Eliot publishes *Notes Toward a Definition of Culture*; *The Cocktail Party* opens.

1950	Thomas publishes *Twenty-six Poems.* Eliot wins New York Drama Critics Circle Award and Antoinette Perry Award for *The Cocktail Party* as best foreign play.
1951	Paul Muldoon is born on June 20 in Armagh, Northern Ireland.
1952	King George VI dies; Elizabeth II becomes queen. Thomas publishes *In Country Sleep, and Other Poems* and *Collected Poems, 1934–1952.*
1953	Eliot's *The Confidential Clerk* opens. Thomas dies on November 9 in New York City.
1954	Thomas's *Under Milkwood* is published posthumously.
1955	Auden publishes *The Shield of Achilles*, for which he receives the National Book Award. Larkin publishes *The Less Deceived*, a collection of poems. Carol Ann Duffy is born on December 23 in Glasgow.
1956	Eliot publishes *The Frontiers of Criticism.*
1957	Eliot publishes *On Poetry and Poets.* Hughes publishes his first book of poetry, *The Hawk in the Rain.*
1958	Eliot's *The Elder Statesman* opens.
1959	Hughes publishes *Pike.*
1960	Hughes publishes *Lupercal.*
1962	Eliot publishes *Collected Plays.* Auden publishes *The Dyer's Hand.*
1963	Eliot publishes *Collected Poems, 1909–1962.*
1964	Larkin publishes *The Whitsun Weddings.*
1965	Eliot dies in London on January 4. Heaney's *Eleven Poems* is published as a pamphlet.
1966	Heaney publishes his first book of poems, *Death of a Naturalist.*
1967	Boland publishes her first book of poetry, *New Territory.*
1969	Heaney publishes his second book of poems, *Door into the Dark.* Auden publishes *City Without Walls, and Many Other Poems.*
1970	Larkin publishes *All What Jazz: A Record Diary 1961–1968.* Hughes publishes *A Crow Hymn, A Few Crows*, and *Four Crow Poems* (limited editions) and *Crow: From the Life and Songs of the Crow.*

1971	Muldoon publishes his first poetry collection, *Knowing My Place*.
1972	Auden publishes *Epistle to a Godson, and Other Poems*. Heaney publishes *Wintering Out*.
1973	The United Kingdom joins the European Economic Community. Muldoon publishes *New Weather*. Duffy publishes her first collection of poems, *Fleshweathercock, and Other Poems*. Auden dies on September 28 in Vienna, Austria.
1974	Auden's *Thank You, Fog: Last Poems* is posthumously published. Larkin publishes *High Windows*, a collection of poems.
1975	Heaney publishes *North*. Boland publishes *The War Horse,* her second collection of poems.
1977	Muldoon publishes *Mules*.
1979	Heaney publishes *Field Work*. Hughes publishes *Moortown.*
1980	Heaney publishes *Selected Poems 1965–1975* and *Preoccupations: Selected Prose*. Muldoon publishes *Why Brownlee Left*. Boland publishes *In Her Own Image.*
1982	Boland publishes *Night Feed.*
1983	Larkin publishes *Required Writing: Miscellaneous Pieces 1955–1982*. Muldoon publishes *Quoof*. *The Complete Poems and Fragments* of Owen is published.
1984	Heaney publishes *Sweeney Astray*, a translation of a Middle Irish romance, and *Station Island,* a collection of poems. Hughes is named poet laureate of England.
1985	Duffy publishes *Standing Female Nude*. Larkin dies on December 2.
1986	Boland publishes *The Journey and Other Poems.*
1987	Heaney publishes *The Haw Lantern*. Muldoon publishes *Meeting the British.* Duffy publishes *Selling Manhattan*.
1988	Larkin's *Collected Poems* is posthumously published.
1990	Heaney publishes *New and Selected Poems, 1969–1987*. Boland publishes *Outside History: Selected Poems 1980–1990.* Duffy publishes *The Other Country*. Muldoon publishes *Madoc: A Mystery*.
1991	Heaney publishes *Seeing Things: Poems*.

1992	Hughes publishes *Rain-Charm for the Duchy and Other Laureate Poems*.
1993	Heaney publishes *The Midnight Verdict*. Duffy publishes *Mean Time*.
1994	Boland publishes *In a Time of Violence*. Muldoon publishes *The Annals of Chile*.
1995	Heaney awarded the Nobel Prize for Literature. Boland publishes *Object Lessons: The Life of the Woman and the Poet in Our Time*.
1996	Heaney's *The Spirit Level* is published. Muldoon publishes *Kerry Slides* with photographer Bill Doyle; he receives an American Academy of Arts and Letters award in literature. Boland publishes *An Origin Like Water: Collected Poems 1967–1987*.
1998	Heaney publishes *Opened Ground: Selected Poems, 1966–1996*. Muldoon publishes *Hay*. Boland publishes *The Lost Land*. Hughes publishes *The Birthday Letters*; dies on October 28.
2000	Heaney publishes his best-selling translation of *Beowulf*. Boland co-edits (with Mark Strand) *The Making of a Poem: A Norton Anthology of Poetic Forms*. Duffy publishes *The World's Wife*.
2001	Muldoon publishes *Poems 1968–1998*. Boland publishes *Against Love Poetry*.
2002	Duffy publishes *Feminine Gospels*.
2003	Muldoon wins the Pulitzer Prize for Poetry for *Moy Sand and Gravel* (2002).
2004	Boland publishes a volume of prose, *After Every War*.
2005	Duffy publishes *Rapture*.
2006	Muldoon publishes *Horse Latitudes*, a collection of poems.
2007	Boland publishes *Domestic Violence*.
2008	Boland publishes *New Collected Poems*.
2009	Duffy becomes the first female poet laureate of Great Britain; she publishes *To the Moon: An Anthology of Lunar Poetry* and *Love Poems*.
2010	Muldoon publishes *Maggot*.

Contributors

HAROLD BLOOM is Sterling Professor of the Humanities at Yale University. Educated at Cornell and Yale universities, he is the author of more than 30 books, including *Shelley's Mythmaking* (1959), *Blake's Apocalypse* (1963), *Yeats* (1970), *The Anxiety of Influence* (1973), *A Map of Misreading* (1975), *Kabbalah and Criticism* (1975), *Agon: Toward a Theory of Revisionism* (1982), *The American Religion* (1992), *The Western Canon* (1994), *Omens of Millennium: The Gnosis of Angels, Dreams, and Resurrection* (1996), *Shakespeare: The Invention of the Human* (1998), *How to Read and Why* (2000), *Genius: A Mosaic of One Hundred Exemplary Creative Minds* (2002), *Hamlet: Poem Unlimited* (2003), *Where Shall Wisdom Be Found?* (2004), *Jesus and Yahweh: The Names Divine* (2005), and *Till I End My Song: A Gathering of Last Poems* (2010). In addition, he is the author of hundreds of articles, reviews, and editorial introductions. In 1999, Professor Bloom received the American Academy of Arts and Letters' Gold Medal for Criticism. He has also received the International Prize of Catalonia, the Alfonso Reyes Prize of Mexico, and the Hans Christian Andersen Bicentennial Prize of Denmark.

DOMINIC HIBBERD is the author of *Wilfred Owen: A New Biography.* He is coeditor of *Poetry of the Great War: An Anthology* and *The Winter of the World: The Definitive Collection of World War I Poetry.*

ROBERT LANGBAUM is an emeritus professor of the University of Virginia. He is the author of *Thomas Hardy in Our Time*, *The Poetry of Experience: The Dramatic Monologue in Modern Literary Tradition*, and other works.

HELEN VENDLER is a professor at Harvard University. She has written *Seamus Heaney*, a study of the poet. She has written books on other poets as well, has published her critical essays, and is the editor of the Harvard/Faber *Book of Contemporary American Poetry.*

STAN SMITH was a professor and head of English at Dundee University. His work includes *Inviolable Voice: History and Twentieth-Century Poetry*, *W. H. Auden*, and *W. B. Yeats: A Critical Introduction*. He is also the general editor of Longman Critical Readers and Longman Studies in Twentieth-Century Literature.

ANDREW SWARBRICK has been head of English at the Royal Grammar School, Worcester. He has written books on Philip Larkin and T. S. Eliot for the Macmillan Master Guides series. He also is the editor of *The Art of Oliver Goldsmith* and of a work of Anthony Trollope.

RAINER EMIG was a professor at the University of Regensburg, Germany. He has published *Modernism in Poetry: Motivations, Structures and Limits*, *Ulysses* for the New Casebook Series, and other work.

LAWRENCE RAINEY is a professor at the University of York, where he also is deputy head of the Department of English and Related Literature. He has published *The Annotated Waste Land with Eliot's Contemporary Prose* as well as *Modernism: An Anthology* and other work.

JANE DOWSON is a reader in twentieth-century literature at De Montfort University, Leicester. She is the editor of *The Cambridge Companion to Twentieth-Century British and Irish Women's Poetry*. She also is the author of *Women, Modernism and British Poetry, 1910–1939: Resisting Femininity.*

ALICE ENTWISTLE is principal lecturer in English literature at the University of Glamorgan. She has contributed to *A Cambridge History of English Poetry*, *The Edinburgh Companion to Contemporary Scottish Literature*, and other publications.

TIM KENDALL is a professor and head of English at the University of Exeter. He is the author of *The Oxford Handbook of British and Irish War Poetry*, two books on Paul Muldoon, and other works.

KEITH SAGAR is special professor in the School of English at the University of Nottingham. He is the author of many books on D. H. Lawrence, including *The Art of D. H. Lawrence*, *The Life of D. H. Lawrence*, and *D. H. Lawrence: Life into Art*, and several works on Ted Hughes.

Bibliography

Bahlke, George W., ed. *Critical Essays on W. H. Auden*. New York: G. K. Hall, 1991.

Blistein, Burton. *The Design of* The Waste Land. Lanham: University Press of America, 2008.

Booth, James. *Philip Larkin: The Poet's Plight*. Basingstoke [England]; New York: Palgrave Macmillan, 2005.

Booth, James, ed. *New Larkins for Old: Critical Essays*. New York: St. Martin's Press, 2000.

Brooker, Jewel Spears. *Mastery and Escape: T. S. Eliot and the Dialectic of Modernism*. Amherst: University of Massachusetts Press, 1994.

Brooker, Jewel Spears, ed. *T. S. Eliot and Our Turning World*. Houndmills [England]: Macmillan Press; New York: St. Martin's Press in association with Institute of United States Studies, University of London, 2001.

Cianci, Giovanni, and Jason Harding, ed. *T.S. Eliot and the Concept of Tradition*. Cambridge; New York: Cambridge University Press, 2007.

Coates, John. *The Day's Work: Kipling and the Idea of Sacrifice*. Madison, [N.J.]: Fairleigh Dickinson University Press; London: Associated University Presses, 1997.

Cooper, Stephen. *Philip Larkin: Subversive Writer*. Brighton [England]; Portland, Ore.: Sussex Academic Press, 2004.

Corcoran, Neil, ed. *The Cambridge Companion to Twentieth-Century English Poetry*. Cambridge; New York: Cambridge University Press, 2007.

Davie, Donald. *With the Grain: Essays on Thomas Hardy and Modern British Poetry*, edited by Clive Wilmer. Manchester: Carcanet, 1998.

Dillingham, William B. *Rudyard Kipling: Hell and Heroism*. New York: Palgrave Macmillan, 2005.

Donoghue, Denis. *Words Alone: The Poet T. S. Eliot.* New Haven: Yale University Press, 2000.

Dowson, Jane. *Women, Modernism and British Poetry, 1910–1939: Resisting Femininity.* Aldershot, England; Burlington, Vt.: Ashgate, 2002.

Duncan, Andrew. *Centre and Periphery in Modern British Poetry.* Liverpool: Liverpool University Press, 2005.

Firchow, Peter Edgerly. *W. H. Auden: Contexts for Poetry.* Newark [Del.]: University of Delaware Press; London: Associated University Presses, 2002.

Hadley, Edward. *The Elegies of Ted Hughes.* Houndmills, Basingstoke, Hampshire; New York: Palgrave Macmillan, 2010.

Hibberd, Dominic. *Wilfred Owen: The Last Year 1917–1918.* London: Constable, 1992.

Hoffpauir, Richard. *The Art of Restraint: English Poetry from Hardy to Larkin.* Newark [N.J.]: University of Delaware Press; London: Associated University Presses, 1991.

Holdeman, David. *The Cambridge Introduction to W. B. Yeats.* Cambridge, UK; New York: Cambridge University Press, 2006.

Holdeman, David, and Ben Levitas, ed. *W. B. Yeats in Context.* Cambridge, UK; New York: Cambridge University Press, 2010.

Howarth, Peter. *British Poetry in the Age of Modernism.* Cambridge, UK; New York: Cambridge University Press, 2005.

Howes, Marjorie, and John Kelly, ed. *The Cambridge Companion to W.B. Yeats.* Cambridge, UK; New York: Cambridge University Press, 2006.

Izzo, David Garrett, ed. *W. H. Auden: A Legacy.* West Cornwall, Conn.: Locust Hill Press, 2002.

Jackaman, Rob. *A Study of Cultural Centres and Margins in British Poetry Since 1950: Poets and Publishers.* Lewiston: Edwin Mellen Press, 1995.

Johnson, Trevor. *A Critical Introduction to the Poems of Thomas Hardy.* New York: St. Martin's Press, 1991.

Jones, Peter, and Michael Schmidt, ed. *British Poetry Since 1970: A Critical Survey.* New York: Persea Books, 1980.

Kennedy, David. *New Relations: The Refashioning of British Poetry 1980–1994.* Bridgend, Mid Glamorgan, Wales: Seren, 1996.

Kerr, Douglas. *Wilfred Owen's Voices: Language and Community.* Oxford: Clarendon Press; New York: Oxford University Press, 1993.

Marsh, Nicholas. *Philip Larkin: The Poems.* Basingstoke: Palgrave Macmillan, 2007.

Matthews, Steven. "The Object Lessons of Heaney, Muldoon and Boland." *Critical Survey* 15, no. 1 (2003): 18–33.

Maud, Ralph. *Where Have the Old Words Got Me?: Explications of Dylan Thomas's Collected Poems.* Montreal; Ithaca: McGill-Queen's University Press, 2003.

Merriman, Emily Taylor, and Adrian Grafe, ed. *Intimate Exposure: Essays on the Public–Private Divide in British Poetry Since 1950.* Jefferson, N.C.: McFarland & Co., 2010.

Moody, A. David, ed. *The Cambridge Companion to T. S. Eliot.* Cambridge [England]; New York: Cambridge University Press, 1994.

Moulin, Joanny, ed. *Ted Hughes: Alternative Horizons.* London; New York: Routledge, 2004.

Orr, Leonard, ed. *Yeats and Postmodernism.* Syracuse, N.Y.: Syracuse University Press, 1991.

Parry, Ann. *The Poetry of Rudyard Kipling: Rousing the Nation.* Buckingham; Philadelphia, Pa.: Open University Press, 1992.

Persoon, James. *Modern British Poetry, 1900–1939.* New York: Twayne, 1999.

Picot, Edward. *Outcasts from Eden: Ideas of Landscape in British Poetry Since 1945.* Liverpool: Liverpool University Press, 1997.

Pinkney, Tony. *D. H. Lawrence and Modernism.* Iowa City: University of Iowa Press, 1990.

Roberts, Neil, ed. *A Companion to Twentieth-Century Poetry.* Oxford, England: Blackwell, 2001.

Rooney, Caroline, and Kaori Nagai, ed. *Kipling and Beyond: Patriotism, Globalisation, and Postcolonialism.* Houndmills, Basingstoke, Hampshire; New York: Palgrave Macmillan, 2010.

Russell, Kirk. *Eliot and His Age: T. S. Eliot's Moral Imagination in the Twentieth Century.* Wilmington, Del.: ISI, 2008.

Shires, Linda M. *British Poetry of the Second World War.* London: Macmillan, 1985.

Smith, Stan. *W. H. Auden.* Oxford [Oxfordshire]; New York: Blackwell, 1985.

Squires, Michael, and Keith Cushman, ed. *The Challenge of D. H. Lawrence.* Madison: University of Wisconsin Press, 1990.

Steinberg, Gillian. *Philip Larkin and His Audiences.* Basingstoke [England]; New York: Palgrave Macmillan, 2010.

Stewart, Jack. *The Vital Art of D. H. Lawrence: Vision and Expression.* Carbondale: Southern Illinois University Press, 1999.

Thwaite, Anthony. *Poetry Today: A Critical Guide to British Poetry, 1960–1995.* London; New York: Longman in association with the British Council, 1996.

Tolley, A. T. *My Proper Ground: A Study of the Work of Philip Larkin and Its Development.* [Ottawa]: Carleton University Press, 1991.

Tuma, Keith. *Fishing by Obstinate Isles: Modern and Postmodern British Poetry and American Readers.* Evanston, Ill.: Northwestern University Press, 1998.

Vendler, Helen. *Our Secret Discipline: Yeats and Lyric Form.* Cambridge, Mass.: Belknap Press of Harvard University Press, 2007.

———. *Seamus Heaney.* Cambridge, Mass.: Harvard University Press, 1998.

Wigginton, Chris, and John Goodby, ed. *Dylan Thomas*. Houndmills [England]; New York: Palgrave, 2001.

Wilson, Keith, ed. *Thomas Hardy Reappraised: Essays in Honor of Michael Millgate*. Toronto: University of Toronto Press, 2006.

Xerri, Daniel. *Ted Hughes' Art of Healing*. Bethesda: Academica Press, 2010.

Acknowledgments

Dominic Hibberd, "The Pity of War." In *Owen the Poet.* Published by Macmillan Press. Copyright © Dominic Hibberd 1986.

Robert Langbaum, "The Issue of Hardy's Poetry." In *Victorian Poetry* 30, no. 2 (Summer 1992): 151–63. Copyright © 1992 by West Virginia University Press.

Helen Vendler, "Second Thoughts: The Haw Lantern." In *The Art of Seamus Heaney*, edited by Tony Curtis. Copyright © 2001, Poetry Wales Press and Helen Vendler.

Stan Smith, "The Living World for Text: Yeats and the Book of the People." In *The Origins of Modernism: Eliot, Pound, Yeats and the Rhetoric of Renewal.* Published by Harvester Wheatsheaf. Copyright © 1994 Stan Smith.

Andrew Swarbrick, *"High Windows." In Out of Reach: The Poetry of Philip Larkin.* Published by St. Martin's Press. Copyright © Andrew Swarbrick 1995.

Rainer Emig, "From Eros to Agape: The Philosophy of Auden's Later Works." In *W. H. Auden: Towards a Postmodern Poetics.* Published by St. Martin's Press. Copyright © Rainer Emig 2000.

Lawrence Rainey, "Immense. Magnificent. Terrible. Reading *The Waste Land.*" In *Revisiting The Waste Land.* Published by Yale University Press. Copyright © 2005 by Lawrence Rainey.

Jane Dowson and Alice Entwistle, "Dialogic Politics in Carol Ann Duffy and Others." In *A History of Twentieth-Century British Women's Poetry.* Published by Cambridge University Press. Copyright © Jane Dowson and Alice Entwistle 2005.

Tim Kendall, "Fighting Back over the Same Ground: Ted Hughes and War." In *Modern English War Poetry.* Published by Oxford University Press. Copyright © Tim Kendall 2006.

Keith Sagar, "'New, Strange Flowers: Pansies, Nettles, and Last Poems." In *D. H. Lawrence: Poet.* Published by Humanities-Ebooks. Copyright © Keith Sagar, 2007, 2008.

Every effort has been made to contact the owners of copyrighted material and secure copyright permission. Articles appearing in this volume generally appear much as they did in their original publication with few or no editorial changes. In some cases, foreign language text has been removed from the original essay. Those interested in locating the original source will find the information cited above.

Index